What Would Lynne Tillman Do?

What Would Lynne Tillman Do?

Lynne Tillman

Red Lemonade

a Cursor publishing community

Brooklyn, New York

2014

For Dr. Stanley Grand

Red Lemonade
a Cursor publishing community
Brooklyn
Copyright © 2014 by Lynne Tillman.

Library of Congress Control Number available from the Library of
Congress.

Book Design by Luke Gerwe
Copyediting by Nora Nussbaum

Printed in the United States of America

Red Lemonade
a Cursor publishing community
Brooklyn, New York

www.redlemona.de

Distributed by Publishers Group West

ISBN: 978-1-935869-21-4

Table of Contents

Introduction

Her aura as she moved onto the stage was both casual and nervous. It was clear that she had done this before. She was not going to stumble or fumble to get the audience on her side, but that confidence was matched by a guardedness, an unease, and a way of maintaining a distance that might have been theatrical. I was not sure. In one of her books, she writes of a character: "Once she dreamed, on the night before a reading she was to give, that rather than words on paper, there were tiny objects linked one to another, which she had to decipher instantly, and turn into words, sentences, a story, flawlessly, of course."

She was wearing black; she had a glass of whiskey on the rocks in her hand. Her delivery was dry, deadpan, deliberate. There was an ironic undertow in her voice, and a sense that she had it in for earnestness, easy emotion, realism. She exuded a tone which was considered, examined and then re-examined. She understood, it seemed to me, that everything she said would have to be able to survive the listeners' intelligence and sense of irony; her own intelligence was high and refined, her sense of irony knowing and humorous.

I had not come across anyone like her before. It was May 1990 and both of us were touring what they call the United Kingdom in the company of an English writer. All three of us were promoting books. Although I had been in New York once and had read American fiction and seen the movies, I had never really known any Americans. Thus I could not place Lynne Tillman. All I could do was watch her.

One thing she said made me laugh. When our English friend spoke of London and how hard it was to live there since it was so large and one had to travel miles and miles to have supper with friends, and then, if they moved, one often had to travel farther and indeed farther to see them, Lynne looked pained at all this talk of traveling and said: "Oh, no. In New York, if someone moves more than a few blocks away, you just drop them."

In one of the cities, there was a friend of mine in the audience. The following morning, as we were setting out on a long journey by car, our English colleague having found her own transport, I had a feeling that Lynne was fragile. But it did not stop her asking about my friend. I still could not read her tone and was not certain that there was not an edge of mockery in her voice, perhaps mockery at the very idea of having a friend who lived in a provincial part of the United Kingdom.

I decided it was time to do something.

"Do you like Joni Mitchell?" I asked.

"No," she replied instantly.

"Well, my friend was like Richard in Joni Mitchell's 'The Last Time I Saw Richard.' Would you like me to sing the relevant lines?"

"No," she said again.

As I seemed to be preparing to sing, she appealed to the driver.

I began to sing. (I am not a good singer.)

Richard got married to a figure skater
And he bought her a dishwasher and a coffee percolator
And he drinks at home now most night with the TV on
And all the house lights left up bright.

Lynne Tillman moaned as we drove north. And even when the singing ended, she moaned more in case it might start again. I gave her ample feeling that the risk was high, as I took her though the lyrics of "A Case of You," "California," and "Little Green." Often, I threatened to sing the words out, rather than simply recite them, just to help us on our journey, but even the driver protested. I liked the idea that Lynne Tillman, who I thought then—wrongly, as I discovered—was the coolest person alive, had met me, a boy from a small town in Ireland who was a complete fool and had not learned any strategies to disguise this dreadful and shameful fact. It might not have helped that my reading the previous evening had given strong intimations that I had been trained in the old school to understand the importance of being earnest and that I had not gone to any other school.

During the days that followed, Lynne Tillman got a pain in her back. She often had to lie flat on the ground. Maybe it was caused by the English motorways; maybe it was caused by having to do a reading every night; maybe it was a leftover from jet lag. But there remained a feeling in the air that her back pain had been caused by me. The pain was not improved by my attempting at one point to pat her heartily on the afflicted region and telling her that she would be better soon. But slowly, perhaps because I was reading her book in the evenings and listening carefully to her readings, I was learning that she was a much more complex figure than I had imagined when I saw her first. She was more thoughtful and serious somehow, also kinder and more considerate and oddly vulnerable. And also, more than anything, she was a rich noticer of strange things and a good maker of sentences and phrases.

*

In the 1930s, as the writer Samuel Beckett tried to make sense of himself, he attended a lecture by Carl Jung in London in which Jung outlined the case of a patient, now adult in age, who had not actually been born, whose spirit, or essence, or essential self had not come into the world when the body did. For any writer of fiction, such an idea is fascinating. ("Sometimes," Lynne Tillman wrote, "Madame Realism felt as if she just didn't exist.") For many people such a condition is almost normal; for writers it is almost a regular part of being alive in the world and a central part of the process of inventing character in fiction. In much fiction done in the years after Jung's lecture, there is always something missing, something which has not been integrated. The point is to explore that lovely missing thing, a thing whose very absence may indeed constitute the self, the core, the ache. It is possible that the idea of a personality or a person without this flaw, or this gift, or whatever we want to call it—Beckett liked to call it Murphy or Watt or Malone or Moran or Winnie—is a myth or a dream or an image from an advertisement for something, and that it is the task of novelists to dramatize the gap between the strangeness of being alive filled with glittering and fleeting desires, filled with shattering absences, and the ideal, whole, and intolerable completed person—what we might also think of as creating the credible character. "Identity is such a fragile thing," Tillman's Madame Realism muses in an essay on Freud. In an interview conducted by Tillman for *Bomb* magazine, the artist Peter Dreher remarked: "But maybe, more important, is a feeling that perhaps I was born with, that everybody is born with: that one is somehow floating between thoughts, between literature, speaking, continents, races, and so on. I think, more or less, each of us today, maybe more than a hundred years ago, has this feeling."

This feeling is inhabited with relish and sometimes with shivering awe by Lynne Tillman in her fiction and in her critical writing. Her style has both tone and undertone; it attempts to register the impossibility of saying very much, but it insists on the right to say a little. So what is essential is the voice itself, its ways of knowing and unknowing. An observation; a dry fact; a memory; something noticed; someone encountered; a joke; something wry; a provocation; something playful. This is not, as in Beckett, a way of inviting company to the dark and lonely ceremony of being. Tillman is content to put these items on the page, and hold and wield her tones, merely because they are in the world; they occurred to her at a certain time; they are part of the day and maybe the night. She is ready to admit them because they live in the mind, and she is excited by the mind, its freedoms and its restrictions, how it wanders and becomes voice and how the voice slowly takes on the guise of a presence moving from the ghostly to the almost real, as the pages are turned.

*

There is a game in David Lodge's novel *Small World* in which the highly educated characters vie with each other to name famous and canonical books that they have not bothered to read. (The winner, by the way, has not read *Hamlet*.) For anyone writing now, or indeed for many readers, there is a serious edge to this game. Increasingly, the canon, the accepted list of great and good books, seems like merchandise, something created to be consumed, carefully packaged for you and all your family. The canon seems concerned to hold on to power, the power of the middle ground. Other voices, other systems of seeing, are excluded with something close to deliberation; they are reduced to being marginal, eccentric. Slowly then what is out of fashion moves out of print.

For anyone serious about writing, it is often the book that has been forgotten or dismissed, the writer you found on your own, the story or poem or presence that has been too strange for others, that has mattered most, that has made you in its likeness. Creating space for your own work involves creating space for the work that made a difference to you. This is why artists write essays; they do so to reposition the way we read or the way we respond so that the work they do can be read or seen more clearly. It is the same reason, if there is a reason, plants grow toward light.

Lynne Tillman's essays, and indeed the interviews she has given and conducted, are thus an essential part of her work. Her response to books is daring, sharp; she allows for mystery, beauty, strangeness, but she also allows for complexity, coolness, distance.

She does not accept that there is a mystical relationship between the world and the book. In contemplating Warhol in "The Last Words Are Andy Warhol," for example, Tillman writes: "Books are not mirrors, and life doesn't go onto the page like life, but like writing." Writing, for her, is like writing, if it is like anything, and it probably isn't like anything; words, for her, come from words, they have their own shape and sound. When, in the same essay, she arrives at the phrase "in real time," she knows to ask "whatever that is." Naming for her is re-naming. There are words and concepts that do not connect for her. "Existence," for example, is "a shaggy-dog story." "Redemption," she writes, "from my point of view, is an American disease." And she adds, in her essay on Paula Fox's *Borrowed Finery*: "Contemporary novels have become a repository for salvation; characters—and consequentially readers—are supposed to be saved at the end."

Tillman is, as she quotes the photographer William Eggleston saying of his own work, "at war with the obvious." Some allies matter to her in this war, and they include Jane and Paul Bowles, Charles Henri Ford, Jorge Luis Borges, Walter Benjamin, Paula Fox, Chet Baker, Etel Adnan, Harry Mathews, John Waters, Gertrude Stein, Edith Wharton.

While writing for her does not reflect life, whatever life is, this does not mean that, for her, fiction does not somehow come from the world and is not a strange and angled response in language to what is beyond its pages. She insists, for example, on the importance of the public realm and the place of literature within the public realm, indeed the connection between literary form itself and the shape of politics. "These days," she writes in "Body Parts for Sale":

the west gloats over the demise of communism, the premise being that de-
mocracy and capitalism are synonymous. The demise of totalitarianism from
the left or right is something to be happy about, but I'm left wondering what
capitalism offers, apart from a certain economic system, to the spirit that
haunts our Gothic stories, and to a sense of how society should be run, to a
sense of what common goals can be. Dog-eat-dog and survival of the fittest are
appropriate metaphors for not just the capitalist ethic but also for the produc-
tion of Gothic perambulations. In our country without adequate health care
and housing, a country first decimated by Reagan's criminal grotesqueries and
Bush's new world order, what more credible form is there?

Tillman allows her intelligence to range over many questions. In "Downtown's Room in Hotel History" her analysis in one paragraph of the power and lure of downtown Manhattan for a generation of artists is definitive:

Downtown's shows and parties, held inside a small perimeter, allowed for
quick comings and goings. You never had to stay; you could usually walk
home. This cosmopolitan life, rootless, maybe, sometimes unheimlich, un-
canny, ordained that home wasn't necessarily homey. The city grew fields of the
unfamiliar and unexpected, which trumped the humdrum. The city's virtues
and Modernist values—such as strangers and strangeness—were the small
town's vices and fears.

Tillman has no time for the unexamined sentence, and, since the process of examination gives her prose an energy, the more she thinks the more she can make sparks fly. This, for example, is a paragraph about John Waters, from her essay "Guide for the Misbegotten":

Though irony is mother's milk to him, Waters's quest for genuine communica-
tion inside bullshit-free zones propels him toward worlds with and without
irony. Sincerely insincere, insincerely sincere, authentically inauthentic, inau-
thentically authentic, his work vexes the normative and all the usual binaries.
Oppositional terms can't tell the stories he wants to tell. The mash-up of
in-betweenness sparks Waters's imagination, where insincerity can be sincere,
sincerity ironic. Waters prodigiously exaggerates the deficiencies of false di-
chotomies; each side of the aisle is desperately wanting. All this ongoing worry
about "authenticity" in art and life, his oeuvre suggests, is moot, since human
beings may be incapable of inauthenticity. Con artist Bernie Madoff's commis-
sion of fraud doesn't make Madoff a fraud: he's absolutely Madoff.

Tillman is also funny. "At parties I observe people acting much like dogs," she writes in her essay "Blame It on Andy," "except for sniffing rear ends, which is generally done in private." In her review of a history of shit, she remarks that the author's "tongue is often in his cheek." Sometimes, the wit is unsettling. When she writes, for example, in "Doing Laps Without a Pool," that "fish probably don't know they're in water" and then adds, "(who can be certain though)," I, as the reader, become uncertain. I think about fish, and the sheer tragedy—or maybe sadness is a better word, or maybe even comedy—of their not perhaps knowing something so obvious, so—how can we put it?—clear-cut, staring you in the face. And then I think about certainty. I stand up and move around the room, opening and shutting my mouth like a fish, wondering if I really know where I am, forgetting about fish for the moment. Then I go back and look at the last two sentences Tillman has written in that paragraph about fish to see if there is any comfort there. "Complacency is writing's most determined enemy," she writes, "and we writers, and readers, have been handed an ambivalent gift: doubt. It robs us of assurance, while it raises possibility." That last sentence is very beautiful, but you would have to be not a fish to appreciate it. Or at least I think so. I wonder what Joni Mitchell would think.

*

Lynne Tillman's essay on Edith Wharton's *The House of Mirth* is the finest essay that anyone has written on that book. This essay, "A Mole in the House of the Modern," is also a key to elements in Tillman's own work and indeed to her sensibility as an artist. Lily Bart in *The House of Mirth*, in Tillman's telling, wants something from life that life cannot give her, and it is that desire, "her magnificent desire to be herself," in all its complexity and seriousness and richness, which destroys her for the world but re-creates her for the reader. Slowly, as her power diminishes, another force in Lily, the force released by her imagination, becomes dominant, as voice in a novel becomes dominant over character, as tone and texture over plot.

By emphasising questions of space in Wharton, Tillman focuses on confinement. In doing this, she manages to capture the idea that Lily Bart is trapped in a cell of her own making, a cell which is the only place where someone as original as she can feel enclosed and nurtured and engaged and then destroyed.

In contemplating confinement and space, Tillman considers Wharton's style:

But Wharton is economical about elegance, stringent about lushness, display,
every embellishment. Rarely extravagant. Maybe it's because she understood
position and space, knew she didn't really have much room, no room for
profligacy. She couldn't run from reality, even if she wanted to (and I think she
did), so she had no room to waste, certainly no words to waste. The inessential
might obscure the clarity she sought. She wouldn't let herself go, let her writing
go. She understood the danger, she understood any form of complicity. Her
often privileged protagonists fatally conspire with society against themselves,
become common prey to its dictates, helpless to disown or resist what they
despise in themselves and it in it. Wharton was profoundly aware that, seen
by others, she was free to do what she pleased, a privileged woman dangling
the world on a rich string. And she wrote, perhaps explained, early on in The
House of Mirth, *Lily Bart "was so evidently the victim of the civilization*
which had produced her, that the links of her bracelet seemed like manacles
chaining her to her fate."

As with any serious piece of critical writing, Tillman's version of
Wharton, while remaining true to the original, also tells us a great
deal about Tillman's own procedures as a novelist, her own scru-
pulousness, for example, her own refusal to take easy options,
her knowledge that her characters are alone and that the style in
which they are rendered arises from thought and strategy, from
a willed and intelligent examination of the available possibilities,
and the full knowledge, as Wharton writes, that "we are hampered
at every turn by an artistic tradition of over two thousand years."

—Colm Tóibín
September, 2013

A is for Andy

I'm going to speculate about some of the issues raised and some of the ideas I found compelling and daunting in *a: A Novel*. *a: A Novel* is a narrative based on 24 audiotaped hours in the life of Warhol superstar Ondine, an articulate, funny, volatile man. When Pope Ondine acted in *Chelsea Girls*, his performance exceeded, crossed—even violated—the supposed boundary between life and art, a line Warhol wanted crossed. It's blurred, if not effaced, in his only novel, *a*.

I've written this essay as a list, a shopping list in paragraphs. Warhol liked to shop. I don't, but I like lists.

1. "A" is for Art, Andy, and Amphetamine—Ondine lived on speed, and the story is speed driven.

2. Reading *a: A Novel*, I sometimes felt like one of its participants: "Nine more hours to go," said the Sugar Plum Fairy. Time was of the essence—actually it's the essential element in the book. There are just so many tapes to fill, hours to stay awake, and so time's on everyone's mind. The tape recorder's going, a book is being made. The Book is being made. In fact, the last words in the novel, spoken by Billy Name, are: "Out of the garbage, into THE BOOK."

In a way, Warhol through Name is claiming garbage—the minutiae and tedium of daily life, the unedited flow—for literature.

3. *a: A Novel* is a project of—and an exercise in—consciousness and self-consciousness. Ondine and most of the others recorded are not unwitting characters or subjects. They're self-conscious even when they're nearly unconscious.

4. Ondine, the protagonist, sometimes fought against the chains of the tape recorder, a new master, asking Warhol many times to stop it. But Ondine continued to let himself be recorded, as did all the others who questioned Drella's demands in making this novel-book. Maybe they knew they were participating in something new, or interesting, maybe even worthwhile, simply because it was Warhol. Though they struggled with him, they complied. Others may now be horrified by this compliance, believe that everyone in the Factory was manipulated, taken advantage of. They used and were used, perhaps, in every possible sense. But another view is that, given the problems in their lives at the time and their insecurities, which A documents, Warhol offered them something—work or a feeling of significance for that moment or a way to fill time. The tape recorder is on. You are being recorded. Your voice is being heard, and this is history.

5. What about authorship in *a: A Novel*? In Part 2, there's talk about the typists who are transcribing the tapes, and who, in a way, through errors, mis-hearings, and incorrect spellings, contribute to or create the book with the speakers. It's the typists' book. It's

the tape recorder's book; it could not exist without it, just as the novel could not have been born without Gutenberg's press. Or, it's Ondine's book, he's the author of himself, and the protagonist, it's his 24 hours. Or, and I think it is, it's Warhol's artwork, a conceptual and experimental book. Part of Warhol's work was to regularly produce a blur around authorship.

6. Warhol dropped the mirror, let it crack into pieces, and instead held a tape recorder up to life. He saw a god in the machine and used as many as he could—*a* notes the arrival of video, a new toy, to the Factory—and Warhol didn't fear the loss of authorship to machines, when his hand, literally, wasn't in or on it; he constructed another kind of artist, who directs machines, people, uses technology, whose imprint was virtual.

7. *a* reveals realism as a form of writing, a type of fiction, a genre, not an unmediated, exact replica of life, not a mirror image. Books are not mirrors, and life doesn't go onto the page like life, but like writing. Warhol's novel is closer to life, reality, than a realist novel. It's mediated by the elements I just mentioned—the apparatus, the speakers, the typists, and Warhol's idea for it—and by the continuous 24-hour frame he wanted to use.

But Warhol was flummoxed by Ondine, who became exhausted or bored after just 12, so the book is not 24-hours straight. At the end of those 12 hours, Warhol asked Ondine for his last words, and he said, "My last words are Andy Warhol." There's a lot of reality in that—and self-consciousness and consciousness. In *a*, reality is gotten at differently, without any of the codes of realism.

8. If Warhol had recorded a continuous 24-hours, *a: A Novel* would have adhered to the classical idea of unity necessary for tragedy, compared with Joyce's *Ulysses*, perhaps, which may have been on his mind, since it stands as the 20th century's representative or exemplary modernist novel. (Bob Colacello says Truman Capote's singular, brilliant novel, *In Cold Blood*, was on Warhol's mind.)

The second half of *a*, instead of being continuous time, is a series of fragments, more out of joint, more out of time—more timeless or against time—than Warhol originally planned, and what started as a modernist novel became a postmodernist one. Warhol taped Ondine's life, whenever he could get it, in all its discontinuous and disjointed glory, or gory, as the wit Dorothy Dean—DoDo in the book—might have put it. He abandoned his original idea, *a*'s purity. But the words "pure" and "purity" appear often.

9. One of the typists was said to have said of the book, "It's worse than Henry Miller." Dirtier, she meant. It's certainly more complex and difficult to read in all senses than Miller. *a* sometimes falls into unintelligibility, into illegibility. When Warhol held a tape recorder up to life, the result was streams of consciousness, many narratives intruding upon and interrupting one another, phrases and anecdotes, wordplay (there's none in Miller), incoherence, coherence, poetry, puns, witticisms (I love Ondine's remark that "charity begins alone"), documentary, bits of all of these. It's not an easy read. None of his work is.

10. *a* challenges reading. How do you read it? Sometimes I heard it, sometimes I thought it was radio, not TV or movies, I didn't see it.

Though I checked Victor Bockris' geographical notes at the back of the book, I couldn't find "place." I tried to stay with Ondine, but when he became very high, what happened to me, the reader? It was a relentlessly strange reading event. *a* felt cerebral and became claustrophobic, airless. It's a book with no space and in which space is a context, an area of contest, in which space is psychological territory that's fought over. The space at the Factory, for instance, was fraught: there were territorial skirmishes, fights for primacy—over who Ondine wants in or out, what the Factory rules were and should be—and all of this is discussed in *a*. In one part, there were so many voices in one taxi at one time and so many interruptions, I began to think about the book as music, as a score. When I did that, I relaxed some, and reading it became less stressful.

II. *a: A Novel* challenges writers because Warhol's idea of what should be on the page allows for the chaos that writers are meant to control, to turn into art. *a* underlines how unlifelike most written dialogue and conversation is. Its most peculiar challenge is to the writerly conceit that writing just pours out of us, from our guts or our heads, without an enormous number of de facto decisions made even before what we're writing came to consciousness or to desire. In other words, we receive language for the page, because other pages have been written. *a: A Novel* wasn't written or conceived for the page in that sense.

The novel follows its protagonist, and in its way, and within Ondine's limits, remains faithful to its structural idea: time. Time's a constitutive element of narrative; it's material. Novelists use time the way filmmakers use cuts, or long shots, close-ups, etc. In *a* the reader is in real time, whatever that is, and every moment is precious or boring. Time and art in a sense are collapsed: Moments are precious or boring both to the reader and the story. Ondine could ask himself: What am I looking for tonight (and he does), what do I want, where do I want to go? (all narratives are journeys). The reader could ask: What am I reading for? What do I want to find?

Boredom tells us something about life's relentless movement toward entropy and death. (Psychoanalyst D.W. Winnicott once commented that he knew when to take someone into therapy—when they bored him.)

12. Warhol wanted Ondine to say everything, to keep talking, to say whatever came into his mind. It's a psychoanalytic idea, and if that's the case, Warhol's the analyst, Ondine the analysand. Robert Polito suggested to me it's also about confessing and confession. Confession mixes with the psychoanalytic, and one reads *a* expecting revelation, which is common to both forms of talking. I read expecting or hoping for discoveries—and found some. Warhol reveals a few secrets, Ondine many, and all kinds of vulnerabilities and fears are displayed—eventually. It's the material that writers would have headed toward more quickly; writers would have edited away most of the other material. But it's not cut out in *a*, it is *a*—the unedited relates powerfully to confession, to psychoanalysis, to not leaving anything out, accepting everything. To me, Warhol's lust for the unedited is the most resonant and mysterious aspect of his work.

13. In another way of looking at *a*, along the lines of Stevens' "13 Ways of Looking at a Blackbird," Warhol's the queer-listening priest, Ondine the queer-talking Pope. An unexpected, moving moment occurred when Ondine said to the Sugar Plum Fairy, Joe Campbell: "You may think I'm not searching, and He—Drella—may think I'm not searching, but I'm searching. Which one of us, who isn't searching, for God?" Joe Campbell was a formidable interloctutor—no wonder Dorothy Dean was in love with him—and induced Warhol and Ondine into making some of their most revelatory statements.

Pope Ondine was searching for God. With this revelation, suddenly his desire to get high shifted into a different gear. In *a* he spoke over and again about beauty and the beautiful, and so, in a way, his quest, his journey, was for the illusory sublime—some kind of state of grace. Taking drugs and listening to opera—especially to Maria Callas—were his ticket to God.

14. Since reason is retrospective, it makes sense that reading *a* as a score, as music, loosened me to its idiosyncratic rhythms. Opera is the soundtrack, the background music, to this book. The opera might be *Tosca*, because of its aria, "Vissi D'Arte." "I lived for art, I lived for love," Callas sings. *a: A Novel* is a record of a life living for art, being recorded for the love of art.

15. Superstars like Edie or Ondine transformed themselves into what they thought was sublime. They were antiheroes performing a mostly unscripted high-wire act. Warhol believed in them, as self-creations, believed in their fictiveness; his belief acknowl-

edged their desires and the power of fiction itself, the reality of fantasy and illusion—and also contradiction, one of fiction's difficult truths.

Another is verisimilitude, likelihood, a similarity to reality. A likely story resembles reality. It may use make-believe to arrive there. His superstars are likely stories, resemblances close enough or odd enough to question stars and stardom, actors and acting. They live inside a narrative that doesn't stop when the film does. Serial, cinematic images, they perform their antiheroics again and again. Their will to be matters, their will to be there matters, and on Warhol's screen, their psychic realities matter most.

16a. In a Warholian world, authenticity is ironic, even a joke, and essences are funnier. Actual histories, biographies, and sometimes bodies were left behind and new ones manufactured in the Factory. Warhol's superstars could march in a parade for those who want to be switched at birth.

16b. The authority or authenticity of any fiction resides in the ability to make others suspend disbelief.

17. Warhol's art questioned what art was, what was expected to hang on a wall, and the same is true of *a: A Novel*. It asks: What do we expect in novels, how should they be written, why do we expect them to conform to certain rules? Whose rules? Factory rules? Recently back in print, *a: A Novel* may be responded to, less vehemently now, the way everything Warhol did in the 60s was—as garbage or genius. Or it will be ignored and its perplexing, vital questions never considered seriously. This novel—and Warhol's

work generally—doesn't provide a walkway down the middle. It's unorthodox, a walk on the wild side.

18. "The last words are Andy Warhol"—he was the last word, maybe, on the 20th century. Though think what he would have done on the Internet. (Is *a: A Novel* the precursor to the Internet novel?)

But are words important to Warhol? I don't know. Talk was. Is talk cheap? He was both a spendthrift and thrifty, even cheap. He surrounded himself with articulate, talkative people—with wits like Fred Hughes, Ondine, Viva—but he was stingy with his words. He often pretended to do a dumb show and often had others speak for him.

19. The last words are Andy Warhol unedited. Warhol started *Interview* magazine and insisted upon publishing unedited transcripts. He wrote an unedited novel. He didn't want to edit his films in the usual sense. Unedited versions came closer to what he wanted, but I'm not sure what that was. He wanted to keep his hands off, or to hide behind the density, opaqueness, of the material, or to let the idea do its work. He wanted to be inclusive, democratic. (After all, he wanted to name Pop Art Common Art.) He wanted something he could never imagine to happen, something he couldn't fathom to occur, and he wanted to be there when it did, to see it or hear it.

Or he wanted the unedited in the way—sort of the inverse way—that John Cage wanted silence. How do we know what to pay attention to; how do we know for ourselves what's important; how do we choose; how do we know if it's art; how do we decide what to see and to read, how can we tell unless everything is there to see and to read.

Being human offers homo sapiens variety, or some elasticity, in social life, though sociologists claim that people's personalities disappear with no one else around. Imagining this evacuation, I see a person alone in a self-chosen shelter, motionless on a chair, like a houseplant with prehensile thumbs.

Diane Sawyer, an unctuous American TV news anchor, once asked a mob assassin: "But haven't you ever thought, 'How can I do this? Who am I?'" The man looked at her with incredulity, then said: "I'm a gangster." Now, it's true that people (a.k.a. human beings) named themselves human and also defined humanity, but this tautological affair entails neuroses: Do we have a natural state? To say there isn't one doesn't quell anxiety, and "just act natural" and "be yourself" remain resilient punch lines to the shaggy-dog story called existence. There are instincts and drives, the basics from which Sigmund Freud theorized—but, oh, the complex array of acts that might satisfy these!

The bandwidth of human behavior includes self-image recognition and cerebration, prized differences from other animals (both premises are currently under investigation). With bigger brains, people have concocted notions about self-reflection and self-awareness, which allowed for "I think; therefore, I am." Not "I think what; therefore, I am what?" One would have thought that might matter.

Human beings have, like other animals, sexual and excretory organs that either share the same orifice or sit near enough to confuse identification by children. In evolutionary terms, apparently, there have been no great improvements. Also, shit still stinks, which, given the horrors humans commit, seems appropriate.

Dominique Laporte's *History of Shit* (1978) narrated the lengths to which people have gone to cover up the smell. But the body finds its way, discharging ugly odors, keeping humans close to their "uncivilized" ancestors. Human violence keeps people as close, maybe closer; it too has likely never changed, only the tools. But violence can't be covered up with perfume. In part, theories about essence and construction, nature vs. nurture, address, directly and indirectly, motives for aggression and cruelty, ethical behavior—or its lack—and the power of the irrational in the human animal.

In the 1950s, American ethnomethodologists Erving Goffman, Harvey Saks and Harold Garfinkel examined tiny units of social life, such as conversation among friends. Seemingly meaningless conventions screamed disaster if not followed: no "hello" back to a friend jeopardizes the relationship. Little miscues caused rips in society's seams. They studied gender, declaring masculinity and femininity performances in need of consistent routines, since people surveilled others for lapses that endangered identity but worse any hope for a life without torment.

Humans act differently in wars, in crowds; they act differently if they think nobody's watching. Punishments and limits—prohibitions on murder, incest, cannibalism—mostly keep people in line, otherwise, humans would be no better than animals, humans like to claim. But all mammals teach their kind and follow rules; they form societies often less violent than ours. Apes, chimps, elephants—the mothers commit years to training their offspring. Wolves, male and female, are ecstatic at the birth of a cub; all guard their young. So, that's no insult: We do behave like animals.

At parties I observe people acting much like dogs, except for sniffing rear ends, which is generally done in private.

"Acting like a human" is a matter of opinion, too. "Did I do the right thing?" can translate into "did I act right?" Some people act better than others; even when being honest, some people aren't convincing. Yet con artists are great at appearing sincere. Being honest or "yourself" isn't necessarily a "natural" state, since the human capacity to dissimulate must always have been necessary for species survival.

I admit to wonder and consternation when people bemoan the loss of authenticity in art, in identity, in life. Andy Warhol is regularly blamed for its supposed absence. He's blamed for everything. I don't know what pure state, unmediated existence, or moment in history to which people can or should return. Homo sapiens call themselves makers and doers, and they never leave well enough alone.

Some people are actual actors. Theater has been around a long time, because it serves several purposes. For one, people can watch others being human, portraying emotions and actions, their consequences and vicissitudes. Which brings me to Ryan Gosling in the film *Blue Valentine* (2010). Gosling embodies an unusually sensitive human to a degree I find unnerving.

He plays the husband in this anti-romance romance—a so-called regular American guy, but one I had never seen on screen or stage. Not a rebel like James Dean or Marlon Brando, standard-bearers of "acting real." No, Gosling's character is content to love his wife passionately, to adore and care for their child; he is ambitionless, happy to have a lame job. This life is enough for him, and he believes it should be for his wife.

Gosling's character might or might not exist offscreen. Still, an artifact, a movie, has proffered a novel image for Americans raised on Horatio Alger and other long-running constructions. In *Blue Valentine*, Ryan Gosling enacts a "real human being" better than most human beings do. I might one day meet such a person. Probably not Mr. Gosling, who would, most likely, not live up to my expectations.

B is for the Bowleses

Nothing is Lost or Found: Desperately Seeking Paul and Jane Bowles

I once read: "All journeys have destinations of which the traveler is unaware." The beginnings of journeys and narratives can be as surprising as their secret destinations. They can start as mysteriously as they end, they can start before one thinks. I was living in Amsterdam in 1972 when I was given a Valentine's Day gift, an anthology entitled *Americans Abroad*. It had been published in The Hague in 1932, in English, and was an out-of-print and rare book. It included well-known American expatriate writers—Stein, Pound, Eliot—less well-known ones—Harry and Caresse Crosby—and many unknowns. The unknowns dominated, the way they usually do. Immediately, I wanted to edit a new one, to represent American writers now, or then. Some months later, I was introduced to an editor who had a novelty imprint at a large Dutch publishing house. He liked the idea. He also liked enormously obese women and had posters of them, nude, hidden in his office. After he got to know me a little, he showed them to me. I remember this very well and the fact that on signing the contract he paid me an advance of fifteen hundred guilders.

I think 1971 was the year I read Paul Bowles' *The Sheltering Sky* and Jane Bowles' *Two Serious Ladies*. I knew that Jane Bowles was ill, in a Spanish hospital, unable to speak her name, and I also knew that Paul Bowles was installed in Tangier and had been since the

1940s. To me, he was the preeminent American abroad (the term is aptly dated), and I was determined to have him in the book.

Writing a letter to Paul Bowles was alarming, and I worked on it for a week. After deliberating, in a circuitous and paranoid way, I decided not to reveal that I was female. It was the era of William Burroughs's vicious or satiric retort to feminism, *The Job*. Burroughs and Bowles were friends; I considered, in a convoluted way, that even though Paul Bowles was married to Jane Bowles, if he was in any way like some of his friends, or affected by their mean-spiritedness, he might now hate women and not want to be in a book edited by one. This might not be true at all—and if it were, why would I want him in the book? But I was in Amsterdam, smoking hash. I concocted a sexless letter, signed it Lynne Merrill Tillman (Lynne is also a man's name; Merrill is my mother's maiden name) and mailed it.

Bowles quickly replied that he'd be happy to be in the anthology. I'd asked for original material; he wrote that he'd send me some, and did. After another letter or two—I've kept all of his letters—I received one in which he inquired if I were a man or a woman, and how he should address me—Miss, Mrs. or Mr.? Otherwise he was "obliged to use Dear Lynne Merrill Tillman." I wrote that I was female, in a letter I hope is lost, and he thanked me in his next letter for setting him straight.

The anthology's publication date kept being postponed, and everything Bowles had given me appeared elsewhere. Finally he wrote that he had no more new or unpublished work to contribute except some poems he'd written in the late 1920s or early 1930s, and, he said, they weren't very good. I wrote that they'd be included even if they weren't very good, because I had to have him in the book. But, I asked, didn't he have anything else, maybe some letters he'd written?

Bowles sent two letters he wrote his mother when he first went to Europe in 1931 with composer Aaron Copland. One told the hilariously anxious tale of his and Copland's nearly missing a boat from Spain to Morocco. The other was written from the south of France, where he was visiting Gertrude Stein and Alice B. Toklas for the first time. I was overwhelmed by my good luck.

Encouraged by our friendly, frequent correspondence—it was now 1976 or 1977 and I was in New York—I asked him for some writing from Jane Bowles. Requesting her work was even harder than asking for his. She was dying when I began the project, and I didn't feel comfortable asking him for her work then or right after she'd died. I didn't want Paul to feel taken advantage of. I thought her death must have been so painful for him that even mentioning her name would upset him. I hesitated a long time. I didn't appreciate then that people usually don't want the people they love to be forgotten. Jane Bowles is often and usually forgotten.

I wanted her desperately. Her novel, *Two Serious Ladies,* was a revelation—a work of genius, unique, subversive. These terms are overused, and usually misused, but are true of this audacious, brilliantly written novel, this masquerade, comedy, tragedy, with its anarchic, singular views of sexuality, marriage, femininity, masculinity, American culture, exoticism. Jane Bowles ignored the worn lines between conscious and unconscious life; she beggared the realist novel with writing indifferent to prosaic notions of reality. Her dialogue is the most particular and idiosyncratic in American literature, as peculiar and condensed as speech in jokes and dreams. I loved and respected Paul Bowles's *The Sheltering Sky*, "He of the Assembly," and "Pages from Cold Point." But Jane Bowles's novel shifted the ground for me—she made the world of writing move. Move over and sigh.

Paul Bowles sent two fragments from a notebook of hers, just a few paragraphs. I was thrilled. With the Bowleses' contributions, I thought, the anthology had a reason to exist. But it was abandoned by its first publisher (the novelty imprint was dissolved) and then again, in about 1980, by its second, a friend who was a small press publisher. One of Jane Bowles's paragraphs was later quoted in Millicent Dillon's excellent biography of her, *A Little Original Sin*, but the other—about getting married and loneliness—has still not been published. Of it Paul Bowles wrote, "I find it a complete mystery, myself."

Our correspondence continued. We wrote about domestic life—collapsing roofs—and dreams we had. He typed his letters on white, crinkly airmail paper. His signature, in black pen, was neat and without any flourishes. I have a couple of letters on green airmail paper written entirely in his legible hand. In one he wrote: "Place seems to have become unimportant."

The anthology receded from consciousness, and I threw myself into writing and co-directing an independent feature film called *Committed*. It was released in 1984, and I was, too, to finish writing *Haunted Houses*, my first novel, which was published in 1987. On its back cover was a quote from the late Kathy Acker that began: "Lynne Tillman, daughter of Jane Bowles." Jane Bowles never had any children, and it didn't occur to me that when the book came out people would think Jane Bowles was my mother. But an acquaintance stopped me on St. Marks Place and said, "I thought your mother was in Florida." One reviewer wrote that "the author mentioned her mother, Jane Bowles," in the novel, and it was a problem. Acker plagiarized texts, wrote characters who invented multiple identities, invoked "her" mother and father, and no one knew what was fact or fiction. It was ironically appropriate that she inadvertently bestowed a legend upon me, a fictitious literary genealogy. On bad days I imagined it was the best thing about me.

I sent my novel to Paul Bowles, hoping he wouldn't be bothered by the quotation about Jane Bowles and me. He read the book, which was very generous of him, more generous than I recognized then. He even liked it. He said it reminded him of a Russian novel, because he confused the protagonists. He didn't mention the quote, and this lack—and the existence of the quote itself—became another layer in the strange and stealthy background of my journey to him. Even his allusion to a Russian novel seemed part of the confusion of character and characters that preceded me and ensued when I finally arrived in Tangier in August 1987.

I wanted to talk with Bowles in person, because I hoped to make a film of *Two Serious Ladies*. It would be my homage to Jane Bowles, and maybe it would bring attention to her work. I could picture the book as a film, its bizarre scenes happily haunted by the ghost of director Preston Sturges, its eccentric dialogue delivered by actors like Lily Tomlin (she'd play Miss Goering, one of the two serious ladies). Bowles thought the film rights had been sold years ago, but he couldn't remember to whom. I found the

41

person I was told was Jane Bowles's agent, who would presumably know. And so starts a terrible story, one I can tell in expurgated form only, to protect others and also myself from further misunderstanding and even the law.

The agent knew nothing about the rights and actually didn't have them, yet involved me in discussions over four months about my buying them. In my first visit I explained that it would be a very low-budget film, and in the last the agent announced: I've taken a look at the story, and it is a little longer than I thought it was. Actually, it's longer than her other stories. So I'll have to ask you for one hundred thousand dollars. Crushed, I left the office.

I was informed by my agent, after she studied the novel's copyright notice, that the book might be in the public domain. I asked the Library of Congress to do a copyright check, in fact three, and each time the book turned up in the public domain. Still unconvinced, I traveled to Washington, D.C., to that great house of copyrights, where I was brought to a room the size of a football field and shown the file cabinet that held the card for Jane Bowles's only novel. The copyright had not been renewed by her publisher in 1973—the year she died. They'd forgotten. The book was like Shakespeare, the library told me.

I wrote the script and, with the Library's authorization, received two grants to make the movie. I was slowly moving forward when one day I received a call from a lawyer who told me his client owned the rights, that the book was not in the public domain in Europe, and that they would stop me from showing the film. Confused, I hired a lawyer, and the sorry story continued.

I met Buffie Johnson, a painter friend of the Bowleses, and visited her in her apartment in SoHo. She offered to introduce me to Paul in Tangier, where she summered. Though I didn't need an introduction—everyone drops in on him in the afternoon and we'd been corresponding for years—I accepted her offer gratefully, eagerly. Buffie had had an affair with Jane Bowles in the 1940s. Jane dropped her, she said, because Jane liked older women, and she and Jane were the same age. Buffie told me that in those days homosexuals married each other and that Jewish people, like Jane, kept their religion quiet. After I commented that Mrs. Copperfield, in *Two Serious Ladies*, could have been code for Mrs. Goldberg, Buffie continued, in a lower register, that before the war everyone was a little anti-Semitic.

A disturbing event happened just weeks before I left for Tangier. I received a copy of a letter Jane Bowles's agent had sent Paul Bowles. It warned of my imminent arrival, that I was trying to steal Jane Bowles's work, that I was, in short, a thoroughly bad character. The letter was meant to deter me, I suppose. But how did the agent know I was going to Tangier? What network was I in, who had betrayed me? All along I'd been writing to Bowles about my dealings with the agent and the Library of Congress, detailing my mostly futile attempts at getting to the bottom of things, where truth supposedly resides. I felt I had nothing to hide. Obviously, I was naive. If I make any money from the film, I wrote him, I'd be happy to give you half. He had not profited from the recent sale of the rights, and the idea that I was in this for the money was grotesquely amusing.

The situation had become byzantine. Everything connected closely to Paul Bowles, I would discover, was and wouldn't be a surprise to him. He knew much worse characters, perhaps, than I could ever be or aspire to—Cherifa, for instance, Jane's Moroccan lover. She was rumored to have poisoned Jane. I didn't believe this and hoped Paul Bowles didn't, either, just as I hoped he wouldn't believe I was the mercenary, flawed character the agent described. David Hofstra, a musician and the man I live with, accompanied me to Tangier. We took a room in the famous—now defunct— Hotel Ville de France. Matisse had stayed there and painted the view out of his hotel window. David and I went immediately to see Buffie. She was waiting for us in the apartment Jane Bowles had lived in years before, just above Paul's. (The Bowleses kept separate apartments.) Then, like a security guard, Buffie escorted us to Paul's apartment, and walking down the stairs, my breathing became stuck in me or suspended. My life was about to change or stay shockingly the same.

We knocked, the door opened, we entered and were introduced to Bowles. He was, he said, about to go to the beach. Would we come back tomorrow afternoon? I handed him the script, we left and I breathed. I didn't know what he was wearing or even what he looked like. If I had an image of him, it wasn't contested by the reality of seeing him. I hadn't seen him. He might be running away from me, I thought, but when he was there the next day, I decided he wasn't. Maybe just stalling for time. (Later I was told that days before, another writer had rushed from London to Tangier, to advise him not to sell the rights. But did he have them to sell?)

He liked the script, Bowles told me; it was faithful to the book. But, he said firmly, I can't help you. My lawyer had asked the other lawyer for evidence, a document authenticating ownership of the rights. None was ever produced. My lawyer believed Paul Bowles could exercise his rights as the inheritor of Jane Bowles's estate, if he wanted. Yet what Bowles had once written me spun another cautionary literary tale. A publisher had gone to Spain to see Jane in the hospital. The publisher asked Paul to leave the hospital room, so he could be alone with her, and when the publisher emerged, he held a piece of paper in his hand. The publisher had gotten Jane to sign something, when she didn't know what she was signing. On this scrap of paper, the film rights to the book rested. That was the story. Bowles never contested the publisher's claim. He lived in Tangier, it was explained to me, precisely because he didn't want to become involved in ordinary and tawdry matters like fights over rights.

Now, a little numb or stunned, with the film out of the way, or dead, I could try to have a good time. There I was, sitting with Paul Bowles in his darkened living room, drinking tea served by the taciturn Mohammed Mrabet, Bowles's companion. I'd read Mrabet's stories, which Bowles had taped and written down. They were published in Mrabet's name, but bore the mark of Bowles's spare, elegant style. Mrabet, I found out later, had once asserted that Bowles was merely his typist.

I greedily listened to Bowles's stories about Jane and himself. In 1943, during the war, when Jane was living in New England with her lover, Helvetia, he told us, he was in Mexico. He was still writing music and needed one of his instruments—a drum. But he couldn't remember where it was. He wrote Jane and asked if it was in Staten Island, or with her in New England, or in their apartment in New York? There was some urgency to his request, and

Jane Bowles sent a telegram in return: Drum not in basement, not on Staten Island, not in New York. Drum can't be found. The day after, the doorbell rang at Jane's residence. It was the FBI.

> FBI: Your husband was in Morocco in the spring of 1942?
> Jane: Yes.
> FBI: And in South America in the fall of that year?
> Jane: Yes.
> FBI: He's in Mexico now?
> Jane: Yes.
> FBI: Why does he travel so much?
> Jane: I guess he's restless.

By now Helvetia, at Jane's request, was burning some of their papers in the fireplace, though it was the summer. But after questioning her a little longer, the FBI was mollified. It turned out that there was a colonel in the army named Drum, and her telegram had been intercepted—all telegrams were read during the war. The FBI thought they might have uncovered an underground group plotting to assassinate Colonel Drum.

In Bowles's darkened living room, above the couch, was a single bookshelf. On it were all of Jane Bowles's books, all the editions, in all the languages into which they'd been translated. The shelf was a shrine to her, and I felt her presence in his life and in the room through her books. I plucked up the courage to question him about her novel. Why had Jane Bowles named one of the serious ladies Miss Goering? Bowles looked amused and said: That was Jane's little joke.

I remember saying, tentatively: I think I've got an idea for another novel. Bowles nonchalantly said, I haven't had an idea in twenty years.

We intended to take him to dinner but didn't. We visited him three times and met him on the street once. We took photographs of him alone, with Buffie, and of Buffie alone. David took some of me and them. Bowles didn't like being photographed and turned wooden. I made him laugh in one and that shot came out blurred. It was too bad. He looked very handsome laughing.

Paul Bowles never mentioned Kathy Acker's quote. I shouldn't have been surprised. Some years before I'd mailed him a story in which I'd quoted a line from his autobiography, *Without Stopping*. He wrote a long letter about it and questioned me on an interesting point of grammar. He never mentioned my tribute to him. His reserve, discretion or secretiveness was impressive, intimidating,or disturbing.

It's unsettling and strange rendering this account and calling up faulty memory to describe my pilgrimage, if that's what it was, to him and the spirit of Jane Bowles. I was as close to her as I'd ever be. Her presence was almost palpable—I wanted her to be there—and always evanescent, like life itself. Even stranger was the sensation I had when I was with Paul. Sometimes I felt I was his daughter, as if that quote had created a symbolic link between us, even a blood tie, in an extraordinary demonstration of the power of fiction. It was a feeling, too, that I got, after my father died, around older men I liked who were difficult to know, the way my father was. I admired Bowles's writing, its inscrutability, lack of apology and explanation, its dark humor, reserve, mystery. He had all of this, too. I didn't know him, I liked him, I didn't know what he thought of me. We laughed together, and I can like or feel familiar around anyone who's funny.

I gave up the film, returned one of the grants, was allowed to keep the other and use it toward writing the novel I'd mentioned to Bowles. It was called *Motion Sickness*, which now seems an appropriate title for the experience of writing this weird history of failure and desire. *Two Serious Ladies* has still not been made into a film.

After visiting Bowles, I began my letters "Dear Paul B." I sent him and Buffie copies of the photographs we'd taken, and he wrote a postcard thanking me. It ended, "Your visit to Tangier was very short, unfortunately. Another time, perhaps?" I haven't returned, but I did fly to Atlanta in 1995 to visit him when he came to the States for an operation. It was his first visit since 1968. I also saw him briefly at Lincoln Center for a concert of his music. These last years he's been ill and doesn't answer most letters. I treasure the ones I have.

—August 1999

Paul Bowles died on November 18, 1999, at the age of 88.

A young American was intent on becoming a writer, and in the spirit of the Lost Generation and earlier American writers, believed that living in Europe, or out of America, as expatriate or alien, was what she needed to free herself or lose herself, and write.

In 1972, I was living in Amsterdam, and decided to edit an anthology of American writers abroad. Paul Bowles reigned as the preeminent American abroad. I told my Dutch publisher that his presence in the book was essential, and assured him that Bowles would definitely be in it. All bravado. I was a complete unknown. Anxiously, I wrote a letter to Paul Bowles, requesting his important participation. Shockingly fast, he wrote back, Yes.

I can't remember what Bowles first sent me. But soon the book's publication was delayed, and whatever piece it was, he had given it to someone else. I quickly and humbly asked for another piece; he amiably sent one along. I really didn't know what I was demanding of such a distinguished, sought-after writer. I knew nothing, I was a kid, and all my ideas about being an editor came from reading literary histories and writers' biographies. I had requested unpublished material from everyone. The long delays continued, and every piece Bowles sent me was eventually published somewhere else.

By the third or fourth delay, and subsequent go-rounds with Bowles and a few other writers, I had returned to America, a prodigal daughter home, because, for one thing, hearing English spoken by Dutch and English people didn't foster my American writing. By now, the correspondence between Bowles and me had grown friendly: we wrote anecdotes to each other, even reported a few dreams, and discussed much more than the putative anthology.

After the first publisher reneged—the novelty division was dissolved—a second publisher came forward to save the book, a friend with a small Dutch press who promised to bring the anthology out, fast. He didn't. I'm not sure how much time passed, but once again I needed to ask Bowles for new writing. Now he had no unpublished work at all, nothing to give; he was very sorry. Desperate, I wrote: Don't you have anything? I don't care what it is. Bowles kindly mailed a few poems he'd written in the early 1930s, noting that they weren't very good, but I could use them if I wanted. He didn't have anything else. Again, he was very sorry.

It never occurred to me that he might have been, with excellent reason, courteously bailing out of my long-sinking enterprise. But I was young, naive, hopeful, and these traits, mixed with others, allowed me not only to ignore that possibility but also to agree with his negative assessment of his poems. Yes, they're not very good, I wrote him. Of course I'll publish them anyway. You must be in the anthology. But, I pleaded, don't you have anything else? How about letters you wrote home from Europe?

Not long after, an airmail letter arrived, on onionskin as ever, but thicker than the one page he usually sent. He, or a helper, had typed copies of two letters he had written his mother on his very first trip to Europe. He had traveled there with composer Aaron

Copland; Copland had been his music teacher, then a close friend. In one letter Bowles tells the hilarious tale of their sailing to Tangier. The second was written after he and Copland had settled in Tangier, about their travails with their piano, and also about Gertrude Stein and Alice B. Toklas, who were their friends. Use the letters if you want, Bowles wrote. I read them over and over, delighted with each line, and also by glimpsing his intimate and sympathetic relationship with his mother; I knew he despised his father. (In his autobiography, Bowles admitted to wanting to kill him.) Now it was worth it, every delay, everything—the letters were jewels.

Over those years, the anthology had gone through many transformations. Mostly I added people: it was hard for me to say no to friends, even those who weren't writers. When the second Dutch publisher stopped answering my letters, I finally gave up, though the book had been designed, typeset, and was actually on boards. I knew it would never be published. Curiously, I took this failure in stride, seven or eight years of work and waiting, making promises and breaking them. By then I was doing other things, living in New York and writing. Maybe more significant, the anthology had come to feel unnecessary to me, a leftover from an existence I no longer had or wanted. I'd done it, and was done with my romance of the American abroad—along with the rest of the world. Being in Europe had helped me unlearn some of what I'd been taught or unconsciously believed. Any writer knows that what's left out is as essential, if not more so, than what's there. Unlearning works that way. I unlearned the model of being an editor like Ezra Pound with T.S. Eliot, the unconscious belief that

America was the center of the world, and that honesty meant saying what I thought and always being direct. (The Dutch and the English, former competitors for world dominance, taught me the wisdom of waiting as well as withholding.) As to new lessons: I learned I could be miserable anywhere in the world. I learned I really was an American.

Bowles and I continued corresponding, hardly ever mentioning the ill-fated anthology. He had suffered much worse fates than the ups and downs of publication, of course, specifically, the slow, sad decline of Jane Bowles and her death in 1972. In some ways I think he was forever amused by something invisible buzzing around him, and that something kept him going. Maybe he was amused just to be alive.

I wanted to meet him and visited Tangier in 1987. There was another motive: I'd written a script and hoped to direct a film of Jane Bowles' novel, *Two Serious Ladies*, but even if there wasn't that desire and wish for his blessing, I would have traveled to Morocco to meet him one day.

Meeting him wasn't anticlimactic, because I'd heard one couldn't really know him. I don't think I had unusual expectations, but I felt anxious, so maybe I did. In a way I believed I knew him from his letters, a writer writing; and in the flesh, he was the person who wrote those funny, smart, ironic letters. He spoke like his letters. His apartment was kept dark, shades drawn; Mohammed Mrabet stood in the shadows, appearing only to serve tea, and Paul's writing could be exquisitely cruel and dark. But he had a sunny smile and liked to tell stories and laugh.

I saw Bowles twice more. First, in Atlanta, Georgia, in the spring of 1994, when he traveled there for a heart operation. A number of us, devotees, acolytes, friends, acquaintances, writers, artists—I didn't know what scale he weighed me on or how to measure myself—flew down for a party in his honor. I shared a hotel room with Cherie Nutting, a photographer and the manager of her Moroccan husband's joujouka band. (They later divorced but she still manages the band.) She and Paul were close, like father and daughter, I imagined; they spent a lot of time together in Tangier.

Thirty or forty people gathered in Atlanta at the home of Virginia Spencer Carr. Carr was writing Bowles' biography (it was published in 2004), and had also arranged for Paul's heart operation. The party was on a Saturday night, some days before it. All night Paul sat in a comfortable club chair, and people came by to greet and talk to him. They sat on the floor, pulled up a chair, or stood above him. He seemed tired and fragile, but he was gracious and pleasant to everyone, looking at us from under hooded eyes. He was probably overwhelmed by the fuss, with these people he knew well, or barely, around him all at once. The last time he'd been to the States, he told me, was 1968.

Paul usually fretted about the mail's getting through from Morocco. He often wrote that he was paranoid about it. He would double-check that I'd received something he mailed. Now he asked, "Did you get the postcard I sent about *Cast in Doubt?*" This was the morning after the party, or the early evening before it; we were in front of Virgina Carr's house. I remember it was light out, a late or early sunlight. "No, I didn't get it," I said. (*Cast in Doubt* was my third novel.) "Oh, too bad," he said. Then he said something I heard but also didn't quite hear, his words at the edge of audibility. A slim, handsome Moroccan man pushing his wheelchair—not Mohammed Mrabet, happily—pushed him on, while Paul continued talking. I think he said he liked it, and something else, or I hope he said that, but I didn't feel I could ask him again, as if that would be craven. Now I'm sorry I didn't.

The operation was a success. It gave Paul five more years. I still wonder why I flew down to say hello or even goodbye to Paul. In retrospect I find my behavior mysterious. I did feel an emotional or literary attachment to him, a man who was detached and puzzling, but more significant to me as a younger writer, I had read his books, admired them and we had formed some kind of relationship. My greater attachment was to Jane Bowles, and he also represented her to me.

The third and last time I saw Paul was in 1995; he was in New York for a concert of his music at Lincoln Center. He had started out as a composer and begun writing fiction after Jane Bowles' brilliant, sui generis and only novel, *Two Serious Ladies*, appeared in 1943. Everyone who thinks about their marriage also ponders how his novel, *The Sheltering Sky*, especially its very successful publication, affected Jane. Her novel was a succès d'estime; his drew wider acclaim. Jane Bowles never wrote another novel, and some blame him. I don't. There was nothing simple about either of them together or singly. And no one cause could ever explain her not finishing any writing after 1949.

For the concert—a night I won't forget, at least I believe I won't—my date was Charles Henri Ford, another sophisticated, elderly and former American abroad, a poet, artist and filmmaker. I watched Charles and Paul greet each other, Paul in his wheelchair, Charles bending down to talk to him. Both must have been somewhat stunned, I thought, but both were elegant, world-weary men, casual about the moment and unexpected events. "I haven't seen Paul in fifty years," Charles told me as we walked to our seats. He said it blithely, without any importance, and I wondered if, some night, I might experience something similar.

Paul Bowles died in 1999, Charles Henri Ford in 2002. Their lives encompassed and contributed to the twentieth century, what some once called The American Century. They also lived long enough to see the end of that.

C is for Character

Cut Up Life

Dear Poet
Charles Henri Ford
Did the lake overturn
When Narcissus fell in
Become opaque
A mad lake—
Oh poet dear
Please make it clear
And let it recover
The reflected image
Of that foolish lover—
Amazedly

Florine Stettheimer

Charles Henri (né Henry) Ford made his entrance on February 10, 1908, in Hazlehurst, Mississippi, to Gertrude Cato and Charles Lloyd Ford. It was his idea to change the spelling of Henry to Henri. "I was tired of being asked if I was related to Henry Ford," he says, "and a young girl wrote me on lavender paper and in red ink and made a mistake that I liked so I kept it."

Ford's parents, and his father's brother's, owned hotels in various small cities in Mississippi and Texas—Ford was born in a hotel that burned down soon after—and his early life was peripatetic. His mother, whom he compares in his diary with Hamlet's mother, Gertrude, was an artist herself and seems to have been a dramatic, beautiful and compelling character. This primary love led the way to Ford's two great loves—Djuna Barnes and Pavel (Pavlik) Tchelitchew.

All spoken remarks are Charles Henri Ford's to the author in two recent conversations. All other quoted material is from *Water from a Bucket*, unless a source is cited.

Ford met Barnes in New York in 1929, before he left for Paris in 1931, and lived with her in Morocco, where he typed the manuscript of her novel *Nightwood*. "She couldn't spell," he says. His most enduring relationship was with Russian painter Pavlik Tchelitchew. They lived together for 23 years. Ford and Tchelitchew met in Paris, in 1933, at an opening, when Ford was 24 and Tchelitchew, 35. Of the meeting Ford notes in his diary that he wrote Parker Tyler at the time, "I've found a genius." In a powerful way, the diary circles around and is about Pavlik, "his great heart," and their complicated love and long relationship.

His younger sister, Ruth Ford—the diary's "Sister"—was a well-known actor. She debuted in Orson Welles' Mercury Theater production of *The Shoemaker's Holiday* in 1938; performed in plays by Tennessee Williams; had a lead in Jean-Paul Sartre's *No Exit* (translated by Paul Bowles); and received a nomination from the London Drama Critics, in 1957, for her performance as Temple Drake in *Requiem for a Nun*, which she had adapted into a play with William Faulkner. Ruth Ford was married to Hollywood actor Zachary Scott, who died in 1965, and lives in the Dakota, four floors below her older brother.

I loved the Blues before I loved the Poem. Somehow the two loves were from the same source, so it was natural I called my poetry review Blues.

Precocious and ambitious, the young poet launched *Blues,* The Magazine of New Rhythms, in 1929. William Carlos Williams and Eugene Jolas were two of its contributing editors and Kathleen Tankersley Young its associate editor. For nine issues, Ford solicited and published writing from Ezra Pound, Gertrude Stein, Kay Boyle, Harry Crosby, James Farrell, H.D., Kenneth Rexroth, Mark van Doren, Louis Zukofsky, Edouard Roditi, Erskine Caldwell. He was the first to publish Paul Bowles.

From Mississippi, Ford moved to New York, to write poetry and lead *la vie bohème* in Greenwich Village. Ford had published Parker Tyler, the poet and future film critic and writer, in *Blues* and was corresponding with him. They met in person in New York—"I could hardly see his face, he had so much makeup on," Ford says—and soon collaborated on writing *The Young and Evil.* Called by some the first gay novel, published in 1933, banned in the United States and England, it is—like Ford himself—unapologetic, unashamed, poetic, candid and determinedly free of conventions.

> *It's not doing the things one wants to do—even if considered a vice, like*
> *opium-taking—that makes one age, but doing things one doesn't want to do.*

A kind of Surrealist free verse, the uninhibited novel was influenced, in part, by Ford's mentor Gertrude Stein, who took him up when he was first in Paris. When Ford fell in love with Tchelitchew, Stein found less reason to see him; she and Tchelitchew had had one of those famous, furious partings of the way. But in *The Autobiography of Alice B. Toklas,* Stein wrote of Ford: "He is also honest which is also a pleasure."

Along with *The Young and Evil*, Ford is perhaps best known for *View*, the international art magazine he edited in New York, from 1940 to 1947. Europeans Marcel Duchamp, André Breton, Max Ernst—forced into exile during World War II—Americans Maya Deren, Meyer Schapiro, Joseph Cornell, Florine Stettheimer, Man Ray, Paul Bowles and many more found a home in *View's* pages and on its covers. Not coincidentally, Ford begins his diary a year after he stops *View* and ends it shortly after the death of Tchelitchew in 1957.

Since finishing the diary, Ford has produced or invented the "poem poster" (shown at the Ubu Gallery in New York in 2000); published many books of poetry, including a limited edition, unique collage book, *Spare Parts*, and *Out of the Labyrinth: Selected Poems* (City Lights, 1991); directed the feature-length movie *Johnny Minotaur* (shot in Crete, starring Allen Ginsberg among others) and exhibited his photographs, most recently with fellow Mississippian Allen Frame (at the Leslie Tonkomow Gallery in New York).

You have to enjoy what you're doing and do it every day.

Ford has made a habit of doing what he wants to do, and his life is dedicated, as much as anyone's can be, to poetry, art, and the pursuit of pleasure. He usually adheres to a self-imposed, rigorous routine, and now, just short of 93, he writes haiku poems and makes collages daily. When I visit him on a brilliant fall day, October 1, 2000, one of the day's haikus is on his disk:

Men too have a

> *change*

of life
didn't Marcel

> *Duchamp*

> *have it twice*

***

I first read Charles Henri Ford's diary in the late 1970s, and again in the late 1980s when I urged him to have it published. He didn't want to bother. He was writing poems, making collages and photographs; not one, as the reader will see, to look back with longing or regret.

Those were not the days. These are the days. My days are always these.

I find it pointless to have a nostalgia about the past.

I: "Would you like to be in Rome…where all the pretty boys are?"
Pavlik: "Don't turn the dagger in the wound."

Poetry, genius, love, fame, friendship, beauty, family, character, sex, psychology, youth, and Pavlik, always, are variously appetizers, entrees, or desserts on Ford's menu du jour et de la nuit. His diary is riveting. As it moves from theme to theme, the reader senses a life formed consciously in the present, one lived spontaneously, interrupted and interfered with by memory and the pressure of unconscious thoughts. The reader feels the moment's vitality and presence, and the sorrow at its loss, but not because Ford insists on it. Emotion—disappointment and sadness—is there in the way he writes the day, flying from an idea, sex act, or fantasy, to a line in a poem, a report on dinner talk, a death, an argument, to a question about aesthetics, a worry about Pavlik—then it's all gone, except the memory of it, what he's written down.

A passionate schoolboy who knew what he wanted—and got it. (In the pissoir.)

A shadow falls, a fragment of night; a day goes, a fragment of death. Life and the sun tomorrow.

Many beautiful machines—Tanguy painted. But the most beautiful machine is and always will be the human body.

His diary is beautiful and homely, an epic poem about the dailiness of art and life. It's filled with insights about himself, love, sex, his illusions, delusions; there's silliness, homages to his heroes—Isak Dinesen, for one—and acerbic or reverent considerations of his contemporaries. Tchelitchew comments that Jean Genet, whom Ford finds "solemn and humorless," is "un moraliste—comme Sade"; Ford refers, less perceptively, to "messes signed by Jackson Pollock." The diary is loaded with gossip about history's celebrated, with whom Ford has had lunch or met at an opening. When he introduces Djuna Barnes to Tennessee Williams at a party, she asks Williams, "How does it feel to be rich and famous?"

Diaries confirm that life is in the details, and in its passions, all of which Ford includes, all of which are inevitably subservient

to time. Ford's diary is profound not because it marks time passing or spent, but because it is imaginatively and definitively of its
time and in it.

I asked Parker (in a letter) if he thought posthumous fame is any fun and he
replied it might be to posterity.

Go back to music, rhythm, as Yeats did, for a renewal of inspiration in poetry.
"Go back" in the sense of renewal—

Pavlik's summary of how I spend my time: "fornication and fabrication."

Like histories, diaries are accounts of the past. Unlike histories,
they are not written retrospectively, and subjectivity is their central claim to truth. Faithful to the subjective, the diarist's words,
Ford's eyes and ears, conduct the reader through the world inhab-
its. The reader finds the way back as it was to Ford. His irrespon-
sibility, his understanding of the power of transience—in sex, art,
love—his appreciation of the ephemeral, and his desire to have it
all, anyway, for as long as he can, carry us with him.

Years of work, a burst of glory, and it's all over.

Up at six and found a feather in my bed, as though, while I was sleeping I'd
been a bird.

Pavlik told me—in 1933—that I had been sent to him because his mother died.

What is called history comes to us as a transcription of the evanescent. A radio announcer's excited play by play of the Tony Zale–Marcel Cerdan fight becomes a monologue written by a Surrealist. The now-famous 1948 *Life* photograph of poets at the Gotham Book Mart—Ford, the Sitwells, Marianne Moore, Tennessee Williams, Delmore Schwartz, W.H. Auden, Elizabeth Bishop, Stephen Spender, Randall Jarrell—was first, in the diary, an occasion for a gathering. The photograph documents the group, contributing to the historical record—these poets were there, those not, some are forgotten now.

Ford's commentary about the group offers another record, a personal view that instantly affects the august photograph. He complains that Gore Vidal is in it, that Vidal is not a poet, and the reader can see the tension the photograph does not image. And then there are Ford's musings about Christine Jorgensen, the G.I. who in 1953 underwent the first highly publicized man-to-woman sex change operation.

> *Why is everyone always foolish enough to think that a sexual partner will make life happy?*

> *I took a terrace walk and saw the most brilliant falling star. I always make the same wish: Love.*

A diary tells us what its author was thinking about then and how it was thought. It is different from a history, because it is an itinerary of lived attitudes, a catalogue of attitudes. Attitude is in the air we breathe, and we don't always think about what we take in and give out. Ford's ideas are his and not his, and, as a matter of history, the expression of attitudes allows a return to the past that so-called objective accounts can't. Ford lets us conspire with him, breathe with him.

A record of himself is all any man records.

Being jerked off—if done by the right person—leaves no regrets.

Characteristic of our age (Henry James' The Turn of the Screw a forerunner)—more and more interest in the perversity of children…to shock now, the child must be involved—Example in painting: Balthus, more shocking than Dali…The child is all.

The contemporary reader may be surprised by Ford's anxiety over the effects of masturbation—"I recover from self-abuse"—or disturbed or pleased by his ecstatic evocations and lust for teen-aged boys, by his openness about his desires generally. Maybe the only thing in life that doesn't change, apart from the certainty of death—though these days that seems to be changing—is desire. Only its articulations and the environment in which it is felt shift. Ford's freedom or constraints, his prejudices or lacks, gauge his moment and ours.

***

But I look too good to ruin: I wish my twin would come along and I'd kiss him.

I don't know how my character will come out in these notes and memories, but I think we usually are to others what we are to ourselves.

The literary diary is a strange form. Was it written to be read? Maybe. Probably. Is it self-conscious? Necessarily. Ford's diary was written to examine himself and others, and in a way, its self-consciousness is its raison d'étre. Preciousness is stripped from its self-consciousness by Ford's sardonic, unflinching self-criticism—he's regularly concerned with his character as well as Pavlik's. (The diary pulses, too, with the impact of psychoanalytic theory on contemporary thinking.) But Ford is unself-conscious about his devotion to the cause of aesthetics and the examined life. And is, in his fashion, devoted to love, writing a love story with its own deliberate ideas about heart.

No one will ever mean more to me—inspire me more—than Pavlik...

The fatal image: Vito's profile as he looked over the terrace yesterday. There it was and there's nothing one can do about it. I wasn't born to live alone.

Pavlik's great heart stopped beating at ten to eight (July 1957).

Ford's diary ends with questions. Does he love Vito? Does Vito love him? Anyway, what is love. Pavlik has died. Ford's days will change. His life has come to the reader in bits and pieces, a collage, or, like his poems, a cut up. It ends the same way.

"This ravaging sense of the shortness of life. . . ." (V.W). I don't have that. I sense, rather, that life will be long—too long.

Charles said something, on that brilliant fall day, about being fortunate or having had good fortune. I teased him about becoming soft. He said, I think a little sheepishly, "Well, it's the right time, isn't it?"

> I shall continue this document until the end of next year, then I vow to continue it no longer. It's a secret vice. Vices should be public.

Houses and people remind me of each other. Both have facades behind whose stone and brick, smiles and frowns, lie other, often hidden aspects. The Hughes house on Lexington Avenue is covered in wisteria. I'm told the massive vine blossoms purple for one week in the spring, and now its gnarly brown branches are naked, obscuring the house, insinuating mystery—it is winter, when nature is under attack by its own elements, stripped to a raw, needy-looking state.

Fred Hughes has lived in the house on Lexington Avenue since 1974. Built in 1889, the four-story house was designed by Henry J. Hardenbergh, who also designed the Dakota, an uncanny actor in Roman Polanski's modern gothic, *Rosemary's Baby*. Hughes's house once belonged to Andy Warhol who, for thirteen years, shared it with his mother. From 1967 until 1987, Hughes was Warhol's business manager, friend, confidante and fellow avid collector. He helped Warhol build upon his fame and realize financial gain from his paintings, for one thing by introducing him to socialites and collectors who commissioned portraits at Hughes's instigation. After Warhol's death in 1987, Hughes played a fundamental role in developing the Andy Warhol Foundation for the Visual Arts and the Andy Warhol Museum in Pittsburgh. He was executor of Warhol's estate, chosen by Warhol to be king, steward of all that Andy had achieved in his lifetime. But fate often treats kings poorly; many suffer and fall. Hughes fell to multiple sclerosis, which was diagnosed in 1984 but did not become active until after Warhol's unexpected, unnecessary death. Hughes has been bedridden since 1998.

The language associated with royalty and lineage fits Fred Hughes like the English custom-made suits he once wore. He venerates the royals, and stories circulate about his English accent— he was born in Texas in 1943—scathing wit, dandyism, elegance, savvy, temper, eloquence and pretensions to being a royal. Like other people who collected around Warhol, or whom Warhol collected like art, Hughes made himself a legend and a superstar. He invented himself much like a novelist might a fictional character. But instead of writing his character, he lived it. Taken up by art collectors Dominique and Jean de Menil, who recognized his astute eye when he was twenty and sponsored his entry into the art world, Hughes gave birth to himself, left Texas and family, and maybe, as in fables, never looked back.

An abundance of desires and tastes overwhelms me upon entering this house. On the first floor, Warhol's portrait of Prince Charles appears to greet if not oversee the visitor. When Warhol painted him, the prince was young, unblemished; but recent history has cast its shadow, and the image is now marked by trouble. Turquoise-green, the portrait's background, is the color Hughes selected for the adjoining room's walls—"the arsenic room," he calls it—where the Tudors dominate. A naive portrait of Queen Elizabeth I claims center stage, while a Duncan Phyfe card table, with ornate legs—"dolphin supports"— stands decorously in one of the corners. In the other room on this floor, where Hughes now rests and sleeps on a high-tech hospital bed, a Warhol "blue Jackie Kennedy" in a gilt frame hangs above a Tudor portrait and, separated by a great, elaborate mirror, the pair repeats on the other side. The American and English royals keep Hughes company, their coupling a visual pun that might amuse him.

Objects—Russian, English, Mexican, Native American, or hailing from New Orleans—fraternize in the house, sharing space across time and culture. Near the staircase, a twentieth-century American naive or outsider painting of a snake charmer stops me: She's a black woman, in a green leaf-skirt, with a green snake clenched ferociously in her teeth and another wrapped around her arm. But my eyes dart everywhere, and everywhere there's something unusual. I'm drawn to some pieces more than others, or perhaps must simply focus my eyes someplace.

In Hughes's former bedroom on the second floor, a Northwest Indian spoon and a mask from a Jemez Indian tribe arrest me, then a cabinet—bursting with too many Mickey Mouses, a Pee Wee Herman—almost screams with plaintive joy. Arranged or deranged, crammed together behind glass, the toys are poignant. They seem like effigies—George Washington on a horse, Mortimer Snerd. The cabinet holds a menagerie of memories and gives a sense of how, when recalling resonant childhood, associations overflow uncontrollably.

Moving away from the colorful old toys, I spy a silver bowl containing antique magnifying glasses. I love magnifying glasses and wonder why Hughes does. A man who treasures detail might cherish an object that can make the finer things in life bigger.

Yet the glass also exaggerates flaws. Hughes is a person, I've read, who sought and demanded perfection; the magnifying glass suggests the scrutiny necessary to achieve it.

Everything has a place here, a reason to be where it is, selected for its color, shape, design, history, visual pleasure and, like a writer spinning a story, Hughes knows that each object in its place makes, like every sentence and word, a world unto itself, but juxtaposed with others, cobbles together new worlds. Looking at the three pieces of statuary near the bed—a Chinese or Japanese Genji, made of wood; and two female figures, nineteenth-century English, cast from Canova originals—I think: Maybe he didn't become a novelist because he loves excess. Nothing succeeds like excess. But a writer throws away so much; one excludes, pares down, crosses out. Omissions are as significant as what's on the page. Hughes wanted everything around him, all his ideas and possibilities, and he bought and exhibited as much as he could. About his wishes and hopes, he was voracious.

From Hughes's room on the first floor, the voice of his registered nurse travels in and out of earshot. He's reading to Hughes from a biography of Napoleon. Of all his senses, Hughes's hearing functions best now, and the nurse reads to him daily. Hughes likes biographies especially. From them, perhaps, he can get a person's measure, learn how others' beginnings and ends may have been radically different, hear how they failed or thrived, and lose himself in details of lives he might have written—collected—for himself.

On the top floor, in the study, is a magnificent Wooton secretary, a desk from 1876, with many compartments and divisions, a warren for secrets. Near it hangs Warhol's *Portrait of an American Male*, an unknown and typical Midwestern-looking American man. Hughes calls him "Mr. Nobody." Perhaps it's on the wall in deference to Warhol, whose fascination with the rich, famous and powerful was matched by an equally strong interest in anonymity and powerlessness. For a time, the Automat was Warhol's favorite restaurant; and according to Bob Colacello, former editor of *Interview* magazine, he wanted his early work to be called "Common Art," not Pop Art. But "Mr. Nobody" might also be hanging in Hughes's study as a reminder: A fictive fellow knows how fragile identity is, how difficult to maintain, and that the possibility of failure hangs over any self-creation.

Few of us, I think as I leave his house and look back, live out our fantasies as fully as Hughes has lived his. Now housebound, unable to move, often unable to speak, he's visible in what he's collected. These things are who he is now. Hughes resides in his portrait of the Duke of Buckingham by Daniel Mytens, Indian masks, carved human skull, Stieff Mickey Mouses, Lichtenstein painting of George Washington, stuffed reindeer head, Cecil Beaton self-portrait, dressing table by Quervelle, Zuni Pueblo masks, early-nineteenth-century American silhouettes, wreaths of dried flowers, nineteenth-century Russian sofa (purportedly once owned by Tsar Alexander I), photograph of art dealer and friend Thomas Amman, nineteenth-century mahogany sideboard, twenty-seven pairs of shoes neatly arranged in his dressing room, silver collection, Wedgwood vases, Audubon prints, eighteenth-century costumes (which he once wore), black painted wooden screen, nineteenth-century petit point Aubusson pillows, photograph of his father as a young man, twentieth-century African funerary marker, Venetian glass . . . If things could only speak, I think.

C is for Cool

Chet Baker could break your heart with his romantic trumpet sound and melancholy way of phrasing a ballad. With his *Rebel Without a Cause* looks, Baker's sound and image could hook you "in about 20 seconds," an ex-girlfriend tells Bruce Weber in *Let's Get Lost*. Photographer/filmmaker Weber, who was 16 when he became a Chet Baker fan, calls his movie "a loving record of the time" he and his crew spent with Baker. A compelling and disturbing homage to a jazz great who got hooked, in his twenties, on heroin, *Let's Get Lost* also celebrates the American jazz scene of the 50s and 60s.

Weber's eye fixes on beauty and style in the movie as it does in his art photography and his commercial work for Calvin Klein and Ralph Lauren. In those ads, young men very much like young Chet Bakers flirt with young women—images that evoke time passing and the heartbreak of romance. A sense of the fleeting moment and the vulnerability to heartbreak pervade *Let's Get Lost*. With Baker as its enigmatic star, the movie follows beauty and brilliance turning tormented, distorted and sad. Baker is the cool, romantic guy who stepped from day into night to live in semi-darkness. Shot in black and white, sometimes with a hand-held camera and always with startling immediacy by cinematographer Jeff Preiss, the movie lingers with Baker in *film noir* shadows.

Preiss recalls, "When Chet didn't want to be filmed, he'd just walk into a spot that wasn't lit."

To Weber the film is "about that thin line between love and fascination. We take into our own lives what the people we admire give us and we fantasize about it. Sometimes the fantasy is so far out of reach that when we meet that person he can't live up to it." Bruce Weber realized a fantasy. He filmed Baker in recording sessions, interviewed his ex-wives, children, lovers, the musicians he played with. He collected footage and thousands of stills of Baker, created scenes with actors and actresses for Baker to star in. Says Weber, "We spent a lot of time with Chet. And when we first met we were taken in by the romance of his music and the way he looked, and a little bit of his lifestyle when he was young. Then we realized we took it on ourselves because we kind of fell for him and we wanted to change him. But Chet never disappointed me, personally or musically."

Weber's fascination with Baker showed itself in his first film, *Broken Noses* (1987). Its protagonist, Andy Minsker, a young boxer, looks just like Baker when he was Minsker's age. Minsker appears in *Let's Get Lost*, too, sitting next to the jazzman, who, at the age of 57, shows the results of a lifetime of addiction in 1968. Baker was badly beaten up and lost his teeth—a disaster for a trumpet player and an event talked about several times in the film. His damaged mouth affected his career as well as his looks. It was three years before he could play again. According to Weber, Baker's image "helped him get by when nobody listened to his music. There was a mystique around this guy, who was incredibly good-looking and cool, especially for a white musician. He was vain but he never wanted anyone to know it. He was the kind of guy who would never look in a mirror if there was anybody slightly in the neighborhood."

Weber sometimes foregrounds Baker's music in sessions or gigs, or uses it as ironic background to enactments or interviews. Baker sings "Just Friends" as an ex-lover talks, in close-up, about their relationship. Weber "wanted to make it seem, with all the close-ups, that the viewer was in the front seat. You look back and see Chet in the car." Baker's in that car or in a restaurant, haunting the film as he haunts the women who loved him. They talk about his charm, his unreliability. His children, now grown, say they hardly ever saw him. In one scene, the camera pans across Baker's mother, children and estranged wife while he sings "Blame it on My Youth."

The camera pursues Baker, who usually ignores its gaze. Nodding, his eyes frequently closed, he sits uneasily in the frame. *Let's Get Lost* studies its subject but is just as much something to be studied, chasing as it does its elusive object of desire. At the end of the film, Weber asks him, "Will you look back on the film as good times?" It's an uncomfortable moment. Weber suddenly exposes his own need. Baker comes to attention and looks steadily at the camera. "How the hell else could I see it, Bruce? Santa Monica. That scene in that hotel . . . in the studio. On the beach. It was so beautiful. It was a dream. Things like that just don't happen. Just a very few." As much as anything else, it's his comment on the movie he's in, a movie that achieves its intensity by looking for, and at, a man who spent much of his life getting lost.

Earlier in the film, a young man begs Baker to sing to people who might never hear him again. "I'm not dead yet," Baker answers. But he's dead now, having met an end that his friends might have expected and feared. Weber says Baker never got to see any of the footage. In May 1988, his body was found on a street in Amsterdam. The police say he committed suicide or fell out of his hotel window.

D is for Dictionary

Appetist [ap-pa-tist] n. A well-adjusted enjoyer of food, frequently used in reference to women, occasionally men. A person with a healthy desire to eat; a person who does not worry excessively about food intake; a person who does not diet constantly; someone who enjoys food thoroughly and in moderation.

Catful [kat –ful] adj. A human being whose behavior is reminiscent of a playful or contented cat.

Catfeasience, catfeasient [Kat-fee-zens/zent] n., adj. Willful, arbitrary and malevolent behavior reminiscent of a cat who scratches furniture, doesn't use the litterbox and is generally incorrigible, as in, If he continues to curse me at parties, his catfeasience will force me to leave him. As an adj., she carried herself with a catfeasient air that drove many away.

Hateless [hate-less] adj. Constitutionally, genetically, or environmentally incapable of severely irrational or violently negative reaction. In the past, derogatively connoted, see: Pollyanna, idealist, idiot. Today, it is considered that one who is hateless may be a secular saint. Very rare, as in: Nelson Mandela is basically hateless.

Hyperchondria [hi-pur-khon-dree-a] n. The state of feeling physical-ly sound; an experience of total, thorough well-being, one in which a person has no physical or psychological complaints; a condition in which one feels superhealthy or superfine; an overabundance of health; in extreme cases, hyperchondria may indicate delusion, but the person will not want to acknowledge a problem.

Intergaze [in-ter-gaz] v. A look which passes between two people or more that occurs in passing or during intense moments; a visu-ally understood look of instant recognition; a quick appraisal; a fast acknowledgment between sympathetic equals, as in: During dinner, his nephew and niece intergazed and decided not to ap-proach him about their father, his prodigal brother.

Jellyrollreversal [ghel-ee-row-ree-vur-sul] n. A gender reversal or role adaptation; primarily domestic; a gendered adaptive variance; an agreed-upon gender variation, as in: He takes care of their children, she goes to the office, but their jellyrollreversal is no compromise. Probably a combination of two terms, bon temps rouler (let the good times roll) and jellyroll (a donut-like pastry whose center is filled with jam). During the 1970s, Americans sought words and expressions for new living arrangements. It is believed that *jellyrollreversal* was first used by a musician, who, in the late 1970s, upon noticing a man in an apron diapering his daughter, retorted, A jellyrollreversal.

Liberal [lib-a-rul] adj. Cool; hip, able to chill; free and freedomlov-ing; uninhibited and unrestricted, as in: The guy is a liberal danc-er. Or, Yo, that's liberal!

Multitidian [mul-tah-tid-ien] adj. Many events or things that occur over and over, usually in a day. Regular repetitions that are accepted in a day, as in: I was used to the multitidian phone, but now there's the cell.

Plaintitude [plen-ti-tood], plaintitudious [plen-ti-tood-i-nus] n., adj. The sense of an action or act that, performed daily, is fulfilling to the actor in its regularity; a sense that ordinary routine is sufficient, as in: The plaintitude of breakfast consoles me.

Protemporary [pro-tem-pur-ee], protemporaneous [pro-tem-po-ran-ee-us] n., adj. An advocate of the new and passing; a person who is not fixed in attitudes or habits; of a group who supports and extols the passing whims and fancies of its day; at its extreme, bordering on anarchy, as in: She follows no dictates that I can discern, her protemporaneous style is too fast for me. Not to be confused with contemporary, which emphasizes a blending into and with one's time. Closer to atemporality, in flavor.

Pseudoist [soo-doe-istl] n. One who supports falsehood and falsity in all things; one who is always false; a person incapable of telling the truth; one who believes in the superiority of lies, as in: Donald Rumsfeld's portrait, like Dorian Gray's, is hidden in a room, a wreck, since it is that of a mean, persistent pseudoist.

Superreflection [soo-pa-re-flek-shun] n. The state of pondering a thought; a condition of introspection; the most intense kind of thinking in which thought mirrors thought, as in: At times like these, Gwen insisted, her superreflection caused a kind of vertiginous insight.

Supertidian [soo-pah-tid-ean] adj. An annoying excess of mostly unwanted events that occur daily, as in: It would be one thing if there were fewer of them, but supertidian right-wing talk show hosts infect my radio even when it's not turned on.

Unscriptive [un-skrip-tiv/ly] adj., adv. A description of behaviors, attitudes, and ideas that have a unique and independent cast; generous attitudes that appear to come from nowhere; unbiased thinking; a desire for openness and intelligent communication. Unscriptive acts were first noticed in the 1950s, in experiments with LSD. In current usage, unscriptive talk and acts are not related to drug-taking, as in: Bill Clinton, at his very best, discoursed unscriptively about history, reproductive rights and race relations. But George W. Bush is, to the country's chagrin, never unscriptive.

E is for Etel and Eggleston

In the late 1980s, I was phoned by poet and critic Ammiel Alcalay, who urged me to hear Etel Adnan read the next night at the Graduate Center. He told me Adnan was an Arab-American poet, playwright and painter, born and raised in Lebanon. Since he had never urged me to attend an event before, I decided to go. The lecture hall was filled. I remember Edward Said and his wife were in the audience. Adnan took her seat behind a table at the front, and, from the moment she began reading, her passion, great intelligence and sensitivity to language and form felt palpable. It was a rapturous night, during which I said to myself, I'm so glad I came. Imagine if I'd missed this.

Adnan writes about exile and place, women and men, war, nature, paying homage to the beauty, complexity, and even the horrors of our lives. She is a philosophical poet, whose range is extraordinary. She the author of, among others, the acclaimed novel *Sitt Marie Rose*, which was translated into ten languages, including Urdu and Bosnian, and the epic poem, *The Arab Apocalypse*. Her paintings have been exhibited internationally and are included in various museums and collections. Adnan's plays have been produced in San Francisco, Paris, Caen, Argentina, Dusseldorf and Beirut, her poetry set to music by composers such as Gavin Bryars, Henry Threadgill, Tania Leon, Annea Lockwood, and Zad Multaka. Her latest books are *In The Heart Of The Heart Of Another Country* and *The Master Of The Eclipse*.

After I heard her read that night, I made contact with her. I saw her twice in NYC, when she was on her way to Paris. I phoned her there a couple of times, and we maintained an infrequent correspondence. I read her books. Her partner, Simone Fattal, who is the publisher of the Post-Apollo Press, always sent me her new books; and Etel always signed them affectionately. Having the chance to talk with Etel Adnan for Bidoun, at length and in her home in Sausalito, was a gift.

LT: You've written that you can never separate experience from theory.

EA: We don't just speak out, we order our thinking. If you call that theory, you can't escape it. If one means, rather, that one speaks with pre-decisions, that this is my way of speaking, I will conform everything to that style and approach, it is not only bad, but it also doesn't work. It is why, sometimes, my work seems to go in many different directions. It could be harmful, but I can't do otherwise. But to do that doesn't mean not to have direction in one's thinking or to be lost. I want to accept things as they come and see what to do with them.

LT: One's own experience of the world might always fall into a category or theory one believes.

EA: I accept contradiction when it happens. Today I may say something philosophical: if I can talk of the idea of Being separated from objects, then I can also say there is no Being outside manifestation. One month later I might write its opposite and be aware of it. That doesn't bother me, because I seek new connections. Of course, you must have some few points of reference in your life.

LT: War is a enduring point of reference for you.

EA: I have become politically nonviolent. I've reached the point that, for myself, it is right. I will not compromise that. On other matters I feel a kind of absolute, if we can use that word. I do not accept the sexual abuse of children. But I have very few of those absolutes. Everything else is in flux.

LT: I admire various kinds of writing, if I feel there is an intelligence behind it, that the language is closely handled, in whatever form the writer chooses.

EA: I don't privilege one approach to another. I don't privilege it within my own works. Some people are prisoners of the decisions they make.

LT: It's fascinating in *Sitt Marie Rose*, your novel about the Lebanese Civil War, which started in 1975, the varieties of style and forms you chose. First, what does "sitt" mean?

EA: Sitt is an Arabic word, used in Lebanon and Syria mostly, and Egypt, to mean "madam"; it's not formal. A girl of five years old in conversation can be "little sitt so-and-so." Sitt can also be for married or single women. It's a colloquial way to address a woman. It carries some respect.

LT: How did *Sitt Marie Rose* come about, when did you write it?

EA: I wrote it before the end of 1976. The event it's based on occurred in early '76. The Christian Phalangists kidnapped a woman whose real name was Marie Rose. People immediately recognized her when the book came out.

LT: You wrote it in French.

EA: I was in Paris and had read in *Le Monde* about Marie Rose Boulous' being kidnapped. I knew she was already dead. I became upset, wanted to write it down; as you are a writer, you know one discovers through writing matters that wouldn't occur to you otherwise. I wanted to find out—all cultures include violence—which forms the Lebanonese culture has taken. We don't know any human group in history that hasn't been violent. I don't believe any nation is better than any other on that score. But what attracted me to this violence was my knowledge: the young men who kidnapped, tortured and killed her, I had grown up with them. I knew Phalangists, and she was Christian too. Through her they wanted to teach a lesson to the various factions. People use religion to excite people and send them to war, like Bush with the word "democracy." It's dogma misuse. The Phalangists were, in their minds, defending Christian values, but in fact they were defending their power against the Muslims. There are orthodox Christians in Egypt, Syria, Lebanon. The majority of Christians in Lebanon are Catholic, so they had links with Rome, and the French, a Catholic nation. The French created a place where these Christians would have their own country—after World War I when the big powers carved up the Middle East. But if everybody were Christian, the new country would have been too small. So they included territory inhabited by Muslims. This is the key to the Lebanese problem—the Christians of Lebanon say, and it's true, the country was created by the French for them. But after two generations, the Christians found they were no longer a sizable majority. Today they are not the majority. It's the source not of hatred but of the antagonism in Lebanon.

LT: Your novel shifts and flows, from politics with its varied discourses, through voices and styles. One of the brilliant inventions is the deaf-mute schoolchildren.

EA: What you call a silent majority.

LT: [laughs] They are taught by Sitt Mary Rose, they don't speak; she is the only one who is kind to them. The four male characters, who represent various factions of the Christians, speak; they are all anti-Muslim. Sitt Mary Rose is sympathetic to the Palestinian cause.

EA: Which was why she was killed.

LT: The deaf children are presented "speaking" in the first person. Throughout all the formal changes, I was able to understand where I was, who was speaking; you included politics but didn't re-create politics per se. You reimagined everything. Desire, impressions, feelings.

EA: And the description of the state of war in a specific place. Politics is such an important part of our lives, whether we like it or not. Why shouldn't it enter novels? In poetry, people mostly avoid politics. They think it's not poetic. But the Iliad is a political work. I became an American poet by writing against the Vietnam war, I joined the movement by writing against the war, spontaneously. I feel the first thing is to be true to oneself. Now you will say what if you are a monster and are true to yourself? [laughing] If you're a monster, you're going to be true to that self anyway. But a movement of poets against the war didn't happen about Iraq, which is as monstrous a war and as long. Why? We are in a period when there is, funnily enough, more poetry being written in proportion to the population than during Vietnam. Poets have followed the general apathy of the Bush and Reagan years.

LT: Maybe that speaks about where poetry is in terms of its relationship to society. Some writers may feel themselves at a great distance.

EA: It's because of the kind of poetry they are writing—a very abstract poetry. They are discovering new forms, by complicating form and by avoiding anything that would smack of a message. And, like all great writing, it can defend itself beautifully.

LT: In Virginia Woolf's essay, "The Death of the Moth," she observes a day moth, which lives 24 hours, and watches it die. By looking at it, she understands the struggle to live, the finality of death.

EA: You're right, one can express anything, in the most unexpected way.

LT: What I want to claim is that fiction and poetry need not be specific to a political event to embrace the effects and depredations to life because of war, violence, injustice.

EA: No. I went to Iraq twice, and, in spite of Saddam's dark side, there was great vitality, artistic vitality—it had the biggest readership of contemporary Arab literature. Iraq had great painters, musicians. It was the most dynamic Arab country for some 30 years, with an excellent medical system, the best in the Arab world. So the destruction of it . . . Simultaneously, Saddam was an excessive character. You were for him or against him, no in between. In that sense, he was a total dictator. Still, something was happening there. There was the same oppressive rule in Syria, but without the counterpart in culture Iraq had. When America attacked Iraq, each time they moved, they destroyed it. I didn't feel my best friends, poets or non-intellectuals, really cared. Though when you think about it, there is so much going on in the world, and Americans cannot care for everything. But this is something that America started and did.

LT: There's a passage from *Sitt Mary Rose*, which, though it came out here in 1982, could have been written now. \

> In this society where the only freedom of choice, when there is any, is between different brands of automobiles, can any notion of justice exist and can geno-cide not become an instable consequence.

It articulates the horrible sense of possibility of genocide.

EA: Hatred can lead to genocide. You don't win, so you will to-morrow, or after tomorrow, but you'll keep going; there is no real rationale to it. The U.S. is not immune, but prosperity made America relax. If this financial crisis goes on, ten people will fight for one job, and race or religion might lead to: "how come the Chi-nese and the Latinos have a job and I don't?" To a degree American prosperity created a certain benevolence. America is interesting, everything is true about it, and its opposite is true. There can be an atmosphere of benevolence, but the word "socialism" is taboo. In one way we have a people's country, there's no aristocracy. We have a democracy in many ways, really. But people are horrified by universal health care, which Europe and Canada have as a mat-ter of course.

LT: I believe that Existentialism is an important philosophy to you.

EA: Yes, I went to Paris as a student in 1950, Sartre was the great thing, and I had not heard of him in Beirut. It was like a miracle. I had come from a culture where we lived on a more basic level. My father was highly educated for those days, my mother was not. We had no books at home. My mother had the Gospels, she was a Greek from Smyrna—Greek Orthodox. My father was a Muslim from Damascus in the Ottoman empire. He had the Koran, he knew it by heart. Amazingly, the books existed on a shelf next to each other. So I have no problem with coexistence. I grew up with it. People finished their education, if they were lawyers they went to law, but that generation didn't have books in the home. In Paris, everything was new, astonishing, until I was 30. I was in a stage of discovery for 13 years, until I started teaching, which gave me a distance from reality. I was immersed in reality until I was 30.

LT: How do you mean "reality"?

EA: In the present, that type of reality. When I read Sartre, I was floored because I'd attended French Catholic schools, they were the only ones you could go to, and they hammered us with religion: you're moral because you follow religion. Sartre said you could be moral without being religious.

LT: Did you hear Sartre speak?

EA: No, but his philosophy changed my life. Its second idea was about responsibility, and that is empowerment. I didn't have the word or concept then, but it's what existentialism offered people. Coming from a Catholic school, I know firsthand that you are meant to follow the church, the priest, then you are a good person. You go to confession. By saying you are responsible, you are your decisions. I think that's liberation. It's not "Obey and shut up."

LT: I'm curious how your parents met. A Muslim from Syria, a Greek Catholic from Smyrna.

EA: They met during WWI, in Symrna, in the street. He followed her. They got married. He already had a wife and three children in Damascus, but he didn't tell her. She was so poor that, for her, it was a fairy tale. He was governor of Smyrna, a top officer; he'd been Ataturk's classmate, because though my father had been stationed in Damascus, the sole military school was in Istanbul. Then the war was lost, and my parents went to Beirut. From there it was downhill.

LT: They were poor, but you were well educated.

EA: I was educated because I went to a French school. But about my social class: I didn't identify with the rich or the poor, though my father's family in Damascus were among the top families. My mother was extremely poor when she grew up. She used to say there were only two jobs in Smyrna for women. To pick up grapes for raisins or be a prostitute.

LT: You often write about prostitutes.

EA: If mother hadn't married my father, she may have been one. She was 16 when he met her. Then the Greeks in Turkey were in concentration camps. Not like the German ones, more like the Japanese camps during WWII here.

LT: How did they let you go to Paris?

EA: My father was dead by that time. It broke my mother's heart. I was 24 when I went. I had a French government scholarship for three years.

LT: How did that happen?

EA: I worked from the age of 16. I was the only child. We needed money. I cut school for a year, and one day I was crying in the office, and my boss, a Frenchman, asked, "Why are you crying?" *Because everybody goes to school and I don't.* He said, "Why not? I'll help you." But I said, *I work all day, there are no night classes. But I could take morning classes.* He let me come to the office at 10am instead of 8, I made it up at night. I finished the whole program in two months instead of eight and received a baccalaureate, which allowed me to go into the third year of a French school that specialized in literature. I quit the first job and found one doing almost nothing, for a man who wanted to write a novel. He thought if I just sat there, he would write it. He didn't, for two years, but I was paid every month. I read books in his library. [laughing] In the

French school, Gabriel Bounoure taught us Baudelaire, Rimbaud and Verlaine. He wanted literature to be free from the Jesuits, and he taught poetry. Thanks to him we got an enlightened education. He's the one who encouraged me to apply for a scholarship to Paris. I told him my mother didn't want me to. When I told her, she went crazy. I was her only child, and I'd be in a foreign place. But I went.

LT: You were very brave.

EA: Brave in many ways, but also brave with no sense of the future. It was day to day bravery.

LT: It raises the question of developing character, your character, and how you respond to others, and fashioning characters in fiction.

EA: Some people have hardships which kill them; others are made so bitter they have no hope. But hardships can also, in some cases, become experiences one can grow from.

LT: Often in your writing, there are questions of liberty and madness. In *Of Cities and Women*, set in Barcelona, in the Ramblas, a woman walks down the street completely naked.

> *After she passed me I saw her from behind, and was wondering if she was really naked. She was. She continued down the avenue probably heading for the red light district. . . . Was this a scene of absolute liberty or of insanity?*

I don't know sometimes what I'm seeing.

EA: That's interesting to say you don't know what's happening.

LT: I'm wary of making judgments, generational ones, in our day this or that. Nonetheless, what is being free or insane—crazy—what's possibility or breakdown.

EA: They're both such flexible notions. We don't know completely what we mean by freedom, especially when freedom is used as a nuisance to others. We also don't know really what insanity is.

LT: We don't know what the benefits or disadvantages of certain behavior are or will be.

EA: Insanity, as a category, has mostly disappeared. But how do you run a society between these two notions, both boundaries, which in effect include disorder. To implement law, what do you do when you have power? How do you use it? Stop? How to integrate contradictory rights?

LT: In your poetics, you are very free. In writing about women and femininity, in *Of Cities*, you employ the epistolary form.

EA: Because it gives one freedom. I wrote it, because my friend Fawwaz wanted me to write a paper on feminism.

LT: You mention cities, experiences in them, think about politics and philosophy, love, aesthetics, painting, how women are depicted compared with men.

> Several questions come forward at the same time, pushing each other. Calling us or escaping us. Should we wish for the acceleration of this process, which is that women become more like men, or should we rather hope for the metaphysical distinctions what man and woman to be maintained without the maintenance of the immemorial inequalities that we know? Always and still present.

You›re so succinct, discussing a complex issue very much with us. I'm not an essentialist, but how do we maintain difference(s) and reduce inequality?

EA: I have no answer, but it is a genuine question.

LT: It's also similar in regard to varieties of cultures and societies, religions: can we respect differences with, for lack of a better word, globalization?

EA: The trend is toward uniformity. Obviously women have been acculturated to use their femininity, men their masculinity. I don't think that we want to keep everything we have called "the feminine." We need societies to maintain what I'd call a metaphysical balance, the different qualities of masculine and feminine. Aggression is part of life, but we also need a counter-aggression. We need men who are against war, as much as women, though there are more and more women for war. We need diversity and balance in the sexes.

LT: It's in your writing, though I don't know if I've read the word as such: forgiveness.

EA: Goodness of the heart. That is the core of Christ and Christianity. Everything else is an invention of his followers. When Jesus said "I am the son of God," he didn't mean it the way it's interpreted. In Semitic languages, in Arabic, to be a "son" is an everyday expression. For example, a man might say, "Young man," take him by the hand, then say, "My son, do you know what time it is?" To be the son is to be accepted. It's a friendly word. When Jesus said "I am the Son, Father," he meant I am accepted, and what I say is agreeable to the Father, to God. He spoke in Aramaic, older even than Arabic.

LT: In *The Arab Apocalypse*, an extraordinary epic poem, I noticed the word "sun" throughout it. I'd never read "sun" presented in so many ways.

EA: As a child, I had a strong sense of the presence of the sun. In the summer, the sun is very vivid in Beirut. I was fascinated by the shadow my own body made, when going for an afternoon swim. In my 20s, I heard the French say that Arabs were the children of the sun, *les enfants du soleil*. It was said with disdain: Arabs were irresponsible, grown-up children. And I remember walking into the mountains of my village, never wearing a hat, being very aware it was hot, feeling surrounded by the sun like a thief by the police. As I said we didn't have many books, and not having brothers and sisters, I was more involved with noticing what was around me.

LT: In all of your work there's a strong emphasis on nature and relationship to a sense of place. It's as if to lose one's place, to feel in exile or be in exile, focused you.

EA: You're absolutely right. My relation to place is also a desire to know where I am. When I arrive somewhere, I want to know, where's south? My partner, Simone, asks, "Why do you bother?" I like to be oriented. I grew up as an anguished child, partly because of not having brothers and sisters in a society where I was marginal. My father, an Arab from Damascus, living in Lebanon, I was born and raised in Lebanon, my mother was Greek. The French were ruling Lebanon, so we were also marginal in relation to a colonial power. And my parents were a mixed marriage, there were few. I think I compensated by trying to know always where I was.

LT: *The Arab Apocalypse* takes a unique approach to writing on the page, you use signs, lines, curves, symbols.

EA: The signs are there as an excess of emotion. The signs are the unsaid. More can be said, but you are stopped by your emotion.

LT: The word "stop" is in capital letters throughout. As in, "Stop This War."

EA: I wrote *The Arab Apocalypse* when Tel al-Zaatar was under siege. Tel al-Zaatar is a neighborhood in Beirut, where 20,000 people, not all Palestinian but mostly Palestinian, lived basically underground. The Phalangists and their allies attacked in '76. Maybe the fighters in the camp had some advance notice and left. But the women, children, and old people who remained were slaughtered. It was worse than Sabra and Shatila.

LT: Worse than Sabra and Shatila?

EA: It was as bad and worse. There was only one well, so women would go there for water. Maybe 20, to make sure one got back; they were surrounded by snipers. *The Arab Apocalypse* is about Tel al-Zaatar—the hill of thyme—but its subject is beyond this siege, which was the beginning of the undoing of the Arabs. This war was the sign of disaster coming, that by mismanagement and mistakes, the Arabs would undo themselves.

LT: The form and content of *The Arab Apocalypse* are imaginatively fused.

> *A sun and a belly full of vegetables, a system of fat tuberoses. A sun which is SOFT. The eucalyptus. The Arabs are under the ground. The Americans are on the moon. The sun has eaten its children. I myself was a morning blessed with bliss.*

What's produced is a sense of survival, even in the midst of atrocious conditions and behavior.

EA: I started this book when I lived in Beirut. It's 59 poems, the same number as the days of the siege. I could hear the bombs from my balcony. For 59 days they didn't let any food in, water, nothing.

I saw a manifestation of pure evil. In metaphysics there is no word for that. I saw evil.

LT: In *Paris When It's Naked*, you quote Delacroix, who said he had to satisfy "something black" in him. It relates to your saying that violence or evil has no one country.

EA: We have institutions, we try to control it. Or, we decide to unleash it. But there is evil in every person to different degrees; evil is part of being.

LT: I think of it as cruelty to other people, to life.

EA: And oneself. Power creates a temptation to be abusive. Nations who feel immune, or superior, sure to win, are not wise. Like the Bush administration, a folly of arrogance. In nature, there is danger too. Because the sun is dangerous. It can kill you, burn you. But the sun is also life.

LT: *The Arab Apocalypse* is a superb example of a poem that pays attention to poetics, and place, war, politics—literally, what happens in the city.

EA: There is the presence of war in almost everything I write. Beirut's importance is because of war, it's a child of WWI. In 1920 we had refugees from Armenia. WWII brought foreign armies, not bloodshed; Beirut profited, because when armies are around, there's money. In '58 a little civil war started. In '67 another batch of refugees. In '71 the Israelis bombed the airport. In '75, the start of 15 years of civil war. In 1982, the Israelis entered Beirut. There were other Israeli incursions, constant bombing of the south. Beirut was done and almost undone by war.

LT: *The Arab Apocalypse* is like a Jeremiad.

EA: Yes. It's pessimistic. I sometimes think I'm an optimist because I always advise myself to go on, overcome. But my vision of the world is pretty dark. I try not to forget the good of this world—not only good people, but the sunshine, the trees. There is also happiness in this world.

LT: *In the Heart of the Heart of Another Country* is written in paragraphs. You said you chose paragraphs, because the nuns gave your class a word from which to write a sentence, but you wrote a paragraph.

> *A person. People here to portray there is a person who loves me to death. Not to my death or hers, but to the death of the person I loved. . . . I wonder who invented the ugly word punishment. It was probably God, who established the word and the deed.*

From the word "person," the paragraph leads to an unexpected end, to the possibility of people hurting each other.

EA: Not the possibility. My heart had been broken. It's full of allusions to my biography.

LT: In the paragraph "Place," you wrote:

> I moved from city to city, traveled from person to person and then I tried to
> define myself through writing. But that doesn't work. No, not at all. It adds
> fiction to the fiction I became. . . . I'm in a disorienting wilderness.

I want to focus on fiction itself. I think you're trying to make a
place from writing.

EA: There is a sense of exile in everyone. We are exiled from each
other, to a point. It's what relationships are about—to close that
gap as much as possible. Writing is a dialogue with that deep feeling. Some feel they came from somewhere. They have a strong
illusion of belonging. Other people, or groups, have a special rest-
lessness and understanding, a nomadic spirit. We're so used to it,
we don't know how to be without it. Everything has its advantages. I don't envy a French peasant in a village—I'm happy that
she's happy, but I can't figure out that happiness.

LT: You've said history is incorporated in individuals.

EA: We are the result of history, more than we know, we think we
are free from it. Nietzsche said, "If you believe in freedom, you are
stupid, but if you don't feel freedom, you're doomed." You function in relation to the entire moral code that is based on responsibility and, therefore, freedom of choice.

LT: In *Sitt Marie Rose*, your protagonist maintains her freedom by not trading places with her Palestinian lover. She won't let him be killed instead of her.

EA: She chose to die, she didn't want to die. The Phalangists offered to trade her; that would have been treason to her.

LT: Sitt Marie Rose was an extraordinary woman. You represent women and their place in the world, not just in the Arab world, and also in terms of feminism.

EA: I am a feminist, first because I was a rebellious child. I was not a conscious rebel, but an instinctive one. I couldn't get along with my mother. I wanted to do what I wanted to do, like taking a taxi in Beirut when I was sixteen—girls didn't take taxis. I took a particular pleasure in it. I wouldn't walk in the streets, I'd always run. I didn't want to get married; I thought marriage was a prison. I became more politically involved, when I attended Berkeley. Society is conservative, you always have to behave. I was a natural rebel.

LT: I was intrigued by your statement that you fear Western civilization.

EA: Conquering is always at the expense of somebody else. Western civilization behaves as if it offers redemption—the Israelis were the last example of that. They came as Westerners, Europeans, but Western civilization, like all civilizations, had invaded others, but most of the other civilizations tried to integrate the indigenous people—the Romans had emperors who were Arabs.

Alexander wanted to join East and West. The Chinese had many ethnic groups. The West is the most racist of civilizations. It eradicates the conquered people. For example, Belgium was responsible for twelve million Congolese deaths. When the West couldn't eradicate outside its boundaries, it eradicated within, as Germany did. Western civilization speaks about itself as a model, but it has a very dark side.

LT: You became a pacifist. What are other great changes in you?

EA: I had no interest in politics until living in Paris in 1950. Israel was just being created, it didn't exist in my head. In 1956, at Berkeley, I joined the Arab Students Association and met a young Palestinian woman, the first I knew. My position then was that Palestine had to be liberated, in any way; we had to win that war. Until the Oslo Accords, ten years ago, when I decided I was not against peace. Oslo was a turning point, it made me a pacifist. I still believe the Palestinians have a cause, but I believe it is natural that we live together and build anew.

Writing also changes me. I don't lie when I write. Something happens, and I must discover it. Writing forces one to go to the bitter end of what one thinks.

In Michael Almereyda's beguiling film *William Eggleston in the Real World* (2005), Eggleston said of his own work: "I am at war with the obvious." The photographer had been filmed, in 1976, answering a question at the opening of his retrospective at the Museum of Modern Art, New York. Eggleston takes shots at the obvious: a misbegotten window display; cheerless interior decoration; a shuttered house. He pictures forgotten spaces, in sidelong glances at American culture's apparent failures or throwaways. He shelters so-called ordinary life, the unremarked-upon objects. Eggleston appears to be a romantic figure from the old school: courtly, handsome, alcoholic, not going quietly into that good night. He wanders in front of the camera, there, not there. Almereyda records Eggleston elusively, letting him hide in plain sight. There are few direct questions, while inter-titles mark the date, event and location. Scenes shift slowly, nothing's rushed, Eggleston rarely says anything. His son, a photographer himself, assists him wordlessly or in code, present when needed, otherwise invisible.

Almereyda's portrait of an artist assembles through a wily accretion of images, with no dramatic "plot points" or "arcs." The viewer creates his or her own narrative, senses what the story might be and, as in any compelling narrative, things don't or can't add up. Almereyda's approach to Eggleston's art and life is subtle, and though Eggleston has declared war on the "obvious," his work is also. Eggleston's images quietly dismiss received ideas of beauty and importance. In his eye, ugliness is no sin, beauty no virtue; they are just cultural and social attitudes that shape perception.

In the film, Eggleston's nights were very different from his days. Alcohol's effects settled on him and his friends, and rattled any identifying cage I might set him in. The movie's lack of comment clarifies the trouble with explanations: they can become heavy-handed guides or judgments. Instead, Almereyda allows encounters and moments to multiply or divide, one incident subtracts an assumption or augments another. An unexpected figure enters into the slippery sum: Eggleston's wife of many years, mother of his children, doesn't appear until close to the end of the movie. An elliptical interview with Eggleston by Almereyda occurs even closer to the end, reframing the artist's image again.

Stories about artists and writers, in novels and movies, usually rely on grating stereotypes, characteristics repeatedly exaggerated in representation. My favorite example comes from a movie Hollywood never released, a life of Franz Schubert. In it, friends beseech the composer more than once: "Why don't you finish 'The Unfinished'?" Hollywood is also the source for the term "the reveal." On a certain page in a script, the heart of the story—usually transplanted during multiple rewrites—should manifest itself, enough so that even on the dullest of minds something can register.

I once wrote a joke-poem to myself, and called it "Do the Obvious." "Do the obvious / you won't forget it / do the obvious /

you won't regret it." (Refrain: "Don't be afraid to be boring.") Living holds few subtleties. There's birth and death, obviously. And everything in between. Teachers of writing and art tell their students, whose hopes must not be crushed—at least not completely—"It's not what it's about, it's how you do it."

It's about expectations, everyone remarks, and desire. I heard a story about a guy from Texas, a Jimi Hendrix fanatic. He was with a friend looking at an art book. The Hendrix guy saw a picture of an Andy Warhol *Campbell's Soup Can* work and exclaimed: "God, that's stupid." His friend said: "What you expect to see there is just as stupid."

All attitudes and positions—positive, negative, neutral, informed, uninformed—betray us. "My education," Franz Kafka wrote, "has damaged me in ways I do not even know." I agree, and here want to substitute the word "culture." It, too, damages in ways we don't know.

The mayor of Tijuana, Carlos Bustamante, tore down La Ocho, the city's filthy, infamous jail, a holding pen for big and small criminals, including American college boys. They were arrested after a night of drugs, alcohol, or sex with a prostitute; they had to pay $2,000 to get out of jail. Mayor Bustamente defended La Ocho's destruction: it represented "the darkest side of Tijuana's history." Speaking for that dark side, a well-known chef and restaurant owner, Javier Plascencia, countered, "It was ugly, but it was ours."

Which brings me to the terrible loss of artist Mike Kelley in January. Kelley was from Detroit and witnessed the collapse of America's Motor City. Early on, he was part of a group called

Destroy All Monsters, school of art, rock, performance. Kelley's treasury included private obsessions, public frenzies, disgust, American bathos and sub-cultural storage units. Poignant, psychologically raw, stunning, his work did damage to what's "obvious" and in "good" or "bad" taste. Kelley didn't destroy all monsters, but he recognized many of them.

F is for Fox

A Conversation with Paula Fox

Paula Fox was rediscovered in the mid-1990s, when Jonathan Franzen found her second novel, *Desperate Characters*, at the artists' colony Yaddo. Franzen, enthralled, wanted to teach the book, but there were few copies around. He contacted Fox and wrote about it and her for *Harper's*. An editor, Tom Bissell, read Franzen's essay and contacted Fox. The rest, we like to say, is history. But history, in all cases, is made by many hands.

Fox's novels have been reprinted, and she is having a writer's second birth and life. Fox and I were paired to read at the National Arts Club in 1999 by the series curator, Fran Gordon. That night, Fox read from *The Widow's Children*, her third novel. I listened, ecstatic. Why had I never heard of her? I bought *Desperate Characters*, *The Widow's Children*, and *Poor George*, her first novel. I hoped to interview her. Now, this interview in *BOMB*'s 25th-anniversary issue.

This provenance exists to register how strangely books live and die, and travel, how idiosyncratic their routes, how capricious a writer's career, how haphazard a reader's chances to find her books. Great literature disappears all the time. After his death, Chaucer disappeared for over 200 years. Every writer a reader loves, with few exceptions, or who is touted now, will be buried forever or a while. Writers sometimes make it their job to unearth other writers. It's not just altruism.

Fox is the author of six brilliant novels, two breathtaking memoirs and 22 children's or young-adult books. To me, it is indubitable that Fox is one of America's greatest living novelists. Her exquisite choices of her narratives, her exquisite choice of language and imagery, her formidable intelligence, her acute observations, her honesty about the trouble with existence here, or anywhere, makes reading Fox a genuine experience. If you let it, her writing will ravish you, even devastate you.

Lynne Tillman: You're a profoundly psychological writer, and also socially and politically engaged. In your first novel, *Poor George,* George Mecklin thinks, "We live on the edge of disaster and imagine we are in a kitchen." Absolute Fox! How did George come to you? How did you decide to write a male protagonist?

Paula Fox: To answer the last part first: I didn't even think about it. It would be false naïveté to say that I didn't realize what I was doing. I did remember hearing, on NPR, in a time of extreme feminism in the late 1960s, a woman being interviewed who said, "Imagine! A man writing about a woman!" I thought of Thomas Hardy, Marcel Proust. I thought, Of course, this kind of extremism accompanies everything that has to do with human affairs, as we see in contemporary life. What engaged me most in writing *Poor George* was a story I was told in about three sentences by someone I knew casually. He said, "I heard this story about a man who took a boy into his house . . . ." I thought of things that might happen. I didn't actually think; a story grows, with me, in a series of images. I have acute memories of the past. I can remember the wrinkles in my father's jacket, when he was lighting a cigarette, 65 years ago. I can see the wrinkles, the cigarette. I have a very visual memory. I started visualizing a place where George lived, and, from there, I invented a whole life for him. But one always writes about one's self in a certain way. There's no way you can write about anything that you know as well as yourself. In a certain sense, whatever is imagined is always based on an inner sense of self. Now, I don't know what that means, particularly after reading in the *Times* today about all the discoveries about the brain. I don't know where the invention of stories comes from. With the violin, you have to begin with some kind of musical ability; you can't sing without an ability to sing. Then you need training. I think you need training for everything.

LT: Before you wrote *Poor George*, had you been writing short stories?

PF: Yes. I've been writing since I was seven. I wrote my first story ever, when I was seven, about a robber who comes into a house and kills everybody, but miraculously they all come alive. Actually, I sent out a lot of stories in between working for a living. I kept getting them back, except for two, which the *Negro Digest*—which is what it was called then—published. I was in my twenties, and they tried to find out if I were black.

LT: Was it because you write black characters?

PF: Yes, that's what I was writing about: black. I didn't feel any constraint about writing about anything, except kind of ordinary constraints of life. It seemed to me that the tracks hadn't been made yet, in certain areas—by me. So, I made my own tracks, not that there weren't lots of tracks around.

LT: There's a fearlessness in your work. As you just said, you didn't feel those constraints. Most white writers do.

PF: I think it's not fearlessness as much as a kind of innocence. I think it was fixed in my mind when I was very little. There's a scene in *Borrowed Finery* that occurred in my brief time with my parents in Hollywood. I had locked myself out one night, my parents were at a party, and I stayed with neighbors. When I came back the next morning, my father had brought home a different woman from my mother. I said, "Daddy, daddy," coming up the stairs to his room. He rose up in the blankets—you know what a man looks like with blankets falling off of him—and in a rage. He grabbed me up and rushed downstairs with me, into the kitchen. There was a black maid ironing. He raised his hand to spank me, and she said, "Mr. Fox, that isn't fair." She rescued me. It must have taken so much courage for her to do that in 1929. I was very struck by that. I think what it did was, it instantly opened a kind of corridor, so that I went down it. Not because I was fearless, but because it was there. It just presented itself.

LT: All of your novels are about justice and injustice.

PF: I feel very strongly about that.

LT: In *The Western Coast*, your third novel, Annie's friend Cletus, who's black, is beaten up. It's a horrible scene. Annie's relationship with him changes, because he can't continue to have the same feelings he had about white people after that.

PF: Cletus is based on a dear friend of mine who is dead now. He had a white mother and a black father. He didn't get beaten up. The ease between Annie and Cletus is based on my relationship with him. You take certain things from life, then you enlarge or diminish them. You ornament them or leave them plain. You strain out the truth. Years ago, when I was looking at a manuscript of mine that was on the floor, turning the pages, suddenly this brain bulb went off. I thought, I have to try to tell the truth, even when it's *and* and *the*. This was around the time that Mary McCarthy had claimed even Lillian Hellman's *ands* and *thes* were lies. My own thought is that we can't know the truth, but we can struggle for it, swim toward it, fight for it.

LT: Toward the end of *The Western Coast*, which takes place in LA during World War II, Annie drives cross-country with Mason White, a black soldier. She gives him a lift to Texas and sees the racism in America—they can't go into many places.

PF: That happened to me. I picked up a black soldier, and we were thrown out of a dozen places in Texas, so many bar-cafés in these little one-store towns. These old men—everybody else had been drafted—they'd be rattling their bones at us. I said, "But he's a soldier, how can you?" They said, "Well, we got our ways down here." I remember the idiocy and limitation of what they said. I didn't feel it at the time to be an idiotic limitation. I do now. I felt it then as a wall that wouldn't give way. I just knew it would never give way with those people.

LT: You have a visual memory and write powerful visual images. In *Poor George*, you write of George's distress and his troubled relationship with his wife, Emma: "There was a boiling sea of acid in his stomach—he longed for a pill. She dropped a cup and the handle broke." You can see him agitated, their tension.

PF: I think that also there's a certain thing that happens—that there is silence between actions. There's so much silence in our lives, despite all of the terrible noise every day. There's an awful silence in between things.

LT: You leave a lot of space between characters, and inside characters' minds. It makes for a lot of anxiety.

PF: I know, in writing it too.

LT: In *Desperate Characters*, your second novel, and *Poor George*, the middle class isn't allowed to enjoy its comforts.

PF: No! That's why I'm not read!

LT: In *Desperate Characters*, Sophie Bentwood can't enjoy eating in the garden of her Brooklyn house because of a wild cat. George Mecklin's house is invaded by the delinquent teenager he sort of adopts. The Bentwoods' summer house is vandalized, which goes back to your first ever story about robbers.

PF: But the Bentwoods don't miraculously come alive; they're not killed. I took a rather uneasy pleasure in writing about a family who were getting eaten, getting eaten to death, for being so opulent and luxurious. Summer people.

LT: The neighbors are enraged at them. George Mecklin's also enraged. You write, "George felt as if his own personal army had just fixed bayonets." He's a teacher, supposedly civilized, a middle-class man. Much of your imagery about him, your metaphors, uses militaristic language and is violent.

PF: I think it's what certain people in this country would use; I wouldn't say, "with his cutlass drawn." The militaristic imagery seems apropos to me. I have a certain sense of what suits and doesn't suit in my range, inside of my range.

LT: Like Edith Wharton, you're able to make inner worlds visible through external objects. The cup's handle breaking, the image of a personal army in him. You internalize through what's external, to create a psychological space. Did you read her?

PF: She and Henry James, whom I admire a great deal, didn't have as much effect on me as Willa Cather and Thomas Hardy. I love two of Cather's books so much, *Death Comes for the Archbishop* and *The Shadows on the Rock*. Of course, there's George Eliot, whom I love. D.H. Lawrence was a great favorite of mine, I have read him over and over. His blood and sex ideology gets in the way of his finer observations and philosophical musings. I think ideologies are terrible for people—any kind. We have to be very careful to avoid them, and sometimes we can't.

LT: Your characters give way to their ideology, to what they're in, or fight it—feel oppressed by the middle class or against it, like Otto Bentwood's partner, Charlie, in *Desperate Characters*. Otto tells him there's no alternative. In your novels, there's a sense that they're living inside something. Some fight it, some don't.

PF: That's a very accurate description. I never thought of it exactly that way. But I don't think about my books in a way that a very good reader would think about them.

LT: How do you think about them?

PF: I see things I like in some of my children's books. I like the section about Paul Robeson in *The Coldest Winter*. It's very hard for me to say. There's something I think about age that makes you feel, there's a certain sense, that you've done what you could do to ameliorate the condition of life, and it's very limited. Unless you're Madame Curie.

LT: In *The Western Coast*, you approach World War II and the Communist Party in America through Annie's experience of them. She's a drifter. One of her lovers, Myron Eagle, says to her, "You must make judgments. How can a person live without them?" That's a central question in your work.

PF: I feel it in my own life. You can't go around with your mouth open, because some buzzard will fly into it. Or some cobra will strike. I think you have to be able to give up judgments, when it's time. But you have to make them too. Otherwise, everything is disorder and chaos.

LT: Max, for instance, in *The Western Coast*, is in the Party, but he steps back from its ideology and observes it. He's an incredibly interesting character because of that.

PF: I think that you have to be attached and detached at the same time—who knows to what extent we can be detached?—but enough so that you can see what it is that you're up to. I had an image once: a lynch mob, a victim, and a mediator. And I was all three. I didn't exclude myself from any group. In some way, that sense of being absolutely susceptible to all of it, to human flaws, to virtues, to circumstances, to experiences—has helped me a lot. Because I tend—as we all do—to close in on myself; I have to keep it, especially when I write.

LT: You never let any of your characters off the hook. You don't write stories of redemption, which, from my point of view, is an American disease.

PF: No, I know, it's "Have a good day!" I wrote recently to the Royal Folio Society in England. I owed them 75 words about Proust. I said that I'd gone one day to Père-Lachaise cemetery and had seen the tomb of Gurdjieff, a spiritual healer. It was covered with flowers and candles, some lit the morning or afternoon I was there. I found Proust's—black marble. And on it a little metal juice can that had contained frozen orange juice, and in it one small bramble rose. I wrote, Gurdjieff said we could reach a higher consciousness and be in control of our lives. Proust taught nothing, but he wrote the most extraordinary book of the 20th century, *In Search of Lost Time*. And he didn't believe in ordinariness. But the childish ideas, that smiley face! It's like naming the atom bomb the "peace bomb." It's a kind of perversity.

LT: In *Desperate Characters*, when Sophie and Otto go for a drive, she sees a poster of an Alabamian presidential candidate. You wrote: "His country, warned the poster—vote for him—pathology calling tenderly to pathology."

PF: That was based on George Wallace. (*laughter*)

LT: Your fourth novel, *The Widow's Children*, like *Desperate Characters*, takes place in a weekend. It's a very disturbed family romance. Laura, the mother, Clara, her daughter, her brothers, all have terrible relationships. The family is supposed to be celebrating. Laura keeps it a secret that her mother has just died. It's an intriguing withholding on her part, and strategy on your part as author.

PF: A lot of things went into that. I don't think in advance about psychology, because then I'd be a psychologist. I think there is an impulse in Laura to keep it private. She was possessive about her mother's death and her mother, in a very primitive way. There are lots of reasons. She wanted to punish her daughter and her brothers. But that was also very primitive—to punish them for everything, for being themselves, for not paying attention to their mother, for neglecting her, for their laughter, for their lives. And then there was a child's secrecy. That is very significant for me: a child's secrecy and horror, because Laura was frightened by the death of her mother. If she didn't say it, then it didn't happen.

LT: Like magical—

PF: Magical thinking, exactly. Her main reason can fit under the subtitle "mischief," of a certain psychological bullying, viciousness, revenge. There are other reasons, but they're less significant.

LT: The Widow's Children is structured in sections: Corridor, Drinks, Restaurant, specific places or times in which we expect things to happen or not to happen.

PF: The corridors of our lives are very different. We pass through them on our way to different places, but they also exist in themselves as places where things happen. In the restaurant, Laura looks around; Clara, all of them, are at the table, and they're moored in middle-class-life comfort. It's the hour of drink, persuasion, assuagement and satisfaction, but not at Laura's table.

LT: The discomfort . . .

PF: It's very extreme, and Carlos, Laura's brother, can't wait to get away, to escape. They all want to escape, except for Laura's longtime friend Peter, who begins to sense, who sees how bad his choices were, but how inevitable.

LT: In the last paragraph of the novel, after Laura's mother's funeral, Peter remembers his childhood.

PF: I remember the last line. He had "known the cat and dog had been let out because he saw their paw marks braiding the snow, and felt that that day, he only wanted to be good." That's a kind of hope. We all wish we were good.

LT: Your characters all want to be good.

PF: Yes, I think that's true. Except for Laura.

LT: Each of your books is quite different from the others, though there are recurrent themes, like justice, injustice, people trying to see their own flaws, wanting to be good, honest. *The Widow's Children* stands out as something unto itself.

PF: It's so dense and compact a book. But I think in the last novel I wrote, *The God of Nightmares* [set in New Orleans], I kind of eased up on pounding away at my themes. That's really my most hopeful novel.

LT: Do you know why?

PF: No, except that it has a kind of easing.

LT: I think it's that, in the text itself, there's forgiveness.

PF: I think that's true. Oh, yes.

LT: There's the protagonist Helen's mother's letter to her. Her mother's dying, and she asks Helen to forgive her. She also forgives Helen.

PF: She says you have to forgive me for myself. Because we're all helpless, the way we are, until we can strike a judgment, a point—that's why judgment comes in . . . . I was just having a very complex thought. I don't know how to speak about it.

LT: At the end, Helen discovers that Len, her husband, was in love with her best friend, Nina, years ago. She feels terribly betrayed.

PF: But after their fight, she passes her hands over his body while he's asleep. Yes, it is forgiveness.

LT: Was your complex thought about forgiveness?

PF: We can't forgive easily. We have to take into account what was done. Various people get treated so badly. People get mistreated all the time. Black people were treated as an entity in a terrible way. We're such primitive creatures that we go by what we see, which is a different skin tone. Part of us is primitive.

LT: Helen leaves New Orleans, marries Len and the novel jumps into the future, when she thinks, "We were no more than motes of dust, drifting so briefly through a narrow ray of light that we could have no history." All of your characters experience that.

PF: Yes, it's a kind of profound life melancholy. But it's offset by feelings of affection for other people and, in this case, particularly for people in the French Quarter, who took Helen in, so to speak. She had such a good time when they told their stories.

LT: The secondary characters are wild, vivid figures. It's a war novel, like *The Western Coast*, but even more so. People go to war, come back, and don't, which is felt in the entire city.

PF: Everything was made very precious by that sense of leave-taking. I just suddenly remembered the black man looking at the ship, and Helen and Nina saying, "What do you think he was thinking about?" Nina says, "Getting away." I did see a black man looking at a ship, while living on the Mississippi. But I don't know if he was longing to get away.

LT: Your fifth novel, *A Servant's Tale*, begins with two words, "Ruina! Ruina!" It covers a lot of time and history. Luisa Sanchez is a character of great abjection. As a child, she comes to New York,

America—El Norte—from San Pedro, where her mother was a maid, her father, the son of a plantation owner. When she grows up, Luisa decides to be a maid.

PF: You know what one of the reviewers said about that? A black woman in the *New York Times* wrote, "Why didn't she pull herself together, go to college, and get a degree?" It's like a corporate person rearranging a book of taxes, when they say it should go here in this column rather than here.

LT: Women writers are meant to write women characters who uplift the sex, like black writers—women and men—are urged to uplift the race. By your having Luisa make that decision, it flies in the face of—

PF: The American Dream.

LT: Horatio Alger, middle-class values. The novel confronts claims and feelings—ideologies—that Americans hold dear. Luisa wants to be a servant.

PF: Americans hold family values dear, even as they're killing their own children. I think that people in terrible situations lie to themselves about the situations they're in. I feel that lying is the great human activity; being right is the great human passion. Because if you're not right, you're nothing.

LT: Luisa marries Tom, a public-relations manager; they met at a political meeting in Columbia University. You feel part of his interest in her is her ethnicity, her so-called authenticity, and his wanting to overcome his middle-class ways. Then he tries to change her. But Luisa will not be changed by anyone or anything.

PF Yes. This is what has happened to her: she wants her childhood back. She doesn't give it up until the end of the book, when she's able to think about something else. She wonders about Maura, one of the boarders in her parents' apartment. Luisa is the victim of herself. She's given everything over to reconstituting, discovering, her own terrible, lovely childhood and her grandmother. That's what she wants. She goes back to San Pedro and discovers that it's all changed, but the old witch is there. Gradually, in that last section, she recognizes it, without being able to name it, but the only way a reader knows that she's recognized it is that she can think of something else, in a way that's absolutely free of everything.

LT: Thinking about a person other than herself gives her the possibility of another future.

PF: I knew that she wasn't going to act the same way afterward. Even though so many years had passed, and she hadn't seen Ellen Dove, her black friend, I thought Luisa would contact her again and see about getting a law degree or something. (laughter) Then there was the last story in The Coldest Winter, "Frank."

LT: One of the boys you were teaching.

PF: Yes. Narcissism is not a good thing to have in the sense that you fill in everything with yourself, and people suffer so. You don't just have to be an indulged, rich child to be narcissistic. In fact, it's the opposite. The poor children. The world's filled up with questions of the self and the sense of the self. It's a dreadful, agonizing torture. And that's what happens to people, it seems to me, who have deprived, difficult, complex lives—when it's very extreme, out of some kind of alarm, everything in one's self—whatever it is—rushes to fill in all the spaces. So I used not the usual, sentimental relativism, that is, something larger than the self, but something other than the self.

LT: That's a very important distinction. You wanted Frank to go to an observatory and look through the big telescope, to see the stars.

PF: I had taken a course with Professor Motz, Lord Motz, professor of astronomy at Columbia. This was in the 1950s. I had a year with him and I couldn't go ahead, because I hadn't been to high school. I had only been there for three months. I didn't have the trigonometry I would have needed. I also couldn't go on with geology, which I loved.

LT: You had only three months of high school?

PF: Yes, pretty much. But I went to Columbia for four years, and managed other courses outside of the science courses. I'll tell you, my father was a terribly irresponsible man. He had a lot of charm, but he was an alcoholic.

LT: In your memoir *Borrowed Finery*, when you were going to meet the daughter that you had given up for adoption, you wrote, "In the face of great change, one has no conscious." You were hoping the plane would crash.

PF: That's right.

LT: When your characters have to face change, they'll do or think anything. Again, you're fearless; your characters don't couch their thoughts. Most writers would avoid their characters thinking what yours do.

PF: My husband, Martin, thinks it's because I didn't go to college. (*laughter*)

LT: Your characters have prejudices. Again, white novelists mostly shy away from writing about race, which is obviously a major subject.

PF: Yes, it is. It seems so important to me. My friend Mason Roberson, who was a writer and part of the Harlem Renaissance, lived in Carmel for a while. We used to have very funny phone calls. He wrote continuity for Sam Spade, and one day he called me up when I was living in San Francisco. He said, "I have a question to ask you." I said, "Shoot." He said, "What's 'shortnin' bread'?" (*laughter*)

LT: You also write about your mother in *Borrowed Finery*. You go to see her after 30-odd years, when she's dying. She offers you a family photograph, but then she hides it under her bed covers.

PF: She was such a savage that she didn't try to conceal anything about herself, though she concealed the picture very effectively. There was something remarkable about her that way; she would never pretend to be anything. I spent very little time with her, but once when she was in New York, with my father when they first came back from Europe, she was in a little brownstone on the East Side. I remember looking down a flight of stairs, and there was a brown, straw baby carriage with a hood. She looked down at it and said, "You know, the woman whose carriage that is killed her baby last week. Isn't it interesting to look down and see that carriage?" She was a terror for me. Any creature can give birth and walk away, and I thought that's what she'd done.

LT: Maybe the one thing you got from her of value was her honesty.

PF: Exactly, that's what was remarkable about her. She never tried to be any different than she was.

LT: I want to ask you about friends, groups, if you saw or see yourself as part of a literary movement. So many literary histories make assumptions about writers in that way.

PF: No, I don't feel that I'm in any particular group or movement. It's hard for me to feel that I belong to any group. That's a limitation for me, in myself. It's partly because I was always on the outskirts as a child—of my own life, in my family. As a writer, I feel like one voice among many. I hope that I don't dishonor the art of writing as I am passing through. It's my hope that I don't damage it in any way.

LT: Was it a struggle for you, the response to your books when they came out, and your novels going out of print?

PF: It was, but I've gone on. When *The Widow's Children* was turned down by Harcourt Brace, by Bill Goodman, who had taken *Poor George* on, he said it was the best novel I had written so far, but that my track record was very poor. That was a terrible thing—the track record idea. Of course, what else is new? This is a country so nakedly based on money. Other places try to conceal it.

LT: You said you didn't want to dishonor writing. That would be impossible. Your writing is truly wonderful. You are a great writer.

PF: Thank you. That's lovely to hear. I don't know what to say.

LT: Are you going to write another novel?

PF: I'm working on a short novel. It's called *A Light in a Farmhouse Window*. It takes place in contemporary France. There's a little part of it that goes back to 1321, when heretics occupied some small villages in the Pyrenees. They were the Cathars, and they were, like the Albigensians, completely wiped out by the Dominican priests. I'll tell you one story that I use: A Dominican priest was describing a village late at night to some horsemen, a gang, and one of the Crusaders tells him there were only 20 heretics in the village. The total population was 200. The Dominican priest said, "Kill them all. God will know his own."

After September 11, reckoning with Paula Fox's memoir, *Borrowed Finery*, is intellectually consoling. Like most people, I'm roller-coasting: Nothing means anything, everything's urgent, life's precious or, obviously, expendable. Her memoir asks: What does another life tell us? How is the manner in which a life is written significant?

Fox's life has had its fair—or unfair—share of painful incidents, alarming events, betrayals, bad parents. But thinking and writing against the current American grain, Fox doesn't deliver cause and effect dicta; she doesn't blame others or luxuriate in neglect, succumbing to the narcissism of victimhood. Instead, she shapes her memoir with a light hand, clearing an unusual path to her psychology and history. Connections she might have forged to establish the story, as she does in her novels—though there too she masters the art of underexplanation—are mostly absent or understood by indirection. The reader connects to and makes sense of, or doesn't, her psyche and worldview.

I once was surprised to find out that Paula Fox writes children's books. Not after reading the preface to this book. She launches her memoir with a parable, using a suit, clothing— *Borrowed Finery*—as a trope for fashioning and rendering a self. The opening prefigures a work about human mysteries rather than revelations. It signals Fox's exception to conventional wisdoms, reminding me of Paul Bowles' elegant, enigmatic Moroccan stories.

"In that time I understood mouse money but not money," she writes, whimsically characterizing her early poverty. In one sentence, Fox ensnares the adult, who is somehow forever a child, to suggest that no one is ever completely removed from childhood's fantastical realm and claims. In her preface too she touches on materialism, capitalism, and proposes that the life she will construct in writing might be the sum of a subjective struggle between culture and politics.

Fox doles out the past in episodes spanning people and places. She leaves them and returns, leaves again. The book divides into sections: "Balmville," "Hollywood," "Long Island," "Cuba," "Florida," "New Hampshire," "New York City," "Montréal," "New York City," "California," and "Elise and Linda." The reader hasn't seen the name "Linda" before.

There are many kinds of surprise in *Borrowed Finery*, not the least Fox's circumspection and reserve. Fox omits a lot—she never mentions becoming a writer, when she first published, any of that. We know, from how she reports listening to adult conversations when she was a child, that she loves words and ideas. We have a sense of the way she sees and pays attention: "Behind the door that closed off that uncanny space, I pictured Auntie, lying on her back in her bed, her eyes opened wide and unblinking, smoking cigarettes in the dark." Those who know her human-suspense novel *Desperate Characters* will notice that Fox was once bitten by a cat. She makes profound use of a cat bite in the novel, not unlike Shakespeare's use of the handkerchief in *Othello*. But like Edith Wharton, who in "A Backward Glance" never mentions her divorce from Teddy Wharton, Fox is reticent, and what she withholds, she forces the reader to embellish, to fill out the suit she's designed for us. In the end, Fox doesn't tailor easy resolutions or cozy notions about redemption.

Looking through reviews of American novels, even a casual reader might be disgusted by how often the concept of "redemption" appears. Contemporary novels have become a repository for salvation; characters—and consequentially readers—are supposed to be saved at the end. Paula Fox avoids pious niceties. She claims a reality most American readers want to avoid—the possibility of failure, when good acts don't replace bad ones in symmetries more appropriate to bad fiction. In Fox's fiction, defeat and failure are normal.

Like her novels, her memoir is exceptional, not because she's had a unique life, though she has probably, or at least a difficult one, but then who hasn't. It's how she chooses to represent it; how she manufactures meaning through style, with measure and intelligence. Her memoir is generative and evanescent. It speaks to the way life comes and goes, with its beauties and tragedies, through its balletic recording of transience and impermanence. Fox's graceful writing and integrity give comfort in these darker days.

Paula Fox's *The Coldest Winter: A Stringer in Liberated Europe* contests not just a book's usual designations—major, minor, big, small— but also its genre, in this case, the memoir. Fox is a great American writer, the author of several brilliant novels—including *Desperate Characters, The Widow's Children* and *Poor George*—and a recent auto-biographical work, *Borrowed Finery*. Her arresting, unique style and her profound understanding of character and situation transform a putative memoir into an assemblage of philosophical tales. Fox writes of incomprehensible acts and alarming histories with an earned, uncanny, and special wisdom.

Like other American writers, Fox sought out Europe as a test-ing ground for her fledgling writer's life. It was "a time when I imagined that if I could only have found the right place, the dif-ficulties of life would vanish." But the year she leaves is 1946, she is 23 years old and life abroad is framed by the harrowing landscape of post-war Europe. World War II and the Holocaust pervade almost every meeting she holds and every place she goes.

In London, when England was still on rationing, wealthy and celebrated English people and American expatriates befriend her. Their class and sumptuous houses provoke her wonder about those who imagine their property "reflected their praise-worthy character, not the ease with which they spent money."

Unlike many earlier Americans abroad, Fox must earn her living. She lands a job as a stringer for a left-wing newspaper owned by a peer, Sir Andrew, who hopes to present an alternative and challenge to Reuters' dominance. He assigns Fox to Paris, to cover a peace conference at the Palais du Luxembourg. But Fox reflects primarily on the effects of the recently ended war, a changed, saddened Paris and human wreckage.

Fox's novelistic eye tracks the odd habits of a fellow female boarder in a Parisian pension, with whom she partners in bridge. Then she notices a "faded blue tattoo of a number" on the strange woman's arm. A love affair ineluctably embraces the war, too; her lover is a Corsican politician whose wife suffered torture to protect him. The lovers' desire collapses under the burden of their own ethical indictments, "her bravery never far from our minds." One of the people she interviews drives her to his apartment for dinner with him and his wife, and Fox studies his shabby sheepskin jacket. Without being asked, the man explains that "the jacket had kept him warm" for three years in a concentration camp. The jacket, she writes, "seemed to me the brown carcass of an animal that had fought in vain for its life." Her qualification "in vain" alerts the reader to a struggle of lifelong despair.

In thoughts stunning as camera flashes, Fox knits her past together. She presents startling images and unforgettable stories. She compresses narrative time, moving fluidly from the young Fox to the older one, to measure first reactions and impressions against the insights of retrospection. She is honest, more severe with herself than anyone else. "I knew so little, and the little I did know, I didn't understand. My ravenous interest in those days was aroused by anything."

Sir Andrew assigns her to Warsaw, where "to walk . . . was to feel the cold and desolation and silence of a city of the dead." Here and elsewhere, Fox encounters people who pose great paradoxes and enigmas. There is troubling Mrs. Helen Grassner, a Jewish-American, middle-aged woman, who searches Poland for Jews and who grieves, because she didn't lose any of her family in the camps. With her, some other journalists and three Czechs who'd been in camps, Fox tours the Polish countryside, courtesy of the Polish government. They visit "a former vacation estate of a Prussian aristocrat," now a home for traumatized children "who had been born [or spent some time] in concentration camps . . . [though] their parents, without exception, had been murdered by the Nazis." A 19-year-old man, formerly a member of a Young Fascists organization, follows her one night and, in shadow, whispers of his thrill at watching executions. She rushes away, feeling disgust, hatred, and also a little sympathy for his abject, ruined life. Much later, working as a tutor for institutionalized, orphaned teenagers in New York, she remembers the children born in camps, their "stunted little weeping figures."

Chekhov's stories come to mind, his portrayals of ethical dilemmas, human ugliness and pathos, their unquestionable beauty and compassion. *The Coldest Winter* accounts for a year or so in Fox's life, but even more it asks how and why her or anyone's experience matters. Fox's past lies between and within the lines of other lives, her history inseparable from the greater one, and nothing she reports is reduced to a truism or general statement. Now, as she looks back, the endurance of memories is a mystery, haphazard as life itself.

In this and her novels, Fox chooses words so splendidly a reader must contend with how language can and cannot allow events and emotions to be rendered. Notably, Fox marks tragedy and "outrageous fortune" with a delicate hand. The enormity of the Holocaust is, in a grave sense, beyond words, so the fewer the better. By her discretion, this reader thought often of Primo Levi's writings and teachings. The uncaptioned photographs that are interspersed sparely throughout the book add to an idea of memory's elusiveness, and how very much more is forgotten. The pictures may be of a person or place Fox has just mentioned. Or, untitled, they may suggest that Paula Fox's experiences, the people she met, places she visited, can also represent those lost to history, unsung and anonymous. Her "year over there," she writes, "had shown me something other than myself."

F is for the Future

1995

You asked how I'm spending my time when I'm not watching the OJ trial. On the Internet at a friend's house. Testing my limits in the screen/face of seeming limitlessness, testing the machinery before I buy into it totally or semi-totally. (Reminds me of an aristocratic English guy I knew who was asked, after he crashed his car into two police cars, why he'd done it, why he'd wantonly wrecked those cars, and he answered: I was testing my machinery. His machinery worked—his grandfather's a lord, he wasn't in Bow Street jail even an hour.) My digression, association, isn't really wack; it's part of what the thing's about—relating, associating, digressing. As well as limits. Because while you seem to be homing in on or sensing the infinite, "accessing" an infinite variety, inundated with choices, threads and threads, you can feel powerless or powerful, depending upon how you navigate in a ocean/ notion like, the infinite is in a machine on your desk. Some people might develop a cortisone-type high, imagining everything in the machine is them, they can master the course/ship; others will get lost at sea, devastated by how much they can't do. I have both feelings. (You know I question the idea of access anyway.) Remember when I bought my computer years ago and fell in love with the delete key, wanted to delete everything. Sea metaphors—you "navigate" on the Internet. A new frontier, discoveries are expected, a journey, a narrative, and some new terms specific to it. I like seeing the way old words appear in new contexts as new clothes. Weirdly predictable material in a new world is expected. Remember how carrying a Porta-Pak was going to change everything? It's important to believe you redo it all with new techie toys, I guess, so even if the Internet carries old problems, it adds possibility, promise and dimension, some new problems, has effects no one can absolutely predict. Obviously your own little world is instantly changed, how you spend your time, whom you meet and what happens to you in cyberspace. You might learn to have different expectations, when people talk the talk, cyberspeak, a telegraphic shorthand. But how will sociality change—did the telephone change how people relate to each other, do we know? How will people's minds change or be changed? Technology and science are already so embedded in our thinking and lives, maybe it's impossible to recognize it. I keep remembering Wittgenstein's horror of science, his fury at the growing dependence on it.

Traveling into libraries, cool; I hated returning books (but library as physical space, as possible sanctum, will be missed; the idea will be missed). The ability to "access" knowledge replays the old Information v. Knowledge prizefight. What's knowledge? I can see, so can you, the movies, mixing animation with live action, the cyber world entering the "real" world, boring. A TV sitcom with the nerd at the computer, all the trouble he—maybe she—gets into. You know. But what's interesting is you can't encompass it, you ride it, surf it (I skim it), you choose. (You have to pick Echo, Panix, Netcom, America Online, Compuserve, one of the delivery systems first, which reminded me of another great

146

divide: IBM or Mac.) Immediately arresting and annoying, to me, overwhelming, the magnitude. What you decide to look into and lurk around, voyeuristically, is self-evidentiary. (Watching trials has changed me. I get worse all the time.)

A showbiz gossip group—"Keanu Reeves' publicist, Robert Garlock, has just issued a release stating that Keanu has never met David Geffen and Keanu is not gay. . . . Any comments, folks?"

A group around dry cleaning—"All of my suits have cleaning labels that say 'Professionally dry clean only.' Has anyone ever heard of an amateur dry cleaner?" "Actually, yes: there used to be, and perhaps still are, coin-operated dry-cleaning machines."

"The Extropians"—"The Extropy Institute now has an official home page and a gopher site as well. Extropian interests include transhumanism, futurist philosophy, personality uploading, critical analysis of environmentalism. . . ."

(I love the use of the word gopher; the hiddenness of cyber-places realized by a furry, furtive animal is futurist anthropomorphism.)

"Alt.Baldspot"—"Oh, my shiney head, my achin' baldspot. I'm writing to ask all of you what is the best baldspot shining method. . . ."

See, one Alt.Baldspot member imagines he can reach "all of us."

People join groups just for flaming, flaming's a raging element of apparent endlessness. The term's telling. Compare it with "Sticks and stones will break your bones, but names will never harm you." Flaming's more abstract, even if you think about fire, maybe a play on "reaching out," which involves the idea of touching but also implies a larger, nonphysical embrace. (*NYPD Blue* uses it too much lately.) A galaxy of sex discussions/groups—"alt. sex.bestiality.hamster.duct tape" is my fave. Haven't mentioned the serious conferences, haven't gotten serious, yet. I did go into a house, "a virtual community," LambdaMOO, and moved from room to room, trying to talk to somebody, but everyone was asleep, virtually.

So, I'll go on it, get E-mail, and become involved in a few conferences. Maybe you're already doing it, like sex, or you're not, because what is it, anyway, or you're apathetic. I don't know. I'm curious, not driven or obsessed, yet. It further marks and divides an already divided world, haves v. have-nots, and being literate or not is evidence of access, obviously, and disposition and more. A thing that seems limitless is all and nothing, what you make of it, like everything else. Massiveness, its volume, if not depth, is attractive and repulsive. I'm living approach/avoid anyway.

Alt.yours.

Thinking about F.T. Marinetti, I'm reminded of an incident in London. Some years ago a play based on Kafka's diaries was performed there by a fringe theater group. Their space was on the 8th floor of an office building. The elevator operator, noting the floor I wanted, complained, "Everybody talks about Kafka but no one does anything about him." What does one do with Marinetti? An anarchist, a poet, an innovator, a fascist, an antifeminist, a super patriot, a drum major for war, a "master" of the manifesto, as he was called, the progenitor of the Futurists is no easy figure or influence to gloss in a few words or in many words.

With the first Futurist manifesto, published in 1909 on the front page of *Le Monde,* Marinetti gave voice to a movement that understood the impact of the machine, that ecstatically embraced technology, war and the idea of progress, a movement that saw itself as the new incarnate. The Futurists cried "Burn the museums." Marinetti demanded "parole in liberta," free verse, free words, words freed from syntax. The sculptor Boccioni was "nauseated by old walls and palaces, old motives, reminiscences." Marinetti claimed the automobile over Samothrace. But in their uncritical belief in progress, the Futurists took off with some 19th-century baggage, brashly landing at the doorstep of a new century, ours.

It's this aspect of Futurism that may be carrying undue weight for its position at the start of the 20th century when modernity was burdened with trying to become modern. To "make it new," as Ezra Pound exhorted. In the 30s movie, *The Twentieth Century*, the train conductor—the name of the train is also the 20th century—keeps repeating, when there's any problem, "But we're on the 20th century," and passengers insist, "But this is the 20th century," The movie asks ironically, What makes one modern (or for that matter, postmodern)?

Through *The Futurist Cookbook*, published first in 1932 and just now translated into English, Marinetti and others propose recipes for modernity, manifestoes for the table. They polemicize against traditions of all sorts, particularly those of the bourgeoisie, offering Futurist maps to the entrance of the new. There's a recipe for "The Excited Pig, formula by Futurist Aeropainter Fillia," which calls for "a whole salami, skinned, served upright on a dish containing some very hot black coffee mixed with a good deal of eau de Cologne." And one for "Words-In-Liberty, formula by the Futurist Aeropoet Escadame," which needs "three sea dates, a half-moon of red watermelon, a thicket of radicchio, a little cube of Parmesan, a little sphere of gorgonzola, 8 tiny balls of caviare, 2 figs, 5 amaretti di Saronno biscuits: all arranged neatly on a large bed of mozzarella, to be eaten, eyes closed letting one's hands wander here and there, while the great painter and word-in-liberty poet Dopero recited his famous song 'Jacopson.'" Or there's "The Steel Chicken"—the flavor of steel is an important ingredient in any machine lover's diet—"the body of the chicken mechanized by aluminum-colored bonbons." And my favorite, by

Marinetti, "RAW MEAT TORN BY TRUMPET BLASTS; cut a perfect cube of beef. Pass an electric current through it, then marinate it for 24 hours in a mixture of rum, cognac and white vermouth. Remove it from the mixture and serve on a bed of red pepper, black pepper and snow. Each mouthful is to be chewed carefully for one minute, and each mouthful is divided from the next by vehement blasts on the trumpet blown by the eater himself . . . The soldiers are served plates of ripe persimmons, pomegranates and blood oranges. While these disappear into their mouths, some very sweet perfumes . . . will be sprayed around the room, the nostalgic and decadent sweetness of which will be roughly ejected by the soldiers who rush like lightning to put their gas masks on."

Trumpet blasts, soldiers and ripe persimmons, gas masks and perfumes of nostalgia characterize the Futurist menu of the 1930s, a tempting mix of militarism, sensuality, art and nature. The *Cookbook* aims for a "culinary revolution . . . changing radically the eating habits of our race." As in the earlier—or first wave—Futurism, speed, motion, light and liberty are part of any dinner, constant companions. Futurist cooking will be "tuned to high speeds like the motor of a hydroplane." Marinetti promises eating that is art, "the art of self-nourishment, which "like all arts . . . eschews plagiarism and demands creative originality." These are prime ingredients of Modernism, taking into the equation, or recipe, that an "art of self-nourishment" is by any other name reflexivity.

"Since everything in modern civilization tends toward the elimination of weight and increased speed, the cooking of the future must conform to the ends of evolution." Pasta is banned. Pastasciutta, "however agreeable to the palate, is a passeist food because it makes people heavy, brutish . . . sceptical, slow, pessimistic. Besides which patriotically it is preferable to substitute rice." The Futurists are for risotto, or "totalrice." Rice is light, good for speed and action, and, it's noted, there's the Italian rice industry to consider as well.

Marinetti deploys food to construct "the modern man," the new subject, to build him from the inside out, where food is what one ingests as metaphor and fuel. Futurist Marco Ramperti asserts: "The allegorical Italian has always got his avid mouth wide open over a plate of tagliatelle when he isn't dangling dripping strands of vermicelli down his greedy gullet. And it's an offensive image: derisory, grotesque, ugly . . . Our pasta is like our rhetoric, only good for filling up our mouths." Since Marinetti's the poet who advanced the idea of "words-in-liberty," it makes sense that food might be seen as rhetoric, freed from its traditional position as just food, or that using certain words and dropping others, like dropping pasta and adding rice, might signify departures and surprises, changes in thinking, changes in being.

In the new diet, taste alone certainly isn't enough. Like art, food must strive to interact with its environment, and the environment itself, like the cuisine, must be shaped to serve higher ends, the evolution of society Marinetti calls for. At a Futurist dinner all the senses must be engaged and taught to renounce the habits that dull pleasure. Between bites one might be squirted with perfume while an airplane motor roars, the music of machines. Under a Futurist regime, where knives and forks are passe, eaters could be asked to touch continuously the leg of the eater next to them or, when having "Fillia's Aerofood . . . composed of different fruits and vegetables," to eat "with the right hand . . . while the left hand caresses a tactile surface made of sandpaper, velvet and silk. Meanwhile the orchestra plays a noisy, wild Jazz . . ."

Their antic dinners and wild proclamations are meant to be taken with a dollop of the zany, the movement itself sometimes appearing to be what Oscar Wilde may have had in mind when he conjured up "zanies of style." Though where there's style there's content, and Marinetti isn't content with jokes. He defines Italian Futurism of the 30s as "the renewal of Italian pride, a formula for original art-life. the religion of speed . . . spiritual hygiene . . . the aesthetics of the machine. . . . Convinced that in the probable future conflagration those who are most agile, most ready for action, will win. . . ."

At the Holy Palate restaurant, sometimes known as the Aluminum restaurant, site of Futurist dinners, one might be served "sculpted meat," which is "symbolic of Italian regions." Marinetti demands: "The word Italy must rule over the word Liberty! The word Italy must rule over the word genius. The word Italy must rule over the word intelligence. The word Italy must rule over the words culture and statistic. The word Italy must rule over truth." It's an odd position from the man who called for words in liberty, words freed from syntax. But not an odd position for a fascist. Words in liberty become fixed, their meaning subsumed by a new syntax, one created by the State. Marinetti was, after all, one of the first members of the Fascist Party. And his own words, not freed from history, resonate with it, tasting the bitter aftermath of the Great War and Italy's sense of betrayal at the hands of the Allies. A past that also, in 1932, included the deaths of many of the leading Futurists, like Boccioni and Sant Elia, a startlingly innovative architect, both of whom, like so many other, had enthusiastically rushed to do battle in that war. In fact it was the Great War that effectively put an end to the most productive moment of Futurism. In this respect, it's not surprising that Marinetti calls for the murder of nostalgia. The Futurist door to modernity, once pried open and walked through, must be shut forever on the past—past failures and past losses.

If Marinetti hadn't written it himself of *The Futurist Cookbook*, it would have been necessary to comment: "It is not by chance this work is published during a world economic crisis." Marinetti's "antidote" is "a Futurist way of cooking: optimism at the table." Significantly the cookbook begins with a parable against despair. In "The Dinner That Stopped a Suicide," Giulio is obsessed with killing himself, as "She" has died in New York—at that time a place of many capitalist suicides—and is "calling" to him to join her. So Marinetti, Prampolini and Fillia, the "Aeropainters," rush to rescue their friend. But another "She" has sent Giulio a message, he tells them, another "who resembles her." Giulio "must not betray death" and says he must "kill himself tonight." "Unless?" the Aeropainters ask. "Unless?" Marinetti asks. "Unless you take us instantly to your splendid, well-stocked kitchens." A hilarious retort to a singular cul de sac or a worldwide depression, and an absurd way out of the devastating effects of the War that ushered in Hitler and Mussolini, as well as killed the earlier Futurism, which was once synonymous with avant-garde.

It's not without consequence, either, that death in the suicide story is represented by She, for women, who are always other in

Futurism (though sometimes [m]other), sit uneasily at its table, occasionally having to eat food shaped like their own bodies. The first Futurist Manifesto proclaimed: "We will glorify war, the world's only hygiene—militarism, patriotism, the destructive genius of freedom-bringers, beautiful ideas worth dying for, and scorn for women. We will destroy. . . feminism." And it's not just coincidence that the call against death also comes from a She, "one who resembles her." This may be reference to capitalism under a Fascist state. But in any case, it's the female body that signifies death as well as renewal. "The fugitive eternal feminine is imprisoned in the stomach. . . . At dawn he devoured the mammellary (sic) spheres of all mother's milk." In the "Geographic Dinner," she's a waitress, "a shapely young women dressed in a long white tunic on which a complete geographical map of Africa has been drawn in color; it enfolds her entire body." This is a neat conflation, woman as Africa, especially Africa, the site then of some Italian colonies. She is colonized and that part of the world is turned into something to be devoured, the waitress, the provider, greedily eaten up like a woman might be by a hungry lover desirous of conquering and overwhelming her. Women here, like food, are figures of speech.

While the first wave Futurists embraced both internationalism and war, but not feminism, the second wave are Italian firsters. They call for an end to Xenomania, defined in the cookbook as "the international cuisine of grand hotels, which in Italy is "submit[ted] to only because it comes from abroad," Xenomanes are anti-Italians, like Arturo Toscanini, who "disown[ed] his own national hymns . . . opportunistically playing foreign anthems," those who don't "promote Italian influence in the world," and who are "infatuated with foreign customs and snobbisms." While the second wave Futurists trounce some traditions, including the earlier Futurists' internationalism but not their patriotism and antifeminism, there remains the traditional belief in an overpowering principle that centers existence. For Marinetti, it not a belief in God but the state, Italy under Mussolini. As Hannah Arendt put it: "The Fascist movement, a 'party above parties,' because it claimed to represent the nation as a whole, seized the state machine, identified itself with the highest national authority and tried to make the whole people 'part of the state.'"

To make Italians into, and part of, a healthy state, Marinetti wants to put the nation on a diet that is not just concerned with food. No more "Xenomania." "No more after dinner speeches." "Elementary patriotism demands that at least half the music on, programme should be by modern or Futurist Italian composers." Like most diet books and cookbooks, *The Futurist Cookbook* is sometimes repetitive, hammering away at its prescriptions for right living, its short announcements like press releases or ads that are trying to sell a product. In this case, the nation. Eating ought to imbue that patriotic feeling. As in, the way to the heart is through the stomach.

And speaking of the heart, the recipe—in fact the cookbook—is a prescription for the regulation of pleasure. While everything in *The Futurist Cookbook* seems to be full of imagination and is funny and clever, not that much is really left to the imagination. We're told not only what to eat but how to and with what feelings, in what kind of restaurant, listening to what type of music and sniffing what kind of scents. The Futurist "New Year's Eve Dinner," for instance, is meant to overturn crusty bourgeois conventions, when "the same elements have conspired to produce a happiness which has been enjoyed too often." So, "everyone eats in compulsory silence; the desire for noise and jollity is suppressed." One may sympathize with the urge to throw away customary and obligatory forms of feeling that seem hollow and perfunctory. But to replace those with others is problematic, to use words like "supress" and "compulsory" means one kind of order is being supplanted by another. In this light it's interesting to consider the Marquis de Sade's *120 Days of Sodom*, his regulation of pleasure written during the French Revolution while he was in jail. A pessimist, de Sade presents a dystopia which took to the extreme the problem of imagining what complete liberty would mean and look like under the law. He translated the furthest reaches of *liberte, egalite* and *fraternite*, where laws insist upon pleasure and turn pleasure inside out, into pain, at least for some. In the midst of a revolution, de Sade questions the ability of any state to provide pleasure or happiness. Marinetti, a man at liberty, whose words are supposedly also "in liberty," sets down a regimen—tongue in cheek—for the right libertinage. The optimistic Marinetti exuberantly ordains a future of aluminum and steel, of controlled anarchy and virility, of art that scoffs at some traditions in search of a genuinely contemporary existence. He doesn't question a pursuit of happiness that looked to the nation for its greatest rewards.

Coming to the end of this century, some of these refrains may not seem unfamiliar. There's the furtive glance back to the beginning, performed like a cat first contemplating its quixotic tail then chasing it. Though since we're at the end of it, and that's supposed to mean something in itself, the way death means something, we're supposed to be at the end of it, the end of the Twentieth Century. Which reminds me again of that movie of the same name, as good a metaphor as any. By now some of the cars have become derailed or separated from each other. In the time after modernism, otherwise known as postmodernism, certain beliefs, especially faith in the new, in progress, in self-referentiality, have come under scrutiny and are in the train station, with a bad wheel or engine. But can anything be left behind and what's in front and what's in back? Does coming to the end of a century have anything to do with an end anyway? Will a postmodern menu offer us something different, other metaphors, like one from column A, column B and column C? Will recipes with generous amounts of asymmetries and hardy dashes of anti-closure not be recipes? My view is necessarily one-sided, seeing the past through the present, my version of the present, seeing *The Futurist Cookbook* darkly, when I might have concentrated on nature versus culture, formal art issues, Futurism's influence on art practices generally, the sheer fun of it. My reading is no doubt compelled by forces from within and without. A recipe may be inscribed in me that I'm unaware of and whose powerful tastes simply, unconsciously, overcome me. Though really, I think to myself, I ought to be at the end of at least this trope.

G is for Goldin

Nan Goldin is a photographer whose work is a record of her life. If this were the 19th century, she might be called a diarist. Her formal compositions have depicted her friends in candid moments—in bars and clubs, funky bedrooms and bathrooms, hanging out, having sex, doing drugs, looking warily at each other, themselves or the camera. Often these characters were estranged from society, but not necessarily from each other, and especially not from the photographer. Anything and anyone Goldin shot were intimate to her. In exhibitions and in books, she has included some self-portraits, a few of which presented devastating views of her own self-destructiveness. But, she suggests, no portrait of her could be complete without the people she loves and what's around her. "The Ballad of Sexual Dependency," the work in which she first documented her friends and herself, her scene, forged a genre, with photography as influential as any in the last 20 years.

Her sprawling new book, *The Devil's Playground* (Phaidon), jars loose memories of her early photographs. As before, she presents what she has and likes in front of her—breakfast on a tray, friends having sex, and young, nude men and women. But now her stage is broader, set in a more expansive world, maybe it's global, and the characters and scenes have changed.

The book opens with large-scale vistas of the natural world and friends dwarfed in it: men in blurred landscapes; fiery red and somber blue apocalyptic skies; single characters floating in placid seas; and the base, or face, of a gnarled, grotesquely green redwood tree. Goldin tells her most recent life story in pictures of places she's been—now, instead of the old bars and clubs, they are romantic countrysides or beaches, elegant hotel suites, balconies and terraces.

Goldin also turns her eye to biological families, a grouping that was absent or infrequent in her previous work, and even includes a series with her own parents and a photograph of her brother. Handsome parents frolic with their lovely children. The pristine portraits of her friends' children nestle against shots of the parents serenely touching and kissing. Goldin hopes to expose unguarded instances of sexual and familial love, maternal and paternal affection.

In one series, a couple and their son roll around on the bed, the parents alternating between attention to the child and each other. In another, Goldin shoots a woman on one bed, a man on another; he's tenderly touching their child's head. A sequence of the couple making love follows, with their child out of the picture. Goldin's mothers are sexual beings, never just maternal. A nursing mother's breast will also be an object in her husband's mouth.

All children wonder about their parents' devotion to each other and to themselves, and compete for their love. Freud said that it was the primal scene children longed to see, that sexual curiosity was the source for the desire to know. Everyone's Garden of Eden.

Any photographer is outside the scene, watching. But wanting to get inside the familial embrace, or, like a child, into its parents' bed, Goldin is necessarily pitched outside the family's frame, and as a result the collection carries a startling melancholy.

The many formal, austere portraits of Goldin's friends add to that feeling. Often they are standing or sitting, darkness surrounding them. Like the photographer, they are solitary, and, looking at her solemnly, they could reflect her singular position. Set in the dark or against a blurry background, Goldin's subjects feel as if they are cut from time, disconnected, not anywhere or in any place. Oddly, place seems unimportant here. Even the book's numerous landscapes seem to represent just an outside to an inside, an impersonal, exterior world to an elusive interior one. Or maybe the pictures document a huge, gorgeous, alienating world.

A section titled "Empty Rooms," which lies at the center of the book, insists on what's lost or gone. Goldin is traveling, staying in hotel rooms, visiting friends, returning home and leaving. There's a portrait of a plumped pillow on a bed, rumpled sheets and two pillows that stand in for bodies that once lay there, a mirror that reflects light only on an ordinary bureau, golden paintings above a bed's backboard, and all are stage sets for memory. Juxtaposed with those images are a photograph of Christian Schad's painting of a masturbating woman, taken in Zurich, and a fire in Napoleon's Elba fireplace. In a way, the two photographs disrupt the narrative flow, but then remind the viewer of other ways to be on your own, by having sex alone or by being an outcast or prisoner.

Hotel rooms usually mark transitoriness and freedom from daily life, but they're haunted by the many bodies that have passed through. The photographs are also haunted by her absent friends, some of whom have died and some of whom are far away. Temporary stations themselves, the empty rooms emphasize the inadequate hold anyone has on life, how it all just goes, finally. So the collection ends with religion and death, which makes sense, since Goldin's work is about how a life spans and spins, sometimes out of control. Fire, skulls and crossbones, skeletons in monks' robes, votive candles blazing. The last image is a tombstone for a 14-year-old: "You Never Did Anything Wrong."

An earlier artist's work comes to mind: Michelangelo Antonioni's movie *Blow-Up*. In it, the photographer becomes a private detective. That transformation—and metaphor—influenced a generation of artmakers. Like Mr. Antonioni's photographer, they wanted to enlarge the event, to get closer to the scene. Goldin investigates intimacy, her large-scale photographs even blow it up. Her work asks if an ineffable feeling or experience can be visualized, and, when it's photographed, if it is available to others. Do we feel it, too? What do we see?

In these photographs, the artist/detective Goldin searches for secret, buried meanings, to find what is beneath the surface of a look that a photograph acknowledges but can't explain. Here, mystery, enigma and sadness shadow the beauty of individuals, couples, children, rooms. Something's missing, something's wrong. Remember: the collection is called *The Devil's Playground*. St. Augustine contended that evil was the absence of good, since God wouldn't create or make evil. The Devil was absence, pure nothing. Maybe what's not here, what's left out or lost, is as significant as what is.

H is for Harry

A Conversation with Harry Mathews

"Everything that happens in these books—the least details of their vicissitudes, their erudite digressions, their langoureux vertiges—are nothing more than the ghostly, frail delineations of the legendary wrestling match in which from the beginning of time we have been engaged with the world of words, signs, meanings, and dreams, in which we call fiction."
— *Avez-Vous Lu Harry Mathews* by Georges Perec

Lynne Tillman: I'm intrigued by your idea that "reading is an act of creation for which the writer provides the means." I wonder how this directly affects your writing.

Harry Mathews: I don't really know that it does affect it, except in some mysterious way that comes out of my experience as a reader. I know, as a reader, that language really doesn't work representationally. And that it's very hard to get away from the idea that it is some kind of representation. I think that probably I only can make use of ideas like that once I'm in the rewriting stage.

LT: An active reader allows a writer . . .

HM: It gets a writer off the hook of subject matter. Many writers think they're not being significant or important unless they're writing about things which are that week or year supposed to be significant. One decade it'll be politics, the next, something else. We have a tendency to feel that the subject matter ought to be big, and often a "big" subject may not be appropriate for a particular writer. The point is that you can write wonderfully about anything. It's very hard, unless one takes a lot of time as I did in that essay, to show how that works. But, for instance, right now we're talking about a particular subject, and I seem to be communicating to you about that subject. By the end of this conversation you may notice that something has happened that has nothing to do with the subject. Probably what really will have happened is some kind of alteration or transformation in the relation between us. We seem to have been having this discussion where I've been talking about my writing or whatever you choose to ask me about, but in fact something else has been going on. I think it's the same in books. Writers should go with what subject matter appeals to them, with what tickles them because that probably will be the kind of subject matter that will give them most access to the process of discovery; of what they are, or the world is, or language is. You must have had that experience as a writer yourself. As you rewrite something, nothing in substance is changed and yet it's not just that you're making it neater or more elegant. It's become something totally different in the third draft. And, in fact, that's what you wanted to say. Even though all the material was there in the first draft, and you got it all down, it wasn't doing what you wanted it to do. Rewriting is so extraordinary, it's where writing, not always, but very often, takes place. That's when the writer becomes the first reader. Becomes a creator. If the reader is the only creator, the writer gets to share and in fact participates in that act of creation in the stage of rewriting. That's when the writer can play creator, too. The old idea is hard to get rid of, that the writers have something to say and the readers are there to get it. I don't think things work that way at all.

LT: In that sense, the author has always been dead.

HM: That's right. There's never been any authors. There have only been readers. The authors are first readers.

LT: Your most recent novel *Cigarettes* seems formally very different from, let's say, your first novel *The Conversions*, although it seemed to me that *Cigarettes* reworks some of *The Conversions'* themes.

HM: The earlier works were misread by a great many readers because they always thought I must be doing something else than what was actually there. And so they kept looking past what was right in front of them. One doesn't have to look for symbols, one doesn't have to look for explanations. You don't need to explain those early books either. I think they are very up front. And one way that they're up front is in the terrific unspoken or apparently unspoken drama that goes on in the life of the narrator, one which is barely indicated but always present. The narrator makes only two or three remarks in the course of *The Conversions*—about his wife divorcing him, for instance—but they're enough to suggest all the things that he's not saying that he should be saying. You can't help being aware, even if you don't know why, that the narrator has been reduced to a point of total fearfulness.

LT: His pursuit of the inheritance, which sets him chasing fragments of an esoteric puzzle that, in fact, doesn't exist, has all sorts of meanings. He's on a quest, a journey. Is he worthy, is he smart enough? A lot of anxiety there.

HM: John Ashbery was one reader who understood this straight off. Many people thought I was being too clever by miles, that I was playing games or just showing off or I don't know what, indulging in a display of erudition. And that really isn't the point at all. All the erudition gets blown up; it all turns out to have no significance whatsoever. In *The Conversions* there's really only one character; the drama you get of one character who can't or doesn't dare tell about himself. I myself find this drama all the more moving by being so painfully, so inadequately expressed.

LT: Which is where your work reminds me of Jane Bowles' *Two Serious Ladies*. In fact, Phoebe, the troubled young woman in *Cigarettes*, asks her father to read to her from *Two Serious Ladies*. I know that people talk about your work mostly in relation to Roussel...

HM: I'm delighted to hear it. I read *Two Serious Ladies* three times and I don't know how she did it. She achieves miracles by just putting one ordinary sentence after the other and she never indicates the way you're supposed to feel about it. That's something which I certainly hold as a model in my writing, but I got that more from Roussel than I did from her.

LT: That "not indicating the way you're supposed to feel about it" is why I think of you in relation to Jane Bowles. How would you describe *Cigarettes* to somebody who hadn't yet read it, or what would you say your project was when you started it?

HM: I had several things I wanted to do. For one thing, I promised myself not to do anything I'd already done in my earlier books. No erudition, no language games. The texture is very clear and if you took each chapter by itself, it would seem very conventional in style. I also wanted the book to be both traditional and modern. I had, almost from the very start, a desire to portray a passionate friendship between two middle-aged women—the friendship between Elizabeth and Maud at the end of the book. In a way, the whole book leads to that.

LT: The portrait painted of Elizabeth by Walter Trale, another character, is so important in the novel. She is at the center and her portrait is a kind of centerpiece.

HM: Actually, the painted portrait doesn't turn out to be very significant.

LT: But it has meaning in relation to people's lives.

HM: It does but it's just a thing ultimately and it's the characters who lay a lot of significance on it. I think it's tempting for readers to do that too. Some people who have written about the book are tempted to see in the portrait a symbol of something mysterious. I think it's symbolic of an object just being an object.

LT: In the novel it seems to be important not because it's essentially important, but because different people desire it, copy it, try to destroy it. It floats through the text as a kind of signifier.

HM: That's true. It's a signifier without any signified beyond itself. It has no metaphysical significance of any kind at all. It plays an important role in terms of the narrative. It's a kind of bait for the expectation, for the desire to find significance. In the end it's just hanging on the terrace being a painting, we recognize its role to be purely narrative and nothing more than that. In a way the portrait is like the huge cultural constructs in my early books, you know in musicology or in art history or theology—they all turn out to be so much hot air. Of course between the opening chapters and the final chapter the portrait serves to remind us of Elizabeth herself, whom we've only known through her effect on three of the male characters. The reader, whether admitting it or not, has probably read the table of contents and seen that the last chapter is called "Maud and Elizabeth." The reader knows after Elizabeth disappears that she's going to come back.

LT: All of the chapters present characters in pairs; each one gets paired with others in different chapters. You date some chapters

1936, and some 1963, which is the reverse of 36. I liked the structure very much; it underscores what things mean in relation to each other and in time.

HM: That's very good. I had general ideas about what I wanted to do, but I had no idea what the book was going to look like. I had invented a design that amounted to a series of empty spaces to fill up. I stared at these empty spaces for two years, watching them fill up, watching them turn into a whole. The story gets told, but it is never told. Whatever it may be, the story of the novel isn't told, just these other stories of the particular relationships.

LT: *Cigarettes* is not only about relationships in a very direct way, but things that have tremendous impact on relationships, like money. Money moves through the text and interrupts lives in very different and fascinating ways. Who inherits it? Do you give it away? Do you squander it? Do you invest it? This too reminded me of *The Conversions*—the hero's quest for the immense fortune. So I wanted to talk about money.

HM: Oh dear, really? I don't have much to say about money that isn't in the book. I guess if I had to say something general about money, it would be that it's completely empty, it has no meaning in it itself, no significance. It's simply in reactions people have to it that it acquires an apparent role. It has no inherent power.

LT: It's used that way in your novel, Maud giving it to her daughter and then taking it back and then giving it again.

HM: And the father giving it to the daughter, giving it and taking it back. Elizabeth, who's obviously been through her share of thin spells (she's broke at the time she meets Maud), finds it totally silly that Maud should get so upset about this. "You're making a problem out of a million dollars"—a million pre-war dollars. For somebody like Elizabeth, and Irene too, money's just something to get when you need it and use for what you need. For the others, money matters to them in some way, it's involved in how they define life as having value or not. Maud isn't a bad person at all, she's a gentle, generous and warm person whom Elizabeth manages to bring out of her state of perpetual reluctance. She's not mean, but nevertheless, she does things which she then bitterly regrets.

LT: I thought that the way in which money figured in people's lives, people with money worrying about money in some way. . .

HM: It's an American hang up, I think.

LT: This is your most American novel, I thought.

HM: It's not the point of the novel at all. But I suppose socially that's true, in so far as it's a depiction of a social milieu.

LT: The novel talks about the meanness, cruelty of people. For instance, Owen is going to discover Allan's insurance fraud. For pleasure. It's a game to him. In your earlier books it looks like games play people, and in *Cigarettes* it's people who play games.

HM: They think they are. It's interesting what happens in connection with Owen's game. It actually cures Allan of his criminality, not because it frightens him, but because he'd finally been caught—appreciated. Owen may turn out to be smarter than Allan is, but at least Owen has gone to a lot of trouble to untangle these very smart frauds that Allan set up and that he's never been able to tell anybody about. Owen acts like a tough macho knocking off another guy and showing him who's boss, but he ends up doing Allan a great favor. Allan gives up this whole secret fraudulent career that he's been pursuing for totally inadequate reasons. At least the reasons he gives sound unconvincing.

LT: Characters in *Cigarettes* are motivated to do things but there's no explanation as to *why* they're doing these things.

HM: They certainly don't seem to know why they're doing them.

LT: Maybe Allan wants to be discovered, wants attention, needs to be bad, those kinds of things, and yet that's too reductive, really.

HM: To go back to your very first question: How does allowing the reader to be the creator work? I could say that the reader has to bring his or her experience to bear to supply an explanation, has to invent some way of accepting these characters and their behavior.

LT: The characters Morris Romsen, the art critic, and Lewis, the would-be writer, have, in *Cigarettes*, a physical sado-masochistic relationship that parallels, in my mind, the relationship of Allan and Owen in which the two men are playing elaborate games with each other that mean, somehow, affection and attention.

HM: I always love to have people find parallels like that. You mentioned earlier that 63 was the reverse of 36. This is news to me, and I'm sure that one could discover an interesting numerical system going throughout the entire book which would also be news to me. It reminds me of my great friend Georges Perec's explanation of *Tlooth*, my second novel. When he translated it into French, he imagined a semantic palindrome running through it. That is to say, some kind of hidden series of statements that could be read forwards and backwards and that he thought determined the course of the book. One piece of evidence he produced was a switch of the letters "m" and "n" in one chapter: *bombe atonique* (a soporific spray) and for*m*ication (meaning ant activity). I told him, you're absolutely right. But I had been totally unaware of doing this. Things like that make me feel that whatever I'm doing must be right, at least as it allows this kind of connections or similarities to manifest themselves. That's a sign there's a whole lot of thought going on of which I'm unaware.

LT: Tlooth seemed the most overtly political of all your works, with its sects, groups, with Jacksongrad being the name of the camp, like a play on Stalingrad, or on a concentration camp or a gulag. But the book begins with a baseball game that also places it in and refers to the United States, spreading the political spectrum left and right.

HM: I'm sure politics is at least implicitly involved, but really the substratum of those first three novels is a religious one. Obviously, in *The Conversions* where there's a sort of white goddess legend. She's black actually but it's still a matriarchal goddess cult. But even in *Tlooth* religion is lurking in all the corners.

LT: The names of the sects, Fideist, Americanist, Defective Baptist, Resurrectionist.

HM: That's right. Elsewhere there are various forms of Christianity, including the Nestorian heresy, which is described in the chapter "Spires and Squares." And then in *The Sinking of the Odradek Stadium*, my third novel, there is Buddhism as well as Catholicism. Certainly politics are present too—it was the middle of the '60s, after all.

LT: I thought about religion in regard to *Tlooth* and then in relation to your work generally. I began to think you were saying that faith in language, as a way to communicate, is like faith in religion. That you have to believe in language, you have faith that you can communicate, even if you're not really able to communicate, as you have in a religion.

HM: I'm very moved by that. Did you know that was how Perec felt?

LT: Really?

HM: I'm glad to know that I ultimately agree with him, having had many arguments with him about the question of how communication actually works in language, of whether communication is possible at all. For Perec, writing was a kind of salvation. It was justification by works. You know that expression, much discussed during the Reformation? And Perec, I think that if he hadn't felt that writing was a vocation in the absolute sense of the word, a calling, like a priest, he would have died even sooner that he did.

LT: When did he die?

HM: In 1982.

LT: Perec was, like you, a member of the OuLiPo. Could you say what it is and give its history?

HM: Thank you. Anything else?

LT: You may want it to be the last question.

HM: Well, you're opening—it's not a can of worms, on the contrary—it's a jewel case full of pearls but there is so much to say about the OuLiPo, especially in connection with Perec, who introduced me to it and through whom I was elected to the group.

LT: Who started it?

HM: It was started by Raymond Queneau, who is by now fairly well known in America in translation, and Francois LeLionnais, a great friend of Queneau's and like him, very interested in mathematics, an extraordinarily versatile and brilliant man. The OuLiPo was created to satisfy their mutual needs—LeLionnais' case, to form a workshop of experimental literature, in Queneau's case, to carry him through to the end of this extraordinary book he was writing called *A Hundred Thousand Billion Poems*. The book consists of only ten sonnets in which any first line can replace any other first line, any fifth line can replace any other fifth line and so forth which means that it's 10 to the 14th power, there being 14 lines in a sonnet.

LT: Because of the permutations.

HM: The creation of the OuLiPo accompanied his bringing that work to a conclusion. The OuLiPo has had as its purpose the invention and rediscovery of what the French call *contraintes* and we call, for want of a better word, constrictive forms. Rediscovery of forms like the palindrome, the lipogram. The palindrome is something you can read backwards and forwards, the lipogram is writing in which you leave out one or more letters. In both these cases Perec did the most extraordinary work. He wrote a palindrome which is several thousand characters long, in which he describes Perec writing a palindrome—he was a real virtuoso in his language. And he wrote this extraordinary novel called *La Disparition*, "The Disappearance," but it can't be translated that way into English because, like the rest of the book, the title excludes any word that contains the letter "e," a letter that is even more frequent in French than it is in English. Leaving out the letter "e" would mean that the opening sentence of Proust's *Remembrance of Things Past—Longtemps je me suis couché de bonne heure* would have only two words left. Not only did Perec do this tour de force writing without using the most frequent letter in the language, he also turned this deprivation into the subject of his novel and wrote about it brilliantly and funnily and entertainingly.

LT: That's an amazing feat. From what I've read about Perec, his life was forged from deprivation, a World War II experience, parents killed in concentration camps, loss of native country. So that absence and lack were central to his existence, and his choosing to write a book that leaves out something essential like the letter "e" parallels his being left without parents and country.

HM: You got it. Instead of having to deal with this anguishing problem of having had his tongue cut out by history, he deliberately gave up an element which makes writing normally easy, and imposed an extremely harsh rule on himself which he then was able to triumph over. He did it so well that some critics didn't notice. But they weren't very attentive critics. Let me add that in the OuLiPo we also invented a great many forms of our own.

LT: How many people are in the OuLiPo?

HM: We never exclude our dead members, who include not only Queneau and Perec but Calvino. But without our dead members,

I think, if you counted everyone, we have about 15 or 16, and there are 12 who are active. We meet once a month for dinner.

LT: In Paris?

HM: Yes, it's a working lunch or dinner, and we'd better get the work done before the dinner starts. It gets rather too delirious to get serious business conducted after the meal starts. Why don't we have lunch?

After Lunch

HM: I remember earlier in the interview saying that for me rewriting was writing. And I've had two experiences in which that was not the case. The first was the title poem sequence of *Armenian Papers* which I wrote at the end of working days right off and hardly corrected at all, and the other was this book which has just come out called *20 Lines A Day*. It's a collection of my warm-up exercises in which I overcame the terrors that we know of the blank page by giving myself something very short to do: writing at least 20 lines, no less than 20 lines, about anything that happened to come into my head. And the writing turned out to be very interesting even though there was practically no rewriting involved. I just wanted to say that because it's not what I usually do and it never the less seems to have worked.

LT: Was doing the 20 lines like automatic writing?

HM: No, it wasn't. I only did one set of automatic writing and I discussed it in one of the 20 line pieces. It was like automatic writing only in that I set myself a limited task, but it was quite different in that I had a subject which I stuck to. Or several subjects. But the writing was as they say, "off the top of my head."

LT: Certain themes return in your work, one of them, the journey. Which reminds me of Barrett Watten's designation of you in his essay in the Harry Mathews Number of *The Review of Contemporary Fiction*: "Harry Mathews, having chosen exile . . . " I wondered how you felt about that. You've been living in Europe since 1952?

HM: That's right.

LT: How did you see that move then and how do you see it now?

HM: When I first left America I was very happy to leave the country and what I have to immediately add to that is that I didn't know the country and I didn't even know New York City, what I knew was the life of the well-to-do Upper East Side and that life seemed very discouraging to me in terms of what I wanted to do. I was talking to Larry Rivers the other day about that and how, when I went down to what later became my stamping grounds, Greenwich Village, among painters, I felt so out of my element, I felt even worse there than I did among the Upper East Side crowd which was not particularly appealing to me (although of course, there are good friends to be found in all places), so then I went to Europe. It was like a kind of going into exile or might have been interpreted as that, although what it really felt like was going back to a place which was very familiar and which had been sort of mysteriously familiar. I didn't come back to the United States at all for six years and then I came back a little bit, I didn't like it and then I came a little bit more and liked it a little bit more, and of course by then I'd met John Ashbery and through him many other friends here and I was discovering a whole other aspect of New York City and the country. I don't know America very well, I haven't traveled it nearly as much as I'd like to, but that original aversion to it vanished. And in any case, even if my departure might have been a kind of expatriation at the beginning, it never amounted to a separation from my identity as an American. I've never been anything else, I've never thought of myself as being anything else. It always astonishes me when people ask me, "Oh, you live in France, well, do you write in French or are you a French citizen?" First of all, that doesn't happen all that easily in France, it's not the way it is here where people come, move here and do become citizens. I may have had a desire to reinvent myself in terms of being, if not a Frenchman, a person living in France, a person living in Italy, a person living in Spain; I very quickly learned that you never leave home. And I think the great advantage of having gone to Europe and having lived there is that it allowed me to become more aware of my American-ness than I would have if I had stayed here.

LT: How did *Locus Solus*, the magazine that you did with other Americans in Paris, come about?

HM: Only John Ashbery was in Paris. Jimmy Schuyler and Kenneth Koch were living in New York at the time. And it came about because we, all of us, wanted to be published more. We did this sort of self-centered thing, we published ourselves and our friends. I hadn't yet found a publisher for *The Conversions*, my first book. I'd published a few poems here and there, John had published his first book, Kenneth had published one or two books, and Jimmy had published, I think, a novel and a book of poems. But we were all anxious to see more of what we wanted, not only in terms of publishing ourselves, but of seeing writing we liked published. Although this is much truer of them than of me. I was much less in touch with what was going on in America than they were because of the fact I'd been living in France, I hadn't kept up, and I didn't have the contacts.

LT: So you didn't meet Georges Perec until much later?

HM: Yes. In 1970.

LT: Cigarettes is dedicated to him, and it felt especially right because of the ending, with its meditation on death.

HM: A lot of people died in my life, in a very short time. Between 1980 and 1986 both my parents died, Georges Perec died, several other friends died. So as I was writing *Cigarettes*, I had experiences of death which are probably reflected in the book. Historically I dedicated it to Perec because when we met we were both going through fallow periods and then he really climbed out of his pit and wrote this fantastic book, *Life, A User's Manual*, which *Cigarettes* didn't pretend to rival. But the fact that he did it and with such panache and such exuberant diligence, got me out of my reluctance to start a novel again. I was reluctant because of the great difficulty I'd had in publishing *The Sinking of the Odradek Stadium*. I didn't want to go through that again. It had been a lot of work and it ended with a lot of disappointment in years of waiting for it to be published. I said, Georges had a lot of excuses not to write if he didn't want to and he came up with this extraordinary novel, so I should, too. *Cigarettes* has nothing to do with *Life, A User's Manual*, but his having done the book did inspire me.

LT: *Cigarettes'* last pages are very moving.

HM: Did I tell you that the pages about the actor in the railroad station (near the end of the last chapter) were the first pages of the book I wrote and the ones that immediately follow—the concluding pages—were the last? There's the description of this impeccably dressed actor who is hired to be an extra man at social functions, but he's also an extra like an extra in the movies. I cared about him. I really cared about that passage, with the book ending with that description. Let me just read it.

"In such circumstances, I sometimes think that only the residual strength of the dead beings inside me gives me power to survive at all. By that I mean both the accumulated weight of the generations succeeding one another and, as well, from the first of times when names held their objects fast and light shone among us in miracles of discovery, the immortal presence of that original and heroic actor who saw that the world had been given him to play in without remorse or fear."

It's clearly the original and heroic actor of whom I had no inkling at the time I began the book who provides the unheroic actor in the railroad station.

LT: This would be a good place to end, at the end of the novel, but I have the alphabet questions I initially planned to ask.

HM: Ask them all, go ahead.

LT: "A" for art world. In *Cigarettes* there's quite a lot about the art world.

HM: That question could have a very long answer—I was married to Niki de Saint Phalle, and I've known artists all my life. I've been friends with people in the group on both sides—dealers, editors of art magazines, and so forth. I really have no particular insight or attachment other than that.

LT: "B," beauty, there's an elegance, a beauty to your writing.

HM: Beauty is something which moves in after the point of works of art have been lost.

LT: "C," *Cigarettes* the title. Why that title?

HM: The question, "Why is the book called *Cigarettes?*" is a question that should be asked.

LT: "D" is dreams. Do you use them directly?

HM: Occasionally. I think that Phoebe's egg hallucination is a dream I had. And the chapter called "The Otiose Creator" in *The Conversions* was a dream of Niki de Saint Phalle.

LT: "E"—we've gone over this—exile.

HM: Yes, though I've never been exiled.

LT: "F," fantasy, father, fake, any of those?

HM: That's a very interesting grouping you've made. More about you than about me, perhaps.

LT: "G" is games and genius.

HM: Games yes, genius no.

LT: You use games, you don't care about genius?

HM: No comment, please.

LT: "H," horses.

HM: A very good letter. I don't want to find out why but—I love horses. I used to love playing them. My second job, when I was 19, was walking hots at Suffolk Downs.

LT: "I," insurance, a scam in *Cigarettes.*

HM: People are very much concerned in *Cigarettes* with keeping control, and that's got to do with assurance, which is the English name for insurance, and also with taking out insurance, like Allan's wanting the woman to have an orgasm before he does being "money in the bank." They're all into that. To go back to what you said about money, it shows that money isn't just what happens with the money—it happens in all the other things they do.

LT: "J," jokes and jealousy.

HM: Jealousy is no joke. Jealousy is a bad joke. Jealousy is an unspeakable emotion.

LT: Many of the relationships in *Cigarettes*, for instance, between Morris and his sister, Irene, and between the two sisters, Pauline and Maud, depict that unspeakable emotion.

HM: Jealousy is hateful and very hard to deal with and I think it's probably more unspeakable in a man than it is in a woman.

LT: Why?

HM: Sexual jealousy, that is. I don't think I can stand going into it.

LT: "K" for Kafka. Especially because of *Tlooth*.

HM: Not *The Sinking of the Odradek Stadium*? I had an epigraph from Kafka at the beginning. He's finally being read in a way he deserves—one of the most explosively stimulating, funny and unclassifiable writers that's ever lived. And the tremendous effort to make thoroughgoing interpretations of his books, which was the way he was read when I first came into contact with it—treating his work as allegory to my mind sprang from that terrifying ambiguity.

LT: For "L," lines, as in *20 Lines a Day*.

HM: Twenty lines a day keeps the dustbin away.

LT: "M," memory.

HM: Memory is an irresistible fiction.

LT: And then for "O," "P," and "R," the OuLiPo, Perec, and Roussel. "Q" is quizzes.

HM: I thought it was Queneau. Queneau's the only living "writing father" I ever had; and the OuLiPo is my writing home in France; and Perec—Perec is irreplaceable.

LT: "S," sexual difference. In *Cigarettes*, Louisa, the mother of Lewis, is afraid of men, they're incomprehensible to her. And in the chapter "Priscilla and Walter," Priscilla talks about men's fear of women. This fear may be one of the themes of the book.

HM: I think that's true and it seems undeniably true that men are terrified of women and women are terrified of men. The reasons aren't the same, but they're compelling on both sides and totally imaginary. Although, in the case of women's fear of men, men have gone out of their way to provide a lot of evidence for that fear.

LT: "T," translation.

HM: Ahhh. *Vaste sujet!* Maybe writing is never anything else but translation—ultimately, a translation which cannot be identified.

LT: "V," vice and virtue.

HM: That makes me feel comfortably 18th-century.

LT: In *Cigarettes*, people want to do good sometimes, worry about it, but feel they're doing wrong. There's an interplay of good and bad—not great evil. Maybe there's a better "V" we can think of.

HM: No, it's a very interesting one and, after all, that's what came to your mind. In all four novels, virtue is wishful and vice is a mis-interpretation of reality. A misinterpretation of what's there.

LT: "W"...
HM: What was "U"?

LT: Oh, "U"! I missed that. The unconscious. It's perfect that I forgot it.

HM: It speaks its own language which is not what we say or write. I like to invent ways in which I can outwit myself and allow it to manifest itself.

LT: What would be a "W"? Virginia Woolf?

HM: What is "W," just "what." What I haven't said in this interview, and one thing would be that despite apparent appearances, my books have always been written out of passion concern and love.

LT: "X." All the X words.

HM: X is an algebraic symbol. It means what you say it means. Not only what it means. It's a variable.

LT: You play with variables.

HM: So I would say that anything I have said in this interview, the opposite is probably also true.

LT: "Y"? What about yearnings?

HM: It's a word which I think I have used several times and it's a word which has always touched me a great deal—it seems to be what runs life.

LT: Yearnings.

HM: Not necessarily, "Whatever is, it shouldn't be that way." There's also room for, "Whatever is, should be more so."

LT: "Z," zealot because of the sects and religious references. I was wondering where your zeal lies.

HM: You can't have too much of it. You can't have too much zeal, but you can't have too few zealots.

I is for I

A Mind of My Own[1] is the autobiography of Chris Costner Sizemore, better known as "Eve." Sizemore was the case study upon
which *The Three Faces of Eve*, a popular 1957 movie directed by
Nunnally Johnson, was based. Joanne Woodward played Eve,
winning an Academy Award for her virtuoso performance as a
woman under the influence of a mental illness, Multiple Personality Disorder (MPD). In the movie Woodward metamorphosed,
before the camera and without special effects, from Eve Black,
"the party girl," to Eve White, "the mother/wife," to Jane, "the
intellectual woman," enacting a female Jekyll / Jekyll, and Hyde
as constituted through a psychiatric/cinematic lens.

   Sizemore has been dogged by her cinematic representative
"Eve," who made her a celebrity, although no one knew who she
was—Sizemore didn't go public until the mid '70s—and, more
disturbing, neither did she. In a sense her life has been mediated, if
not constructed, by the movie that gave her "fame in anonymity."
Sizemore was supposed to have been cured of MPD by her first
psychiatrists, Corbett H. Thigpen and Hervey M. Cleckley, which
is what *The Three Faces of Eve* portrays; and Lee J. Cobb, playing the
psychiatrist who discovers her illness and works through it with

---

[1] Her books prior to this one are entitled *The Final Face of Eve* and *I'm Eve*.

her, is nearly as much its star/hero as Eve. But *A Mind of My Own* tells another tale: Sizemore writes that it took twenty more years for her to overcome MPD, to become, as she puts it, "unified."

Ironically, Sizemore did not see the movie until November 16, 1974, an event of great meaning to her and her family, and one carefully documented in the book. "My alters" (her other personalities), she writes, "had been barred from its world premiere in Augusta, Georgia, because Drs. Thigpen and Cleckley believed that seeing it could be highly detrimental to the stability of the patient who, they had wrongly claimed, was cured."

Sizemore's book takes up her life after the movie and explains how she worked through her illness with her new analyst, Dr. Tony A. Tsitos, how she strove to bring together her alters, to allow her various personalities to find expression or representation through just one conduit or self. After unification, her newly won self learns the difficulty of existing in the so-called real world. She must make amends with her husband, who has, in a sense, been married to many wives—"whichever one was 'out' was my wife"—and to her children, both of whom, she explains, were given birth to by alters and had formed attachments to their alter-mothers and to others of her personalities. With a new psyche in place, Sizemore now pursues a career as a painter (some of her alters had painted), making work that represents her former illness and current "wellness." In addition to painting, Sizemore actively campaigns for the mentally ill, especially the sufferers of MPD, speaking in front of large audiences around the country as an advocate for their rights and their ability to be helped. She has also worked hard to get MPD recognized as a bona fide mental illness, to make the disorder exist in representation not just as a movie but in the annals of the psychiatric establishment. (In 1980, MPD entered the medical language by way of the APA's handbook, the DSM, as 300.14 Multiple Personality.)

The issue of representation in all its complexity is critical to Sizemore's life, and its multiple meanings show themselves throughout her book, a book in which she speaks of her own multiplicity. MPD itself, understood as an intrapsychic battle waged over mind and body by warring selves or representations, is a condition that embodies such issues. As Sizemore recounts her life she often compares herself with the movie Eve, with whom she seems at times to have a kind of sibling rivalry. (Even after she is unified, she is given presents by her husband and family in the name of that alter.) She likens herself to celebrities—Liz Taylor, for one—in a conscious effort to emulate successful female role models. She presents herself as "cured patient," as "artist," as "writer," as "normal woman, wife and mother," to public, family, and friends. Overwhelming at times is Sizemore's need to achieve representation and to make representations in the world—in all of these guises. "In short, I struggled to be all things to all people." A Mind of My Own showcases a dizzying display of what she has done and who has praised her, making this reader wonder whether the self, once unified, is almost destined to become self-congratulatory.

Perhaps to offset this burgeoning narcissism, Sizemore's preferred mode of writing the self is the quote. Like literary devices, the many alters are in a sense already quotations. These personalities offer their thoughts through Sizemore, as memories and dialogue, or through their diaries and notes. When their voices enter, paragraphs read like sketches for bizarre sitcoms in which characters such as Retrace Lady, Strawberry Girl, or Purple Lady vie for "point of view" or dominance.

But even when not representing the alters, who are in a way the unconscious' quotations, Sizemore writes her life as a series of quotes. Rather than saying what she thinks, she cites herself having said the thought at another time. Or instead of incorporating into her narrative someone else's comments about her, she puts their sometimes innocuous remarks in quotes. The curved marks of punctuation distance the reader from her words and set off the ideas as if they had arrived from far away. The effect is to make the unified self Sizemore so urgently wants recognition for a fabrication of fragments and statements, an aggregate of impressions rather than a seamless unity. It may not be the result she desired, but it is a better reflection of the problems of the constructed self and of representing that self. Overall, the use of quotation attests to her desire for authenticity. In this regard the book's ultimate sentence is striking—again in someone else's words: "Chris Sizemore is real."

Having engaged successfully with the psychiatric institution, Sizemore may be ready for her current entanglement—with the law. Some years ago Sissy Spacek, the actress, expressed a desire to make a film of Sizemore's life since *The Three Faces of Eve*. But Twentieth Century Fox has refused to allow the project to go forward, insisting that the studio owns the rights to Sizemore's life story, which Sizemore, at the time the movie was made, signed over to them. To add to the obvious irony of a fight to own her life story—"claiming my own history"—is the injury that might have been done to her by the psychiatrists who negotiated the contract for her, when they stood to gain as much if not more from it than she.

Sizemore's legal argument is that one of her alters, Jane, signed the contract, and that she was not yet cured of her illness. When it comes to trial, the case will most likely rest upon the issue of her competence at that time. But in A Mind of My Own Sizemore may have logically contradicted her own defense. Asked by the FBI, in February 1982, to evaluate the case of Kenneth Bianchi—the serial murderer known as the Hillside Strangler, who claimed to have MPD—she recounts her position (she thought he was a fake) and also her feelings about the "not guilty by reason of insanity" plea. As to whether a person with MPD "could have determined right from wrong" and "be held responsible for those acts," Sizemore answers, "Unlike schizophrenics, MPD patients do not lose touch with reality, and most of their alters can tell right from wrong. So, yes, I believe he should have been held responsible for his acts." Should Sizemore now be held responsible for the act of a competent alter? Or was that alter incompetent? What's true?

If Chris Sizemore's story reads as much like fiction as "real life," it may be because truth or reality isn't opposed to fiction. Sizemore's "cases" pose truth itself as a complex of representations whose interpretations will always be informed by the institutions that define reality. And Reality and its fraternal twin, Representation, undergo continuous overhaul. Sizemore's struggles within different discourses are played out on a broad field where the battle over, and the critique of, representation is waged. That current field includes movies such as *Everybody Wins*, in which Debra Winger's character flips from one personality to another—raunchy prostitute, wholesome do-gooder, pedantic sadist. Her romantic partner, Nick Nolte, doesn't know what's hit him, along with the audience, which is elliptically clued in, an hour into the film, that Winger's character is more than just whimsical. But her "craziness" is never referred to as MPD or indeed named anything at all. The representation of an unnamed disorder fuses with familiar fantasies and fears of women, conjuring psychoanalyst Joan Riviere's "femininity as masquerade" (discussed in her essay "Womanliness as a Masquerade," 1929) as the horror-movie theme of the '90s. Sizemore might be horrified by this casual usage of MPD, where personality changes become just so many plot points.

"Everybody wins" certainly won't be the outcome of her court case, as it probably won't be the conclusion to the struggle for representation itself.

J is for Jokes

Tompkins Square Park was the site of a tree-planting ceremony in honor of Allen Ginsberg. Ginsberg lived on East Tenth Street, bordering the park, for 30 years before his death in 1997. I went, even though I was, and still am, ambivalent about him. Thirty people were there. One of the poets who organized the event took the mike. He started to talk about Ginsberg; the tree planted for him; Ginsberg's name on a plaque; and the importance of Tompkins Square for the neighborhood. A woman standing on the sidelines screamed: "Allen would've hated this, he would've hated what's happened to the park." In 1989, the park was closed for more than a year, maybe two, after the City forcibly evicted squatters and homeless people from it. There was a terrible, violent confrontation, and, ever since it reopened, cleaned up and refurbished, the police surround the park every May Day, expecting trouble. The poet tried to continue, but the woman kept shouting, then demanded to speak at the mike. "Let her," someone yelled. "Get her out of here," someone else yelled. Quickly, the organizers decided we'd all vote on it: three minutes, yea or nay. She got them. I couldn't stay and left thinking how democratic it all was, how right that a worthy ceremony turned into a fractious happening, an existential monument to Ginsberg. It was complicated and funny, too, like living inside a New York joke: "A Jew, an Irishman, and a black man walk into a bar. The bartender says: Is this a joke?"

Try Again

I gave a fiction reading with the poet Matthea Harvey at New York University's Lillian Vernon House, which lodges its creative writing program. At the end, we took questions. The last to me was: "What would you tell younger writers is the most important lesson you've learned so far in your writing life?" The next night I dined with a friend who's an artist. He and I discussed how—and whether—to answer questions about our work: "I've said I believe in something, an idea or cause," he said, "then someone in the audience says, 'But I don't see that in your work.'"

No one strong-arms you into becoming an artist or writer—most often you're dissuaded—and volunteers who bemoan their chosen gig seem disingenuous. Visual artists are often called to account for their choices and asked to defend their positions. Few occupations other than finance, politics and crime entail this reckoning. Writers and artists may ask themselves why they make art or write, and many feel the pointlessness of their self-chosen jobs, but all rebuttals and answers to their existential questions rest on faith in Art or Literature. Faith itself will be tested.

Art and literary projects regularly fail, but the announcement of mistakes or failures is rare. There's no written history of these failures, unless artists record them. In art, mistakes can be happy, revelatory surprises. Failures are also intriguingly resisted, by people who keep on trying. My dermatologist has researched a cure for cancer for 40 years. At 82, he appears undaunted, but then he is one of many scientists engaged in cancer research. This commonality of purpose and group effort doesn't pertain in the arts. The field primarily supports individual achievement at the cost of a general goal, like a cure for cancer. But pursuing a common goal for art would be misguided.

A comic gets rid of bad jokes, or is a bad comic, though failures might make it into the act, since they're at the heart of funny. Comedy wouldn't exist without failure, especially that of other people. Writers may publish idiocies and artists make dull objects, and some of this work may be celebrated as good writing or art. Some write more and more books, hoping to get it right, often digging a deeper hole to fall into. Success itself can be a rut, since, it's said, it breeds success, so might condemn an artist to doing the same thing forever.

To the question about my best lesson for younger writers, I answered: "Don't expect that being published will make you happy." I didn't mention the inevitability of rejection, luck, money, nepotism, etc. Before my first novel appeared, I'd naively believed that being published would compensate for every bad thing. In those pre-publication days, my writing was for me, I was its only reader, and I could believe it was without sin.

At dinner with my artist friend, I told him I didn't know if artists owed anyone an answer or what a writer's responsibility to readers was, if there was one. The ethics of these peculiar relationships remain conundrums. Notions of service to the field may not matter, if the proof isn't in the pudding. Anyway, writers and artists are not voted in or out by an electorate, though institutions—including collectors, gallerists, publishers, art magazines, critics—do vote but not in a transparent manner, not democratically. It's insisted there is a public for art, but those who remark on it generally presume themselves separate from it.

Working with words and pictures engages artists and writers in a world they didn't make, to which they may or may not contribute. I often think about Samuel Beckett and his agonistic relationship to writing and living. Beckett wrote novels, he wrote in two languages, he wrote plays. Beckett talked with actors, had intentions about how his plays should be performed, specified the props he wanted on stage, in service of communicating the incommunicable. A play is such an earnest art form, as it is written for, acted by and presented in front of living people. Its earnestness also resides in its ephemerality, the precariousness of every performance, tethering the genre to life's temporariness. That Beckett wrote is a thrilling paradox. "Try again. Fail again. Fail better."

Societies find cunning solutions for communicating even the incommunicable. Which brings me to the time I lived in London. I didn't understand the British use of "I don't mind" to mean "yes," "no," "maybe." The phrase seemed to allow for ineffable negotiations between people, though. "I don't mind," I saw, opened a conversational door through which either party could leave, without embarrassment. But it was hard for a foreigner to use, because it's part of a British dance whose subtle moves are learned from childhood. The British also sometimes avoided answering direct questions. I loved that, it was so un-American, and now I sometimes do it in New York, where people expect answers. I change the subject or pretend I haven't heard the question, and watch surprise or chagrin appear on faces. It's a liberation from others' nosiness, a freedom I never expected. I recommend it, with reservations that will be different for each person, discerned only through trial and error.

K is for Kafka

The film shows at the Museum of Modern Art attract a strange audience. Very old people who come to all the shows tend to talk throughout the experimental work or leave. People drift in and out. The serious remain. Very big audiences become small ones. It's a hard crowd to figure.

One night when I was there, before the start of the film, a young man leaped onto the stage and announced that he was an unemployed actor looking for a role in a movie. He pointed to his seat and urged anyone interested to contact him then and there. Smiling, he leaped from the stage and the audience applauded.

We became a more relaxed crowd and I remarked casually to the elderly women beside me, "New York is such a crazy place."

Her answer was less casual. She replied: "Yes, that's because of the Galiciani. The Litvaks are *not* funny." She paused and continued: "The English *are* Jews. Gaelic is Hebrew but no one knew this until Pittman invented shorthand and then without the vowels it was clear that Gaelic and Hebrew were the same. The English *are* Jews." Her hand waved in front of her and she said: "My daughter wrote the best art book ever written. It's across the street at the Donnell Library. My husband invented radar. All the books are across the street." I consider this and the lights dim.

L is for Lamentation

What happened in 2012?

Otto Muehl, the Viennese Actionist, once kept a diary. A whole year was represented by this line: "Extreme Hatred for the Mayor of Vienna." Stealing from Muehl, about 2012 I could note: "Impulse to Slap All Birthers." Through our *annus horribilus*, or the US presidential campaign, some comfort came from thinking about history: people have always been stupid, wrong. Smart people, with generative ideas, occasionally prevail. This cheered me up.

I tend to believe that, before total annihilation, this clever/ dumb species will design ingenious devices to ameliorate the poisonous effects of previous ones. I predict: The end is not near. Believing it, though, could be as reassuring to some as my recourse to history.

Future beings will laugh at us; each generation does about its predecessor. It's an endless competition. The chunky, clumsy, slow things they devised—electrical wires, sockets. Coming soon—tiny memory implants, iWands.

But let's not forget forgetfulness: A normal amnesia overwhelms most of any lived life. Recalling a year, last month? Stray scenes can return in startling dreams we usually forget; vague images surface, slip away.

In 2011, with millions, I watched Egypt's revolution on television: "I'm watching history; history is being made." But what does that mean, to watch an event that will be recorded, remembered, but not to have been in or of it? Anything could have happened in Tahrir Square. Normal disappeared. A few Americans told me they'd have liked to be part of their revolution. I thought, but didn't say: A revolution doesn't send out invitations. The Egyptians weren't "having a revolution." They were the revolution.

2012 rode in on the back of chaotic, thrilling, frightening political events: the clamoring will of people in the Middle East; the fragility of hope, and rebellion spreading; the instability of the euro and Greece's desperation; the Occupy movement's impact; now, street-by-street fighting in Syria, a government slaughtering its citizens, and no stopping yet.

In 2012, on May 1, I gave a reading at the KGB Bar in the East Village, with fellow writer Colm Tóibín. Afterward, a bunch of us had dinner. About 11 p.m., in a funky bar on Second Avenue, I heard a guy, who was peering into his iPhone, whisper: "Bin Laden's been killed." What? The bar turned dead quiet. He said, louder: "Bin Laden's dead." The bartender switched on the television. "Bin Laden's been killed." Colm and I walked outside, told passersby, or they told us: "Bin Laden's dead." I admit to shock, excitement, but more a rush of relief. "Admit" because I didn't expect relief; I didn't know that particular anxiety was lodged in me. What else didn't "whoever I was" know that might inflect or form "my positions" and "my ideas"?

Unique characters, like Marshall McLuhan, envisioned the future, and speculated brilliantly. But no one knows exactly what's

214

coming, or the consequences that will follow. No one knows what artists will do next, either, or why. Maybe perceptive, ludic, didactic, inspiring or dull art, film, writing. Contemporary work usually responds obliquely to its time, which necessarily includes the past, hidden or disguised. I didn't expect relief at Bin Laden's death, and artists may imagine and describe a surprising object from and of its time, with no obvious source.

In 2012, I saw an exhibition of work by Anna Molska at the gallery Broadway 1602 in New York. I remember her video, *The Mourners* (2010), in part because it caught me—thematically, formally, psychologically—and made present what I hadn't expected. Molska asked seven Polish women to participate in a "social experiment." The women were friends, who also had a folk-singing group, and sang songs at funerals. Molksa invited them to use a gallery, once a greenhouse, to do in it what they wanted. She provided neutral-colored parkas as costumes; and, in the windowed, spacious gallery, one wide bench and a white sheet, which became props.

In about 25 minutes, the women created a play: Enacting a funeral, singing to the dead and the living, they danced, roughhoused and laughed. They discussed God and the Devil, telling folk tales and their own stories about dying people. Very early in the improvised drama, one woman said, as if out of nowhere: "The Germans thought they were so smart; but they were stupid." Suddenly the past joined the present and framed it.

Molska's camera observes the group, usually in medium shots; close-ups study their happy, impassive, mournful faces. It watches them listening to each other or fashioning the white sheet into a corpse, which they position on the bench. The women sing to it and, as they sing, an unnerving seriousness settles. Their eyes close. Their voices sound like the only music possible for lamentation. Later, World War II returns, when a woman mentions her father being sent to a camp, and her sympathy for orphans. Tears come to their eyes. The work includes much more than I can report.

What happened in 2012?

M is for Marx

One night Patrick McGrath regaled a group of us with a strange but, he said, true tale: A man went into a bar in lower Manhattan for few drinks, was seen talking to a woman and didn't return home. The man's wife was frantic—he'd never done this before, not come home. A few days passed and there was still no word from him. Then, on the fourth day of his absence, a man awoke in Central Park, dazed; he didn't remember what had happened to him. He was taken by the police or passersby to a hospital. The doctors found, on his lower back, a fresh and healing scar, evidence of an incision. It turned out that the man had been robbed—of his kidney. The hospital was not surprised. This was not the first time they'd encountered it. Body parts are for sale these days, what with organ transplants being a hot new technique and organs very much in demand.

We all thought it was a perfect story for Patrick to tell me— a modern day horror story. We all thought it was really ghoulish business, business for our times.

The tale took on added credibility when on September 23, 1991, I read an account in the *New York Times* of an Egyptian laborer who was selling one of his kidneys in Cairo to the highest bidder, so as to give his children an education. In the Third World, organ selling is a growing market that "relies on live donors and draws donors from throughout the Middle East." The news story was titled "Egypt's Desperate Trade: Body Parts for Sale."

The body as a commodity wouldn't have surprised Karl Marx. But what surprised me, in looking back at the Fetishism of the Commodities chapter of *Capital*, was to see that Marx himself had been influenced by the Gothic—and/or, that the Gothic had been for him a viable way to analyze the commodity form.

Here Marx writes of the mysterious quality of the commodity form. He says: "The table continues to be wood, an ordinary sensuous thing. But as soon as it emerges as a commodity, it changes into a thing that transcends sensuousness . . . it evolves out of its wooden brain grotesque ideas, far more wonderful than if it were to begin dancing of its own free will. The mystical character of the commodity does not therefore arise from its use-value . . . it is nothing but the definite social relation between men which assumes here, for them, the fantastic form of a relation between things. In order therefore to find an analogy we must take flight into the misty realm of religion. There the products of the human brain appear as autonomous figures endowed with a life of their own . . . I call this the fetishism which attaches itself to the products of labor as soon as they are commodities . . ."

A little later in his narrative Marx refers to a hidden secret. He imagines how commodities might speak. In these passages Marx, a Gothicist, refers to the "grotesque," and spices his discourse with "transcends," "mystical," "wonderful," "misty," and "fantastic." He animates the commodity form—anthropomorphizes it, as when he wonders how it would speak and then he goes so far as give it voice or dialogue. The things he imagines so vividly represent the hidden labor and relations of people and in the way he conjures them brings to my mind Mary Shelley's *Frankenstein*, and further the Golem story that Frankenstein was based on.

In that story, the Jews create a man of clay to protect them, to represent them, the most famous Golem that of Rabbi Low's creation in the 16th century. Rabbi Low has to destroy the Golem when he runs amuck and cannot be controlled by his human creator. In Marx's version of capitalism, the commodity form seems to be its uncontrollable Golem. I like looking at what Marx wrote in this section as allegorical, as a kind of narrative fiction that uses as its antihero protagonist the Golem named commodity form.

It's interesting to reflect on why Marx would use the Gothic to talk about and render the effects of capitalism. And, to bring the question up to date: What I am doing in an anthology titled *The New Gothic*. And why does it exist? Perhaps the current enthusiasm for the Gothic, for horror as a genre in the U.S. and England, is in part a reflection of contemporary life, specifically life under postindustrial multinational capitalism, a capitalism under, in and through which we writers labor and produce, and a powerful way of articulating and representing that condition. Inescapably, the new Gothic will also be a handle, a fad, a marketing tool, but this does not alter its value, to me.

These days the west gloats over the demise of communism, the premise being that democracy and capitalism are synonymous. The demise of totalitarianism from the left or right is something to be happy about, but I'm left wondering what capitalism offers, apart from a certain economic system, to the spirit that haunts our Gothic stories, and to a sense of how society should be run, to a sense of what common goals can be. Dog-eat-dog and survival of the fittest are appropriate metaphors for not just the capitalist ethic but also for the production of gothic perambulations. In our country without adequate health care and housing, a country first decimated by Reagan's criminal grotesqueries and Bush's new world order, what more credible form is there?

M is for Mordant

The Final Plot

Some writers believe they control their fictional worlds, and nothing else; others that they are conduits for a story—words arrive, characters write themselves. (Few believe they have no control at all over what or how they write.) But even if one can imagine dying or being dead, one can't represent it autobiographically. The impressions and scenes that can be imagined will have been nourished by others' deaths—those witnessed, heard or read about. (Duchamp's tombstone epitaph, "After all, it's always the other one who dies," means it's always the other's story, too.) The way being dead actually feels, a lack of all sensation, supposedly, can't be described, depriving human beings of certainty about life's afterlife; but, conversely, fomenting, with death's partner sexual curiosity, a drive for knowledge.

Ones who know they are dying, those physiologically at death's door, and also those who pathologically fear death, might want to rush life's conclusion and kill themselves. Suicides, or self-murderers, as the Dutch put it, can select the method, day and hour, and direct the last narrative, up to a point. Despair, significantly and regularly, overrides choice and strips it of volition. And, how being dead feels will also elude a suicide's capacity to know. (Virginia Woolf wrote in her diary that it was "the one experience I shall not describe.")

When death progresses naturally, which can be slow-going, over days or months, unless from a high-impact, head-on car crash, when organs fail fast, depleted of blood and oxygen, there comes a stunning withdrawal: people, like other animals, remove themselves psychically and physically from the known world. A person goes elsewhere, while the body works hard to shut itself down. One is "actively dying," hospice workers say. Death is oxymoronic until it finishes its work.

On ordinary days, a depressive has her funeral to fantasize, an activity that reassures with sad, cozy comfort. When required in actuality, planning it will probably be discomforting. A dying person may type, scrawl or dictate a list of demands or wishes for a service or memorial, exerting a sort of posthumous control. (The list can also be a preemptive strike against the omissions or excesses of fond others). A funeral might be plain as a pine coffin or theatrical. One who is dying might have specified songs, musicians, speakers and kinds and colors of flowers, or, if possessed of minimalist inclinations, wanted no displays or eulogies, just a plaintively beautiful song. (Both may have designated worthy charities.)

For a writer's funeral, words could seem superfluous, though there can never be enough, also. Selecting speakers raises unique problems. Most particularly, eulogizers script themselves. Some will mumble, overcome or shy, while others will improvise on humiliating episodes in the dead person's life. All jokes will be on the dead. (Most people will speak primarily about themselves.) In fantasy, a depressive mourns herself and watches the abstract procession, loving the inconsolation of others; but soon her morbid pleasures are jolted by the awkwardness of social situations, pre-and post-death. Inclusions, exclusions, who speaks first, last? (Funeral rites survive, and have changed historically, for the living.) Planning an actual funeral might allay worry or generate more.

For writers and nonwriters, other kinds of writing than suicide notes can be left behind. A letter might confess secret loves and hates, with recuperative gestures of remorse and forgiveness. Or, it could be a screed against the living. A death essay could be an "avant-fin" manifesto, raving mad, or setting out rational principles for existence. (A treatise on melancholy risks mawkishness and unoriginality.) The essay could haltingly document one's protracted departure (exquisitely incomplete).

Any of these compositions might supply a reason to live fully while dying, but inciting, for writers, a specific anxiety. The final text could cause a cascade of revisionist views of the individual and body of work, staining both, and lasting until everyone who knew the writer had died (considered in Buddhism an individual's "second death").

Most likely, one will have scant energy for planning and writing in the final stages of life. (There are exceptions, who prove the rule.) Meeting death, sometimes called "the maker," though really the unmaker, is essentially debilitating, so its specific conditions dominate and alter the living. A dying person may have no ambition or desire to control anything during the process (in itself unburdening). One's death, though, will likely be written about by someone else or, even more likely, no one. Most deaths go unremarked. So-called "ordinary people" get thousands of hits on YouTube, when killed by a usually docile lion on an ecological safari or pushed in front of a train. (The living identify with the pathos and meaninglessness of random, final endings like these.)

An ignominious death recasts an entire life as unintelligent and witless. A relatively healthy person moves an old, huge TV set or a five-drawer steel file cabinet, which, unbalanced, leans, starts falling, its weight unbelievable, gains velocity, collapses, and crushes one beneath it. (Domestic deaths invariably make foolish last impressions.) An ignominious end is beyond prediction. But the great majority of deaths will be common, following a predictable course indicated by one of several illnesses, resulting in complete organ failure. Sherwin Nuland, in his book, *How We Die*, refutes the contemporary delusion of living forever by defeating the ageing process. He insists, almost too vociferously, that human beings will die sooner or later, because of the wear and tear on the body, also known as old age, which is not a disease. But if one believes people are dying as soon as they are born, then living itself is an illness overcome only by dying.

Near to death, people usually don't speak or have last words, hospice workers say, especially not those profound or pithy final utterances compiled in books.

> Thomas Carlyle: "So this is Death—Well!"
> Aleiester Crowley: "I'm perplexed."
> Ulysses S. Grant: "Water!"
> Emily Dickinson: "Let us go in. The fog is rising."
> Goethe: "More light!"
> Edgar Allan Poe: "Lord help my poor soul . . ."
> Washington Irving: "Well, I must arrange my pillows for another weary night! When will this end?"
> Gertrude Stein: "What is the question?"
> Ludwig Wittgenstein: "Tell them I had a wonderful life."

If a dying person had her wits about her and enough bodily function—swallowing becomes impossible—she might be able to come up with a line or two. But this also can't be plotted. (Spoken and written communications not close to death are technically not deathbed statements.) Withdrawing from life for days or weeks, one is expected to be silent and uncommunicative, or will communicate but be misunderstood. (The writing of Ivan Ilych's death, hospice workers say, is eerily close to how dying people feel; they wonder at Tolstoy's prescience.)

Since what death feels like is unknowable, most people fear it, and dying, particularly in great pain. In this time, as no other before, unless wishing to suffer mentally and physically, a patient can receive palliative care and medicines that make the "transition," a hospice term, from life to death painless or nearly painless. (Many believe hospice speeds death along, but often it prolongs what life is left.) Against all reason, which death conquers easily, a few want to feel pain, not to remain as lucid as possible and say their good-byes, but as self-punishment for past bad acts and guilty consciences.

Hardly anyone wishes "to die badly." In the late Middle Ages, when the concept of "artes moriendi" was formulated, the ideal of "a beautiful death" emerged, and it thrived through the 19th century. "Dying well" has replaced "dying beautifully" and is rigorously enforced by post-mortem judgments. People aren't supposed to struggle at the end, people should be "ready to go" and "accepting," and opprobrium is cast on those who aren't ready and willing, on those who "died badly."

This ultimate indictment glosses and assesses a human being's last trial. (To die smiling makes it easier for the living.) But in the matter of dying and death, mortal judgments, like most received wisdoms concocted of exasperating pieties and galling stupidity, should be eliminated. Only death's uninitiated would espouse these moralisms.

Of death, mortals are absolutely ignorant. The dead, fortunately, are beyond caring.

N is for New York

Whatever facts support their findings, biographies and histories are also inventions that rely upon human imagination and fascination. Conscious and unconscious interpretation, inclusions and exclusions alter our record-keeping. Often memory is cast as "ours," history "theirs," but sometimes the two battle: suddenly you—in this case, I—find your writing inside exhibitions and books that represent a period under investigation.

Since childhood, I have gorged on biographies, real-life crime, and literary and cultural histories: Abigail Adams, Bloomsbury, the Surrealists, Freud's circle, the Cambridge spies, Leopold and Loeb, Americans in Paris. Other lives summoned possibility, freedom, difference; I could imagine people unlike any I knew at home. Then I saw Paris for the first time. Its streets were not paved with bohemians and I realized my bedtime readings were also fairy tales. So there's a beautiful irony to my inclusion in a cultural designation called Downtown.

Under this rubric, an assortment of art, film, video, music and writing from the mid 1970s to the early 1990s has returned for scrutiny and appreciation. There have been two exhibitions, "East Village USA," at the New Museum in 2004–2005, and, in early 2006, "Downtown: The New York Art Scene, 1974–1984," at the Grey Art Gallery, and an anthology, *Up is Up*

But So is Down: New York's Downtown Literary Scene, 1974–1992, edited by Brandon Stosuy. Like others included, I am doubtful about Downtown's significance as well as resistant to being placed inside a "scene," as if living on a film set or behind glass in a diorama at the American Museum of Natural History. Others may see you as part of something of which you feel no part. So, I reject some of the claims made for Downtown, but I'm also curious about its purposes for the present. Given its apparent return or resurgence, Downtown appears, at least, to have been a moment, or had its moment, because it has taken a room in the historical imagination.

Usually a term exists in opposition to another, but what is Downtown's opposite? Uptown makes geographical sense, but Downtown is and isn't a place. It's also a virtual or mental space. Downtown might mean lower class, but most musicians, writers and artists arrived from the upper and middle classes. If Downtown means avant-garde, mainstream would be its opposite and also incorrect, since many straddled both: Patrick McGrath, Ann Magnuson, Dennis Cooper, Peter Hujar, Barbara Kruger, Richard Hell, Richard Prince, Eileen Myles, Nan Goldin, Eric Bogosian, Reno, Spalding Gray, Gary Indiana, Patti Smith, Richard Foreman, to name some. Downtown comprised many disciplines, and there was crossover between them.

Literary readings happened in galleries and clubs, artists formed bands, poets wrote plays, and musicians published poetry. And, during this brief moment in time, without an overarching plan or script, some people acted in synch, or merely coincided, clustering in some of the same spaces, partaking of the same events.

Watergate, Punk, Vietnam, civil rights, women's and gay rights, Minimalism, conceptualism, Warhol, anti-aesthetic and anti-narrative theories, these movements, ideas and events were both background and foreground, a kind of political and cultural geography, for Downtown. Earlier art and culture played an influential role: David Wojnarowicz revered Rimbaud, Kathy Acker plagiarized Dickens, and Cindy Sherman recreated a social history in her "Film Stills." As practiced in various art forms during this time, appropriation was parody and homage.

But styles and practices varied too widely to call Downtown a movement; there was no coherent aesthetic. Cool and hot, figurative and abstract; narrative films; non-narrative video; political art; conceptual and text-based work; graphic sexual photographs; streetwise fictions; gothic fantasy; New York School poems; transvestite; lesbian and gay theater; performance art; AIDS manifestoes: formally, the work was all over the map.

Downtown didn't represent waving fields of wheat, crumbling barns and open skies. It was urban, the city Downtown's trickster muse whose characters' celebrations and problems, visions and traumas, as well as rats and heroin overdoses, were sources and material.

Historically, the city developed along with industrialization and modernism. In early 20th-century New York, Djuna Barnes apotheosized the city as the exemplar of the modem, while in Paris, Walter Benjamin anointed the flaneur, Kazin's walker in the city, modernity's citizen. Ecstatic or frightening, the city became a metaphor of freedom, change and chance. It thrived on speed, just as the Futurists wanted, and had a center, so it could be captured as an image by its inhabitants.

Downtown's shows and parties, held inside a small perimeter, allowed for quick comings and goings. You never had to stay; you could usually walk home. This cosmopolitan life, rootless, maybe, sometimes unheimlich, uncanny, ordained that home wasn't necessarily homey. The city grew fields of the unfamiliar and unexpected, which trumped the humdrum. The city's virtues and Modernist values—such as strangers and strangeness—were the small town's vices and fears.

In a sense, this Downtown of thirty years ago presented America in a new guise. It was no longer small, homogeneous towns complacent with simple pleasures. In Downtown's music, art, writing, the city represented America, as it was. America was gay and straight, women and men, of all major religions, some minor, believers, nonbelievers, with conflicting values, both high and low, whose manifestations suggested varieties of obsession, disgust, beauty, pleasure and despair. Notably, Downtown was overwhelmingly white, though living inside a city that wasn't. Many of us didn't notice our white skin and European stock. Nominally international and without prejudice, debunkers of the so-called real America, Downtown was also American, racially divided like the rest of the country.

Today's city is post-modern; it sprawls; the walker sits behind a wheel; the crowd is Internet community. Modernism was a European and American phenomenon, no matter from whom it borrowed, while post-modernism is resolutely global. Seoul, Los Angeles, Peking, Tokyo and London are exemplars, though New York City has finally embraced its growing boroughs. If I were an historian, I might declare that Downtown signified the last hurrah from the last inhabitants of the last and premier modernist city.

When your work is historicized as Downtown, it sits inside vitrines or hangs on walls with captions that explain it briefly, often inadequately or quaintly. You—I—never see yourself or your contribution that way. I don't know if it matters; my version will be countered by another's. Maybe, as I still do when reading books about the past, people will view Downtown's art and artifacts as escape, lesson, amusement, hope.

Still it's implacably odd to know that lives function for others in uncontrollable ways. Historians can agree about an event's occurrence and importance and dispute its interpretations forever. In the same club at the same time, people tell different tales about how the singer fell off the stage. These contestations engage now in then, in things that might have relevance. We don't always know what's relevant or what history teaches, but it affects us, anyway.

Downtown's inventors contributed some generative, brilliant, and bold objects to consider today, still relevant, I think. And even flawed accounts reveal something about the past. We are all unreliable narrators, after all. Inevitably and maybe not unreasonably, the present will make its own terms with the past.

O is for Outlaw

Here's my pet theory: Right after godfather Paul Castellano was gunned down in front of Sparks restaurant in December 1985, crack spread uncontrollably on New York streets. Castellano's death, like Capone's imprisonment in 1930, triggered mayhem: Wiseguys set out on their own with just enough venture capital and entrepreneurship to start doing business. Later John Gotti reined them in and restored a kind of disordered order. In the meantime, other gangs already in operation—Colombian and Chinese—cashed in on the disarray and brazenly branched out into new territory. There were freelancers, also, reveling in the Mob's temporary glasnost.

Given my parti pris, I was curious to read *Boss of Bosses—The Fall of the Godfather: The FBI and Paul Castellano*, by Joseph F. O'Brien and Andris Kurins, if only to discover that Castellano had been the antidope La Casa Nostra pope. In the early 1980s Castellano dictated "Two Commandments": "No one caught dealing drugs after 1962 . . . could ever become an initiated member of the Gambino family," and "anyone caught dealing drugs, and whose activities in any way implicated other family members, would be whacked." Before his death, some member of LCN were already dealing it, warily. Here were the seeds of discord. It was open season when he died.

One like to have one's pet theories confirmed, which is precisely the level at which this cleverly constructed and predictable booklike docudrama operates. Everyone's predigested versions of the Mob and the FBI are once again trotted down the aisle, a fashion show of mediated wisdoms. Written in short chapters, or scenes, *Boss of Bosses* is the script for the movie of *Boss of Bosses*. O'Brien and Kurins score points with the premise that the Mob learns its line and gestures from movies and book about the Mafia. Their book does too. Reading it one can actually sense representations building one upon another, piling up into mountains of images and words, to create what seems like "real life."

Boss of Bosses recounts the Paul Castellano reign, as told by the FBI men who were responsible for bugging his Staten Island residence and bringing about his fall: An indictment by the government and assassination by Gotti's men. To execute the placement of Gotti's men. To execute the placement of the listening device took months of planning. As the authors humbly put it, "A more crucial quarter-hour would be difficult to locate in all the annals of the fight against organized crime in America." In that 15 minutes the FBI invaded the Castellano residence and wired his kitchen, where he did most of his business.

O'Brien and Kurins report what "O'Brien and Kurins" had to do in order to get inside. In the third person, they reconstruct their dialogues with one another and their superiors, which set in motion the invasion of the godfather's mansion. In reverential detail, they relate how Paul Castellano came to be Boss of Bosses, how his particular brand of wisdom served him well and moved him up the ranks. But there wouldn't be a story without an equally reverential analysis of his fall: He was complacent and out of touch in Staten Island; he wasn't watching his troops; he was home, because he was sexually obsessed with his Colombian mistress/ maid, Gloria Olarte; and worst of all he kicked out his wife, Nina, violating the code any reasonable Mafia chieftain obeyed.

To make the story worthy of being read or filmed, O'Brien and Kurins must construe the Boss and themselves as bigger than life; otherwise they might look too little on the screen. The FBI's bringing in some businessman who heads an illegal corporation isn't as thrilling as bringing in, say, a tragic hero. "Of all recent Mob Bosses, he had the most self-discipline, the most restraint. He kept his ego out of his businesses. He did not make the kind of mistakes—mistakes that generally sprang from character flaws rather than mere tactical misjudgment—that precipitously brought down other Dons. The more impressive Big Paul's track record became, the more he began to haunt the imaginations of certain Special Agents. He was growing into a figure worthy of obsession."

From the FBI agents' point of view, Castellano's obsession with Gloria is central to his downfall. Castellano had been impotent since 1976—"ironically, the same year he became the omnipotent Godfather. The disability apparently had not greatly bothered him until the Colombian maid entered his life." From the tapes they learn that he will undergo an operation—a penile implant—to be able to have intercourse with her, a source of sly humor throughout the book. Gloria is a troubling, salacious punchline, a dirty joke that messes with Big Paul's mind. The writers ask what they think is the Mob's question: "Why did he indulge this crude, sharp-tongued unglamorous woman, this foreigner with her accent and her appalling table manners?" But in their words, she's just a hole: "'You wait and see,' said Andy Kurins. 'He's following that metal dick of his into a cold and lonely place.'" The special agents' "obsession" with the Boss must never be thought of as sexual. A sprinkling of misogynist dialogue and some innuendoes about Gloria function to separate the men from each other.

When they bust him, Kurins and O'Brien given Castellano respect. They allow him time to change into his suit; they don't cuff him in front of his family. On another day, bringing him to court, they escort him to the Second Avenue Deli, for his favorite—a corned beef sandwich on rye. After months of surveillance, the FBI agents are sad to take him in; they've come to like the Godfather. Passing Castellano over to the marshals "they felt strangely like they were giving the bride away at a wedding."

In the current exposition of cops and robbers, everyone is the hero, and everyone the antihero. Besides, if the supposed bad guys don't have stature, the good guys look bad. Castellano has to be heroic, for if he isn't, what are the FBI guys? Just a couple of antihero-worshipping G-men, playing with an underworld figure's civil rights.

From the universe of possible reasons for a book's going out of print, there might be collected an anthology in cultural politics, with a chapter for "unpopular culture." One could imagine Horace McCoy there, as all his work is OP, even his famous-for-a-minute Depression-era marathon dance novel, *They Shoot Horses, Don't They?* (1935), which returned to print, briefly, with the movie of the same name. Collectors know a real find: McCoy's *I Should Have Stayed Home*, sitting in a used bookstore on a dusty shelf, positioned somewhere between Precious and Obscure Oblivion. My paperback copy's cover proclaims it "Hard-boiled," "Perverse," "shockingly Brutal."

The hard-boiled McCoy, if he was—we can't know the real McCoy—might have appreciated his oblivion. Cynicism and despair suffuse his novels, and a sad literary fate might have satisfied his pessimism. In its darkness the hard-boiled school previewed film noir; in its cool toughness it rehearsed the next war and constructed future Cold Warriors. McCoy's writing is also self-conscious and reflexive—modernist—showing the influences of Hemingway and even Stein. His lean, taut style serves the genre, but what's interesting about his novels is their mix of literary forms. His work is not easy to categorize.

I Should Have Stayed Home appeared in 1938. Hitler was threatening Europe, and the U.S. was slowly moving out of the depression, from isolationism toward war. This is the novel's time; its location, Hollywood—the Hollywood of extras. McCoy's truly marginal characters are drawn there by the movie world's promise of fame and fortune, not unlike Steinbeck's Okies in *Of Mice and Men*, who also went West hoping for salvation.

Ambitious antihero Ralph Carston wants it all, but his conscience and idealism stand in the way. Roommate Mona is much more stalwart. The novel begins with her and their mutual friend, Dorothy, going to jail; Dorothy for shoplifting. Mona for objecting loudly, in court, to Dorothy's sentence. Mona's disappearance into jail sets Ralph adrift, and he descends into the abyss: "Feeling the way I did, alone and friendless, with the future very black, I didn't want to get out on the streets and see what the sun had to show me, a cheap town filled with cheap stores and cheap people, like the town I had left, identically like any one of ten thousand other small towns in the country—not my Hollywood, not the Hollywood you read about."

Temptation enters Ralph the extra's life in the guise of an older woman. Mrs. Smithers is "filthy" rich with all the best movie connections. Embellishing this filthiness is how she takes her pleasure—she loves getting slapped around by gigolos. McCoy uses the novel's filmic context by having Mrs. Smithers seduce Ralph with pornographic home movies. Ralph succumbs, not quickly, not completely, and not, finally, successfully—he doesn't get a part but he also doesn't ever give up. And throughout the novel, Mona, as chorus or superego, warns him against Mrs. Smithers and himself; the two extras' dialogues construct a kind of argument about how far and how much are okay in the pursuit of success.

Relatively plotless, though replete with the genre's dark mayhem—suicide, court scenes, jail for Ralph—the story is primarily a journey, Ralph's making his way, or not making it, in the world. In this *Pilgrim's Progress*, the hero's struggle is not with God and the devil but with the secular world. McCoy uses Hollywood as the paradigm, the apotheosis, of capitalist society at a time when the myth of Horatio Alger was becoming a maudlin and corroded irony.

Ralph's battle with his own corruption and loss of principle is key to McCoy's work generally. His protagonists fight the good fight. In *I Should Have Stayed Home*, Mona refuses to be interviewed by fan magazines and rails against them for creating false and insatiable longings. A friend of Mona's, Johnny Hill, who does publicity for a studio, quits his job because a German consul was able to have censored a part of a movie in which "German youngsters [are] drilled as soldiers."

Then, in the reflexive mode, Johnny announces to Mona and Ralph that he's going to write a novel about Hollywood's extras—"the true story of this town concerns people like you—a girl like you and a boy like him. Maybe I'll put you two in a book . . . Understand I don't think I've got any special talent for novel writing." Ralph-in-Hollywood is McCoy's meditation on desire and failure. Through failure may now be the unspeakable of our society, in the midst of the Depression it was an existential fact of life. McCoy's Hollywood is the nightmare machine that produces phonies, monsters and wasted youth, sadness and sadism. He sees failure embedded within the system; there will always be people who don't make it.

McCoy's version of cultural politics is, like the country he's from, contradictory. There's some "conventional" racism, homophobia and misogyny side by side with sympathy for the underdog and hope for a nationwide new deal. Contemporary "conventional" attitudes are as questionable but more difficult to isolate from the narratives—ideologies—that we live. It seems easier to spot offensive or questionable ideas in work from earlier periods, in part because language and style change. Concepts such as "underdog" and "phony" may seem dated in today's parlance and in our nation, as presidents wrap themselves in symbols and commit highly unsymbolic HUD and S&L frauds. And get away with it. It's banal now even to say that corruption is endemic when many are positioned as permanent underdogs, the underclass.

Reading the out-of-print McCoy returns one to the not-so-distant past and to another consciousness. McCoy's sometimes uncomfortable speeches, prejudices and "old-fashioned" language bespeak the U.S.'s disturbed history, its citizens' noble and ignoble values. His writing style itself speaks a very American language, presaging the Beats; long flowing sentences and a moody lyricism alternate with terse, plain speech. Like other American writers from the Transcendentalists on, McCoy eulogizes a disappearing America, its hometowns and daily life transformed by powerful economic and social forces. Hard-boiled despair is personal, political and unpopular. But given our economy, McCoy's lessons on living with failure might come in handy.

In his novella *Tonio Kröger,* Thomas Mann writes, "Only a beginner believes those who create feel." Kroger is a young middle-class German who considers himself manqué both as a bourgeois and as an artist. John Waters might be the anti-Kröger—a well-off, middle-class man whose life and art mock high, low, middle and all their fuzzy gradations. He's an aesthete and an anti-aesthete; he's classy and classless. Filmmaker, artist, writer, actor, Waters revels in spectacle and spectatorship; and the joys of making, being and observing fill the pages of *Role Models,* his 2010 collection of essays. In Mann's terms, Waters might be that rare creature: An artist who feels.

Early in his career, Waters became known for films depicting bizarre characters in outrageous, super-melodramatic situations, as in *Desperate Living* (1977), a gay/lesbian/cross-dressing murder fantasy set in Mortville, a circuslike shantytown. Bakhtin's theory of the carnivalesque nicely fits these films. A contemporary Lewis Carroll, Waters luxuriates in the topsy-turviness of life, and his somewhat more conventional recent films depend, like most narratives, on the reversal of fortune. In *Pecker* (1998), the eponymous protagonist flees instant New York art-world stardom when his photographs of Baltimore buddies and family subject them to unwanted and unsympathetic attention. What dances on the surface in this and other Waters films is explicit in *Role Models*: a concern for art, fun, justice and people.

The essays recount actual and imaginary encounters with ordinary but extraordinary people, as well as with celebrities such as Little Richard and 1950s crooner Johnny Mathis. Their stories, intermingled with Waters' own, comprise a kind of bildungsroman, or even a portrait of the artist as a collage of his influences. Take the chapter on Mathis, which kicks off the book. "I wish I were Johnny Mathis," Waters confesses. "So mainstream. So popular. So unironic, yet perfect." None of these qualities characterizes Waters' own oeuvre; but as he himself asks, "Do we secretly idolize our imagined opposites . . ?" Waters once chanced to see the elusive Mathis but didn't have the nerve to talk to him, and then felt compelled to interview his undoppelgänger. "[Mathis's] appeal is broad and wide, something I could never achieve and he can never escape."

Thinking about the singer, Waters travels down memory lane and unearths other boyhood heroes, like Clarabell, the clown on TV's *Howdy Doody Show*, played by Bob Keeshan, later Captain Kangaroo. "Imagine his life, his schizophrenia," Waters writes of Keeshan. "Am I Clarabell? Or Captain Kangaroo ?" It was Clarabell whose clownish makeup would inspire Divine—Waters's apotheosis and star, the drag-queen actor featured in many of his films, first celebrated in *Pink Flamingos* (1972) for eating actual dog shit on a Baltimore street. Au revoir, good taste, Waters sings, and good riddance.

Role Models pays homage to Baltimore, Waters's muse and hometown, whose culture spawned many magnificent oddballs, as well as the bars and barkeeps who nursed his imagination. In the chapter "Baltimore Heroes," Waters writes, "The good [bars] have no irony about them. They're not 'faux' anything. They're real and alarming." He gravitates toward characters like Esther, a fierce, bad mother with a filthy mouth who slings whiskey and fears nothing, and Lady Zorro, "an angry stripper with a history of physical and sexual abuse with a great body and the face of a man." Waters reflects: "To this day Zorro is my inspiration. . . . Brave. Without makeup. Like Tilda Swinton at the Oscars."

Though irony is mother's milk to him, Waters's quest for genuine communication inside bullshit-free zones propels him toward worlds with and without irony. Sincerely insincere, insincerely sincere, authentically inauthentic, inauthentically authentic, his work vexes the normative and all the usual binaries. Oppositional terms can't tell the stories he wants to tell. The mash-up of in-betweenness sparks Waters's imagination, where insincerity can be sincere, sincerity ironic. Waters prodigiously exaggerates the deficiencies of false dichotomies: Each side of the aisle is desperately wanting. All this ongoing worry about "authenticity" in art and life, his oeuvre suggests, is moot, since human beings may be incapable of inauthenticity. Con artist Bernie Madoff's commission of fraud doesn't make Madoff a fraud: He's absolutely Madoff.

In this vein, Waters prefers second-rate to first—Jayne Mansfield to Marilyn Monroe, "bad" Tennessee Williams to "good" Williams—but he also cherishes Jane Bowles' *Two Serious Ladies*, one of the great American novels of the twentieth century, and the work of Denton Welch and Christina Stead. He's a big reader, a bookworm. "I've jitterbugged with Richard Serra, eaten Thanksgiving dinner with Lana Turner . . . gone out drinking with Clint Eastwood . . . but what I like best is staying home and reading."

Waters's faves cover the map or, to put it differently, map his hybrid values, his "taste." Taste is now a dirty word; theoretically, it's near untouchable. Still, everyone has it and displays it, whether or not they think they do. Over and over in his art and these essays, Waters deftly shoves our noses in it. He's a high-fashion hound whose idol is Rei Kawakubo of Comme des Garçons: "I genuflect to Rei's destruction of the fashion rules." He collects art by Moyra Davey, Mike Kelley and Cy Twombly, no outsider artists, and calls their work his "roommates." But the high-style-and high-art-loving Waters is also a devotee of certain amateur or "outsider porn" moviemakers—without whom, he writes, "I could never have had the nerve to make my movies. . . . Am I a pervert for loving the work of Bobby Garcia and David Hurles? Well, yes, I guess. But a healthy one."

Waters complicates and flouts the boundaries of taste, but there's no disingenuousness in his assault on all guises of high-mindedness. "Parents should understand that their young kids are not like them and need to have the privacy to fantasize both their good and bad desires," he writes. Voilà: the youthful, healthy pervert. He suggests, from his upside-down perch, other alternative moral positions: "Zorro tried in her own misguided way," he writes of the angry stripper's mothering, which even psychoanalyst D.W. Winnicott might not have found "good enough." Happily, the word "transgressive" doesn't dot Waters's essays. One, calling it so doesn't make it so; two, transgression happens when you don't know it; and three, he isn't merely reactive to society's dictates. He does what he likes and embraces his contradictions. So he sports a black Maybelline-pencil mustache and wears Comme des Garçons, but his manner can be as folksy as Will Rogers's, and like that midwestern stand-up comic, he's partial to truthfulness, good-natured subversions and self-deprecation. "The DJ . . . honors my presence by playing Eminem's 'Puke' every time I come in the door."

Waters layers his narratives with fantastic concoctions, but he tells us in the chapter titled "Leslie" that he learned the hard way to discern for himself the fault line between reality, which Timothy Leary once defined as an opinion, and the uses of make-believe in his art. Leslie is Leslie Van Houten, one of the "notorious 'Manson girls,'" who was nineteen, in 1969, when she participated in the murder of Rosemary LaBianca on the orders of the insane, charismatic cult leader Charles Manson. Van Houten has been in prison since then and is now over sixty. Waters and Van Houten became friends, first because of Waters' fascination with the Manson cult, but through knowing her—she lives with great remorse for her crimes—he reckons with his own conscience: "I am guilty, too. Guilty of using the Manson murders in a jokey, smart-ass way in my earlier films without the slightest feeling for the victims' families or the brainwashed Manson killer kids who were also victims in this sad and terrible case."

Any half-sentient artist or writer will recognize this aesthetic and ethical Maginot Line. What is crossing the line? Whose line is it anyway? Should it be crossed, redrawn—and if so, in what way? Waters doesn't proscribe behavior or approaches; the reader can infer from his questions and choices that he continually negotiates art's ambiguous terrain. There are no rules; there's self-rule in art, which is its freedom, and a slide rule for one's mutating sense of good, bad, right, wrong. Inside this collection resides a unique version of art criticism and artistic self-criticism. "Who's the real extremist," he asks, "Johnny Mathis or myself?"

"Tennessee Williams saved my life," Waters announces, calling the playwright his "childhood friend.... I never met Tennessee Williams.... Nobody has to meet [him]; all you have to do is re-read his work. Listening to what he has to say could save your life, too." Art can save lives. There it is, a claim assiduously avoided in our wary art world, so the notion just might refresh and comfort the jaded, even though it jars with experience and reason. Waters doesn't shrink from absurdity—he rambles around in it. "Sometimes," he says, "you have to lighten up." Waters thinks funny. Even when he's arguing that Van Houten deserves to be paroled, he can't help but relieve the gloom: "Initially both my mother and Leslie's were nervous about our friendship. 'Does the Manson Family have to have our address?' my mother moaned when I once had a letter sent there."

Waters is a reluctant ethicist, owing to his overwhelming sense of the ridiculous. He takes the piss out of himself often, but he can't stop offering help. In *Role Models*, there is actually a guide on how to love your misbegotten self. "Cult Leader," the last chapter, reveals Waters as the anti-Dr. Phil for our time. He declares: "I'm so tired of writing 'Cult Filmmaker' on my income tax forms. If only I could write 'Cult Leader,' I'd finally be happy. Would you come on a spiritual pilgrimage with me?" If you do, reader, here's a sample of his ecstatic dicta: "A filth movement ... to the final Armageddon of the elimination of the tyranny of good taste." "You'll need a uniform. A habit. A 'fallen angel' look to intimidate yet attract." "Damaged people make the best warriors." "What you don't see is always sexier."

John Waters, cult leader, hopes to encourage sexual fantasies, to have his followers feel no shame, take risks and die by "spontaneous combustion." Anyone who reads this collection, highly recommended for all sorts of minds, dispositions and school libraries, would do well to join.

P is for Points of View

Tennis, with actual winners and losers, contents me and other workers in fields of indeterminacy—artists, musicians, writers—where first prizes declare arguable standing. Choosing sides is often wrong but not in sports. In this year's US Open, Novak Djokovic beat Rafael Nadal as if Nadal were an ordinary mortal. I was torn between them, and miss that action. Fortunately, since art can be long, sports short, I'm absorbed in *Diane Arbus: A Chronology, 1923–1971* (Aperture, 2011), a book of her beautifully written diary entries, letters and work notes.

Sides formed early about her enigmatic, brilliant photography. At home, Arbus's photographs upset my father, viscerally. I experienced them, as an adolescent, the way I did Franz Kafka's *The Metamorphosis* (1915)—identifying with uncanny strangeness, fascinated by what I didn't understand. Some of what Arbus had imaged—people once referred to as "freaks"—was usually kept from sight. In the 1960s, families still institutionalized their "mentally retarded" or "insane" relatives. Various art critics and civilian viewers over the years have thought Arbus cruelly exploited unsuspecting subjects. Some felt she went slumming.

There are English words whose definitions confound definition. Words such as "exploitative," "ambitious" or "pretentious," when applied to art and writing or their creators, form blurry impressions, subjectivity shaping them. Mindful of Virginia Woolf's dictum, in her 1937 essay "Craftsmanship," that "words don't live in dictionaries, they live in the mind," I know recourse to a dictionary definition won't clarify much that is significant to me. Words live in usage, with connotations.

Lewis Hine, among other documentary photographers, pictured desperate people in desperate conditions. His photographs presumed what I'll call a "benign-looking contract" between viewer and viewed. "We" viewers were expected to feel sympathy for "others" and their stricken lives. Specific assumptions shaped the spectator as well as those imaged. Hine's subjects existed primarily in one dimension, which might indeed overwhelm other aspects of their lives, but it was likely only one way they saw themselves. Still, Hine had a specific purpose in shooting them as he did: to expose terrible poverty, appalling slums. I can't imagine that he was grilled about intentionality then.

Any discomfort I experience looking at a Hine feels simpler to explain than my discomfort with an Arbus, because her purpose was various, ambiguous, dimensional. Deprivation, lack or difference in her work, which encompassed many living situations and conditions, is generally psychological, cultural and physical, often genetic. There is no consensus about—and in looking at—the characters she pictured. No consensus in part because how "normals" perceive "stigmatized" people, and vice versa, is an ever-evolving process. (See Erving Goffman's *Stigma: Notes on the Management of Spoiled Identity*, 1963, which Arbus read.) Goffman called these interactions "mixed-contacts." There was also no "social-looking contract"—my term—codifying how viewers should look at her photographs. Still isn't.

"Someone told me it is spring, but everyone today looked remarkable, just like out of August Sander pictures, so absolute and immutable down to the last button [. . .] all odd and splendid as freaks and nobody able to see himself, all of us victims of the especial shape we come in," wrote Arbus in 1960, in a note to her friend, the artist Marvin Israel. Arbus recognized the precariousness of her interests and knew her terrain was treacherous. Curiosity, identification, fear, discontent with her upper-middle-class origin, and fascination with what she was not, caused her to seek and embrace difference. Her characters aren't posed in shadows. They look directly, baldly, at the camera. Her photographs don't take a recognizable side: she is not moralistic or judgmental. Her most infamous or celebrated images reside in the interstices of ethical positions, since the eye of a wavering beholder is also a judge.

A viewer might be thrown contending with *Identical Twins, Roselle, N.J.* (1967), girls who are common or normal and also different. Or, by Arbus's representation of an upper-middle-class white family in their suburban backyard, *A Family on the Lawn one Sunday in Westchester* (1968), which appears to have landed in *The Twilight Zone*—"nearly like [Harold] Pinter but not quite" she writes in a letter. Or, by *A Jewish Giant at Home with his Parents in the Bronx, N.Y.* (1970): giant man and parents stand in the living room of a small apartment and compose an unbalanced image, one that also upends the nuclear family and makes it "other," even perverse.

Risking ambiguities, Arbus vigorously subverted the subject/ object position, shoving the viewer onto her soft ground. She interrogated looking, aggressively, and made looking itself controversial.

A naked gaze forced the viewer's look to rebound onto itself, which may not make a pleasant picture. Consciously, unconsciously, viewers hold points of view and attitudes about what's pictured. If it is hard to look at or turn away from an Arbus photograph, it may be because viewers experience unwanted or unclear impulses—disgust, loathing, fascination. Arbus's photographs work with and against self-disguise.

Art-conscious characters know that, early in the 20th century, Marcel Duchamp threw the seminal art screwball, but his work provoked a mostly sectarian response, testing institutional limits and aesthetics. Arbus's photographs ripped up the "benign-looking contract." There is no social contract anymore.

Do "others" see themselves as "other"? No, she or he is not marginal in his or her life. And, whoever "they" are, they probably view and shoot too. Anyone can "exploit" anyone on TV, and many do. So, "willing" or "unwilling" participation begs new ethical definitions. There's power, advantages . . . I'm longing for an elastic dictionary. Fortunately, it's football season in the US. But the concussions suffered in that game . . .

Decade-ism

In work and love, people get boxed in, edged out, ruined; others find acceptance, win prizes and are vied for. A few are venerated, even adulated. True meritocracies are rare. Talent aside, whatever it is, human beings, like other animals, favor their own, cautiously adopting outsiders, especially those who will keep treasure close. A sociologist once told me that the only outcome your college statistically and reliably predicts is your marriage partner.

Our aggressive species has its survival methods, which usually relate to competition. Class, race, ethnicity, religion, sex: These categories for exclusion and inclusion were long ago transformed into naturalized or so-called civilized mechanisms. Snobbery persists based on these dubious categories. Self-described snobs, necessarily deluded, sit on top of this survivalist heap, priding themselves on their taste. "Taste," in this instance, connotes "good" but everyone has taste or preferences. "I prefer not to," declared Bartleby. He had no taste for copying anymore.

Calvin Tomkins' book, *Marcel Duchamp: The Afternoon Interviews* (Badlands Unlimited, 2013), is my latest friend. Tomkins met Duchamp in 1959 to interview him for *Newsweek* magazine; over time, the art critic and artist became friends. Of Tomkins' many books, two earlier publications are on Duchamp: *The Bride and The Bachelors* (1965) and *Duchamp: A Biography* (1996).

Duchamp talked to Tomkins about taste: "Taste is an experience that I try not to let into my life. Bad, good or indifferent, it doesn't come in. I'm so against interior decorators . . . You don't have to be happy or unhappy about it, you see? . . . Taste can't help you understand what art can be."

Taste is a five-letter word no one discusses. Mentioning it, I notice friends and colleagues look at their menus or their nails. Mumbling begins, then silence. I'm not kidding, completely. People like to believe their sensibilities, approaches or attitudes have been educated, nurtured or expanded beyond mere taste, "bad, good or indifferent." It is also a matter of taste not to appreciate taste.

Duchamp distinguishes between the "onlooker" and the artist. "The priority of the connoisseur or whatever you call him isn't to speak the same language as the artist [. . .] But don't say the artist is a great thinker because he produces it. The artist produces nothing until the onlooker has said, 'You have produced something marvelous.' The onlooker has the last word on it." Duchamp holds that these formations—artist and onlooker—perceive the same object differently, having very different aims. But the onlooker will determine the worth and fate of the art(ist).

Conversations among artists and writers about work often center on "how to make it work." Craft, materials and considerations of space regularly come into discussion—work talk. Periodontists see diseased gums, wherever they are, just as musicians and composers hear with other ears.

I regularly question my preferences. Why I like or dislike writing, a photograph. I don't trust experience, even if it has shaped me; I don't fervently trust what I think or believe, while I believe it still. A pox on absolutes! I could trace a genealogy of what I think and like, which is, to some extent, what I was exposed to, taught, made conscious of, and decided not to be or accept. Tendrils of difference and objections sprouting rebellions and self-discoveries—I could list them. But I couldn't create an order for my character, and hold it/me to a neat line. (When I learned to write, I wrote fast, not on the lines, only below or above.)

My preferences change and change again. Once I believed, doing studio painting with Ron Gorchov and Doug Ohlson, that the figure would never return. Once, involved in showing and making experimental films, I believed Hollywood movies were uninteresting. One night, watching a structuralist-materialist black-and-white film of its celluloid grain, I asked myself: "Why am I watching this?" Like Bartleby, I preferred not to, anymore. Whatever I've "renounced" resides somewhere, pinging and ponging, because ideas live on, more or less alive in different moments. Being for or against something now is less interesting to me than understanding what it does, how it does it, and why it's being done.

Which brings me to the art world's obsession with decadeism. The so-called literary world stores much less faith on periods of emergence. The new is treasured more in visual art than in writing; the literary world is backward in so many ways, and I will not count them. But a first book comes out in 1991, say, and the year stops being of interest, with the next book, whenever it comes out, which counts more, and then the next. A writer is thought to mature, even to write better and know more. The actual age of the writer matters today as a form of "branding," but the brand becomes old, just as the writer will.

Artists get pinned to a decade. It's as if time had stopped, the artist suspended in it. Artists think in and through their work, during all the decades after the one in which they debuted. If humans weren't perverse, in Postmodernity the "post" would become valuable.

People now live so long, many past 100. Extended middle and old-age pushes youth further and further back in time, making being young really a thing of the past. Something interesting could emerge from that.

Q is for Quiet

At the Microphone

At a conference called "Schizo-Culture," held at Columbia University in 1975, the speakers were magnetic and illustrious: William Burroughs. R.D. Laing. John Cage. The audience—graduate students, artists, writers and freelance intellectuals. Later on, "Schizoculture," organized by Sylvère Lotringer, would be billed as the conference that launched French theory in America.

The gathering took place in a lecture hall or auditorium that seated about 300 people, a raucous, animated group, who heard, for instance, about psychoanalyst Jacques Lacan, and were told that "the unconscious is structured like a language." R.D. Laing said that graduate students were the most depressed population in any society.

All day, men—no women—took the microphone and spoke. There was always a buzz in the audience, whispers, an audible hum of excitement. Then it was time for John Cage. He walked onto the stage and began to speak, without the microphone. He stood at the center of the small stage and addressed the crowd. He talked, without amplification, and soon people in the audience shouted, "We can't hear you, use the mic. We can't hear you." John Cage said, "You can, if you listen." Everyone settled down, there was no more buzz, hum or rustling, there was silence, and John Cage spoke again, without the microphone, and everyone listened and heard perfectly.

R is for Redux

The Rolling Stones, The Academy of Music, New York City, May 1, 1965

During college, I had to invent or reinvent myself every day, create a person who awoke, dragged herself out of bed, and went to class. I was morbidly depressed; life was futile. I had to move from despair and apathy to the shower, then find clothes to put on my naked body, even though for three years I wore a self-fashioned school uniform: Baggy Chinos and a long-sleeved, all-cotton, black T-shirt. A friend living near me on West 96th Street drove a Bucati, and when I could catch a ride on the back, getting to class was easier. She was depressed, too, but more manic, and sometimes she shouted above the engine and wind, "I want to kill myself." I hugged her waist tighter then and felt my own desire to die tested.

I met my other best college friend in a required Introduction to Sociology class. She had a bad attitude like me, she was two years older, not a freshman, very cool, but then she disappeared for a while. "I dropped out," she told me when she returned. She also told me to take studio art classes, and I did. I listened closely to everything she said, because she knew what was really happening; for instance, she knew the night Linda Eastman and Paul McCartney slept together for the first time.

The Beatles were cute, but they were too fresh and sunny for my dark, youthfully jaded, sort of hip character. The Rolling

Stones existed for me and my friend, bad boys for bad girls. The Stones were anti-everything and suited my sensibility. My psychotherapist had asked me, "What do you want to do?" I said, "I want to rebel." "Then," she said, "my job is to make you effective."

The Stones were rebels—at least their songs sounded rebellious—and they appeared effective. They could have whatever they wanted: sex, drugs, cars, houses, more sex, drugs. I didn't question the implications of their being middle class boys, the Beatles working class boys, or what rebellion worked in them. I lived inside my troubled mind, and each day had to awaken in the same bleak and unchanging world and do what I'd done yesterday or something a little different.

Every night for dinner I broiled chicken wings and heated up canned, sliced beets. Like wearing the same shirt and pants to school, I ate the same dinner for three years, unless my knowing friend said, Come on, let's eat out, or hear a band, or see a movie. Later, we shared a railroad apartment in the East Village. She fixed up her rooms reasonably, while I ripped plaster from a wall in one of mine, to uncover the brick, but it turned out to be the outside brick, so I stopped. The plaster lay on the floor of the room. I never cleaned it up; I couldn't use the room anyway, because cold air blew in through the cracks.

My friend found out when the Rolling Stones were doing their first concert in New York: May 1st, 1965, at the Academy of Music. "Satisfaction" wouldn't come out in the States until June 1965, but we were already hardcore fans. We had to be at the Stones' triumphal entrance into our city.

The Academy of Music was on 14th Street between Third

Avenue and Irving Place, where the Palladium would be in the '80s. The first Academy of Music was a grand opera house, built in 1854 on the northwest corner of Irving Place and demolished in 1926. The Stones played the second Academy, erected in the '20s across the street from the original. This one showed movies from the '20s on, but by the '60s, it was mostly a concert hall. Its marquee letters broken, its seats uncomfortable and seedy, its brilliance and glory faded, the Academy of Music was the right theater for the Stones, who were uncomfortable to parents, and seedy and glorious in their own way.

We sat in the balcony, or we sat downstairs; wherever we sat, my sight lines weren't impeded. I'm short and saw everything that happened, and a lot did and didn't. Opening for the Stones, Patti LaBelle and the Bluebelles, which was how she was billed, as a girl band. In their ice blue, space-age costumes and feather head-dresses, with Patti's big voice and their choreographed moves, they rocked. But the audience was indifferent. Stones fans were sullen like the band, and also we were there only for them. Patti must have been onstage an hour, and the audience grew restive. When the set ended, the group received some applause, but they didn't get an encore. They were really fine; we were just lousy for the Stones.

Then nothing, and nothing, and time went by, and no one came on stage, and nothing, and we were waiting and waiting. After a while, someone in the audience roared something, or there was an outbreak of off-the-beat white people's clapping, and a few dispirited, feeble calls for the Stones. Waiting, we turned more sullen.

Where were the fucking Stones.

Forty-five, maybe 50 minutes passed. I don't know how long it was, but still nothing. We were angry already; it didn't take much to make us angrier. Where were the Stones. Where were the Stones. The question was our breath.

People had slumped and settled into their lumpy seats, passive and aggressive both, because there was nothing to do but wait or leave, so we were trapped because we wanted the Stones. Wanting was hell, and while existentially waiting is all there is to do, we didn't like it. There was no clapping now, no sudden shouts for the Stones, just enraged sedentary bodies.

Then they walked out. They just walked onto the stage, as if they were going to the men's room. They had no affect. There was no jumping or dancing or mugging. They walked onto the stage and plugged in their instruments and took their positions. They didn't look at us, not once, except for Mick. Mick came to the front of the stage and sort of said, "Hello, New York." He tried a little, but the rest of the band didn't care. They didn't want to be there, and they ignored us. Mick made another pathetic effort, that's all it could be: "Hello, New York."

Brian Jones sat down on the floor. He was stage right, his head down, blond hair splayed over his face obscuring him further, his instrument lying in his lap. Maybe it was his Vox teardrop guitar or a Vox Phantom. He never looked up, the group didn't look at us, they looked bored, and only Mick exerted himself a little, threw off some energy, but he didn't try long. We were angry, deadened, too, and quickly Mick accepted defeat. Listlessly, the Stones started their first number. Probably they were very stoned.

A matron stood at the edge of the stage, on the same side as Brian, but at the top of the stairs, which was the only way up there, except for leaping. She was a heavyset black woman, about 30—I don't remember any black people in the audience—and she wore some kind of theater or usher uniform. She faced the audience, grim and solemn, with her arms crossed over her chest. The Stones were playing, and Mick was singing, Brian was sitting on the floor, head down, and I don't remember what Keith was doing, but he wasn't crouching the way he does now and uncoiling like a rattlesnake to strike. Charlie Watts was Charlie Watts, steady, imperturbable, playing the drums the way he's always played the drums, and Bill Wyman was himself, unmoving and dour.

There was a kind of stasis on stage, and in the audience. Into the third song, a hefty, dark-haired girl made a run for the stage, and up the stairs. But when she reached the top of the stairs, the matron blocked her. She gave her the hip. The girl flew down the stairs. One move, down she tumbled. The girl landed on the floor, stood up, and walked back to her seat. That was it, that was our resistance. The matron crossed her arms over her chest again and glared at us. The audience became more frustrated. The Stones hadn't even noticed, and nothing happened again, and not one of us yelled or stood up, either, and soon the atmosphere turned solidly against the band.

The Stones played eight songs, the songs were three or four minutes each. They were onstage less than half an hour. They finished their set and walked off the way they'd walked on. They just walked off. No one clapped or shouted, everyone was fed up, pissed off, let down. We'd become the anti-audience, and rose, grabbed our jackets, left our seats and filed out. There was no fighting, no talking. We'd all been rebuffed, like the hefty, dark-haired girl. The audience spilled onto 14th Street, a morose confederacy of rebels. It was early evening.

I suppose my friend and I went out for something to eat. Or maybe I went home and ate sliced beets and broiled chicken wings. Life continued, but something had changed: the Rolling Stones had played New York.

By now, the Stones have changed a lot. Brian drowned, murdered, it's alleged, by his assistant; Mick Taylor quit, so Ron Wood plays lead guitar; Darryl Jones plays bass, since Bill Wyman retired; and Mick's, Keith's and Charlie's faces are cross-hatched and filigreed with event and experience. I've changed, too. For one thing, I have stopped eating wings exclusively, though I eat chicken. I still love beets, but now fresh and roasted, and order them whenever they're on a menu. I still like to wear a uniform of sorts, but now I buy six or seven pairs of the same, usually black pants, about that number of the same all-cotton, long-sleeved T-shirts, and many of the same linen, rayon or silk blouses. I buy everything in different colors. Life isn't as bleak, with some variety.

"Bigness is theoretical domain at this fin de siècle: in a landscape of disarray, disassembly, dissociation, the attraction of Bigness is its potential, reconstruct the Whole, resurrect the Real, reinvent the collective, reclaim maximum possibility."—Rem Koolhaas and Bruce Mau, *S,M,L,XL*

Contemporary writers worry about the place of writing the cultural space for books. The novel is an endangered species, as fiction faces down confessions and "real-life" stories. "True" today means "actually happened," and invention and imagination are dirty words, viewed as suspiciously as communism in the 1950s. More fiction and nonfiction books are published, but most vanish without a trace, so not only writers, but also publishers and editors are depressed. The phrase "return of 1996," the industry's LA earthquake (when books were returned to publishers in record numbers), is repeated like a mantra. The picture is not getting better: "The latest survey from the Association of American Publishers shows that net sales of hardcover books are down by 12 per cent per year to date and books are being returned to publishers at an average rate of 45 per cent," reports *The New York Times*. The context in which books are written and published is unstable, unpredictable, and who knows how to account for taste, anyway.

In the 1950s, when Don DeLillo's new novel *Underworld* begins, there was a notion—the great American novel. It has disappeared and in its place, probably under Reagan, great became big. Publishers publish big or little books: authors are big or little, midlist or midcareer. Big, mid, little don't measure page-length, but how the book will be positioned. Marketing determines "big" or "little" more than the way the book is written, its ideas, length, cost. What it's been paid, the advance, is a variable, but a book with a small advance may become "big," depending upon how it's seen in-house, whether editors and salespeople think it can "break out." If a little book sells, it can become big, the surprise publisher and authors make money from. Martin Amis is reported to have called our big books "Big Macs." In fast-food America, everyone agonizes about fat, but wants to be a big, fat deal. Undoubtedly, we're a nation of size queens.

Don DeLillo understands bigness, economics and capitalism. The underworld of *Underworld*, its base, is economic; its epilogue, titled *Das Kapital*, underscores that. Structurally, or superstructurally, DeLillo's novel makes capital. *Underworld* opens with the 1951 World Series game where the series-winning home run baseball Bobby Thomson hit starts as a fan's treasure, fought for, won, then stolen. It flies through *Underworld's* pages as an underground economic and cultural signifier, its value unifying characters' desires.

The baseball circulates. *Underworld* is, in part, an examination of circulation whether marking a meeting of powerful men at that game—J. Edger Hoover, Jackie Gleason, Frank Sinatra—or the fates of lovers, Nick Shay and Klara Sax, waste analyst and artist, respectively. After an illicit sexual moment, they go their separate ways, taking other into the world as memory.

Memory is another underworld and, in *Underworld*, it functions as a kind of currency. When intact, memory is as hard as Thompson's home-run ball, with its strange history that only fans and collectors care about. Along with the baseball, the atomic bomb, atomic energy, and waste blow treacherously. Taste as human excess and folly must be managed, like memory, and hangs in characters' minds and in the air. If there's an enemy in *Underworld*, it's forgetfulness, the denial of history.

DeLillo's ambition in *Underworld* is to join the history of postwar America as a series of events to certain characters, who are shaped more by circumstance than psychology. Hoover's power and paranoia, the Zapruder film, the firebombing of black churches, the Cuban missile crisis, Lenny Bruce, AIDS, cyberspace— events and things collect and make history. Terrifying weapons, mute objects and traumatic memories proliferate. *Underworld*'s a proliferation, or a collection, of 40 years of great issues and small ones. DeLillo seems to have wanted to put everything he could into it, as if a book could be a time capsule, which demonstrates DeLillo's ongoing concern with what we leave to the future, with history. While history may be a collective memory that must be kept alive, fiction plays its role in keeping records for posterity. Like many writers, DeLillo may be concerned, too, with what his work will mean for posterity.

These concerns are probably being fanned by fin-de-siècle anxiety. DeLillo's previous novel, *Mao II*, focused on the place of the novelist, with a desire, perhaps, to "reclaim maximum possibility" for fiction. Appearing after the fatwa on Salman Rushdie, *Mao II* and its protagonist Bill Gray may have spoken for many writers: "In the West we become famous effigies as our books lose the power to shape and influence . . . I used to think it was possible for a novelist to alter the inner life of the culture. . . Because we're giving way to terror, to news of terror . . . news of disaster is the only narrative people need." His interlocutor argues: "Are you crazy? Writers have long-range influence."

Do writers have long-range influence? Long-range like missiles? Reading *Underworld*, one wonders if the author of *Mao II* decided that for a novel to make an impact now, it must be big in all senses, cover a wide swath of history over many pages, "to reconstruct the Whole." Though the Whole has never existed and the Real is not available, these illusions nourish fiction. Fiction responds to a multitude of losses, fantasies and wishes. *Underworld*'s Lenny Bruce's monologues, reconstructed from Bruce's LPs and DeLillo's memory, and its marking of actual events appear to address what *Mao II*'s Gray thinks novels must do—compete with, or at least challenge, the big, nightly news.

Whether it's a conscious or unconscious gesture, making things big also responds to being scaled back and down, to holes that need filling or to significance that needs restoring, from an America that never was—innocent—to fiction's shaky, minimized place. The circulation of books may be thwarted by capitalism looking for fast profits, but the meanings of books accrue, slowly, over time. Especially fiction. Fiction imagines lives and ideas and doesn't immediately announce its value.

S is for Gertrude Stein and George Saunders

Approaching Gertrude Stein's writing critically is tricky. She strove to reshape literary conventions—syntax, language usage, narrative order and the sense of making sense—so any comment on Stein's choices may already be rebuffed or unsettled in her poetics and practice. Actually, Stein is tricky, even a trickster. This may be why, as I read *IDA* and *Stanzas in Meditation*, both reissued in corrected, authoritative editions from Yale University Press, I remembered John Cale's singing, "Nobody ever called Pablo Picasso an asshole."

Gertrude Stein is called a genius, and through that brilliant lens her writing gets read or is not read, since awe and reverence are regularly met by dismissal and ridicule. Curiously, other writers are called geniuses, but the term doesn't suffocate the reception of their writing as much. Obviously, readers know the extraordinary reputations of Shakespeare and Virginia Woolf, but some prefer Shakespeare's *Richard III* to *Richard II* or Woolf's *Mrs. Dalloway* to *Orlando*. They feel at liberty to discriminate.

Fewer readers imagine they can create their own Stein; many feel she is beyond their capacity to understand. Maybe this happened because she has been claimed as the sine qua non of the avant-garde. But she aligned herself with her time. Being part of the "contemporary composition" is at the heart of Stein's trenchant essay, originally a lecture, "Composition as Explanation." "The only thing that is different from one time to another is what is seen and what is seen depends upon how everybody is doing everything." Stein inscribed novelty and surprise, through her special prose, to explain their appearance generation to generation and theorized why the new in art and writing may first be thought "ugly," then later "beautiful" or "classic." In that same essay, she declared: "No one is ahead of his time." A future artist, Andy Warhol, said, "I'm part of my time, like rockets and television." Uncannily, both Stein and Warhol occupy ambivalent places in American culture. They're adored and also big jokes, both recognized even if only for a single utterance. Stein: "A rose is a rose is a rose is a rose." Warhol: "In the future everyone will be famous for 15 minutes." But people have called Warhol an asshole.

"For Stein," Peter Nicholls writes in his important book, *Modernisms: A Literary Guide*, "language is to be grasped not as a means of reference to a world of objects which can be dominated, but as a medium of consciousness." Stein's works of consciousness depend on a reader's consciousness, and unconscious-ness, to engage them. Otherwise, her writing is flat, dead, the rhythms and her play with words, her biting wit and clarity, lost.

IDA: A Novel was published by Random House in 1941, but excerpts appeared from 1937. The Yale reissue contains reviews from the day and versions from Stein's notebooks, showing the novel's development during those years. Its editor, Logan Esdale, has written an excellent introduction (and notes throughout) containing necessary biographical and textual information. One learns that fame was much on Stein's mind when writing *IDA*, her own and Wallis Simpson's, the American divorcee who became the Duchess of Windsor. Stein's new fame rested on *The Autobiography of Alice B. Toklas*, published in America in 1933. The book became very popular and gained Stein a wide readership and celebrity. With the onset of fame, Stein questioned how her work would be received because of it.

Stein constructs a cubist portrait or skewed biography of Ida, who was born with a twin, Ida-Ida, to kind parents. "It was a nice family but they did easily lose each other . . . her parents went off on a trip and never came back. That was the first funny thing that happened to Ida." Odd, sad and happy events populate *IDA*'s pages, while doppelgängers lurk everywhere: Ida becomes Winnie, because she's winning; characters like parents to Ida come and go, and men who may, or do, become her husbands appear, disappear, reappear. Ida herself leaves and returns, she's often going to another state (a place or state of mind). A reader experiences the pull of freedom, and Ida's contradictory desires—wanting a home, needing to escape; wanting to be known and not. Her identity is in doubt and it's not.

With these radical changes, there's a bounty of tension and release. Words appear and reappear—like her husbands—but syntactically differently, scrambling meaning and Ida too. There's psychological and logistical weight on Ida: whom does she know; what does she know; which dog has died, and where will she live, with whom. Most urgently, who knows her and what does that knowing do.

Ida sat on. She said to herself. If a great many people were here and they all said hello Ida, I would not stand up, they would all stand up. If everybody offered me everything I would not refuse anything because everything is mine without my asking for it or refusing it.

There isn't a better description of celebrity affect.

Release from textual and narrative tension comes, in part, through Stein's remarkable voice, as well as internal and external rhymes, some so childlike one might be listening to a book read aloud. "Well what did Ida do. / Ida knew just who was who. / She did. She did know. . . . There are so many men. What do you call them there. They did not know Ida. / Now then." Also, Ida frequently rests, and "when anybody needed Ida Ida was resting. That was all right, that is the way Ida was needed." I read the word "rest" again and again, and had a weird sensation. The story would sort of stop, and a space opens up where I could disappear like Ida, or stop too. Also, it provides a rest, as in music.

IDA wanders from its theses in its second half. Interrupted by allusions to, and fragments of other texts Stein had written before or during the writing of *IDA*, such as "Superstitions," the novel turns into a repository of fleeting images and ideas that protagonist Ida might hold. Something feels missing and amiss, much as Ida bemoans and muses on missing. "Everybody began to miss something and it was not a kiss, you bet your life it was not a kiss that anybody began to miss. And yet perhaps it was." I love the insertion of "You bet your life." My own insertion was Ida became a pronoun and verb: I da won't, I da will, I da wanna.

Stanzas in Meditation fulfills Stein's great ambition. It's an amazing work, a modernist epic, and Stein is at her playful, philosophical, poetic best. It's a lively, imaginative work, riffing off Tennyson, Shakespeare's sonnets, nursery rhymes, the cultural gamut. Joan Retallack's rich introduction, "On Not Not Reading Stein: Pressures and Pleasures of the Text," reckons creatively and helpfully with the problem I'll call "Who's Afraid of Gertrude Stein?" Retallack also presents Stein scholar Ulla Dydo's important textual discovery: Stein's lover/wife, Alice B. Toklas, forced her to change the verb "may" to "can." May Bookstaver was Gertrude Stein's first lover, and Toklas was enraged finding her name so many times in the manuscript of *Stanzas in Meditation*. (Apparently, Toklas had no trouble reading Stein.) In the new Yale edition, "may" has been returned, according to Stein's original manuscripts. The Stanzas' editors, Suzannah Hollister and Emily Setina, literary sleuths, have done significant work restoring it.

Gertrude Stein suggested that becoming a classic could kill a work of art. I enjoy Gertrude Stein most as a theorist, her ideas startle me, in whatever form they appear. (I call myself an inexpert.) Readers' responses should shift, like Ida, with changing times, to make a book new(er), otherwise it doesn't truly live in the present. If Stein becomes an endpoint for literary invention—a classic—her work can't be read in the present tense. I figure that if Gertrude Stein were alive now, she'd be rambunctious differently. Literature can't stop, and can't rest on its laurels.

And she wouldn't be writing like Gertrude Stein.

Pastoralia

The Puritans proved their worth in the New World by achieving worldly success that, they hoped, demonstrated God's love. But since the Bible told them the meek shall inherit the earth, wealth was an uncertain sign. God could be ambivalent. Failure, like the Devil, could masquerade in a wicked variety of disguises. Anxiety and guilt drove the Puritans, and those were their psychological gifts to America's future. It is this punishing legacy that shapes the wacky world of George Saunders' story collection, *Pastoralia*.

Saunders' exuberantly weird stories recount Americans' mostly futile attempts at self-improvement, the terrible dread of failure—or damnation. His stories appropriate behaviors and institutions that already seem parodies of themselves. They respond to an America where men running for president cite Jesus Christ as their favorite philosopher, either to curry votes or because they haven't actually read any philosophy, and where women vie to marry a multimillionaire on television. They speak about the most prosperous nation in the world, whose citizens don't have adequate health insurance and worry about being too fat to be loved but not about being too self-involved to consider the pain of others.

Saunders showcases Americans' fears, shames and need to be accepted—all resonant reminders of this country's neurotic origins. In *Pastoralia*, his frantic characters move through defamiliarized terrain. They anxiously await punishment for nonexistent crimes and imperfections, suffering for the strange sin of wanting to be happy. His losers are threatened with losing even more—jobs, sexual attractiveness, their illusions, just about everything.

In this collection's title story, a woman named Janet and an unnamed male narrator worry about losing their jobs playing cave people in a historical theme park. The pair are not allowed to speak English: "I make some guttural sounds and some motions meaning: Big rain come down, and boom, make goats run, goats now away, away in high hills." Janet speaks English anyway, among other rules she breaks, and the narrator protects her from the boss. The boss punishes him by withholding their daily food. "I go to the Big Slot and find it goatless."

In *CivilWarLand in Bad Decline*, his first collection, Saunders also represented America as a kind of Disneyland and relied on repetitions and other stylistic devices to hammer home the poverty of a simulated existence. He stripped down his sentences to convey the inadequacy of language to capture the zeitgeist. His insistence on these effects sometimes turned smart into merely clever, inventive into predictable.

But in his new collection, Saunders' tales cover larger, more exciting territory, with an abundance of ideas, meanings and psychological nuance. Saunders can be brutally funny, and the better his stories are, the more melancholic, somber and subtle they are, too. Pathetic contradictions underlie the ruthless drive for success in love and work, and Saunders weaves them into artful and sophisticated narrative webs.

In "Winky," a desperate character named Yaniky is prey to self-help and New Age groups whose philosophies fault the individual for not having it all. Yaniky attends a meeting where people wear white paper hats that mean "Beginning to Begin," or pink ones meaning "Moving Ahead in Beginning"; they are labeled "Whiny" or "Self-Absorbed" and are taught there's "A Time for Me to Win." Their leader tells them: "I was once exactly like you people. A certain someone, a certain guy who shall remain nameless . . . simply because he'd had some bad luck, simply because he was in some pain, simply because, actually, he was in a wheelchair, this certain someone expected me to put my life on hold." He exhorts the group not to let others, as he puts it, relieve themselves "in your oatmeal." Suddenly Yaniky realizes that his sister, Winky, has been fouling his. This dismal epiphany provokes a series of deluded interior monologues that describe yet another geek who won't realize the American dream. But what makes the narrative truly unusual is Saunders's introduction of Winky, whose voice he juxtaposes with Yaniky's in a tragicomic duet for codependents.

'   "Sea Oak" is the sick tale of a man who works in a strip club but who doesn't want to show his penis, even though he'd earn more in tips. After giving the ladies (almost) what they want, he returns home to his dysfunctional family. Saunders mocks that overused generalization in stupefying exaggerations that recall Theodor Adorno's dictum, "Today only exaggeration can be the medium of truth." The stripper's sister, Min, and cousin, Jade, are barely literate single mothers who watch bizarre television talk shows and converse in monosyllabic curses. Their Aunt Bernie, an optimist—or "optometrist," as Jade calls her—acts as a foil to their sullen negativity. But when this Pollyanna dies, Saunders transforms their home into a neogothic haunted house. Aunt Bernie returns from the grave. "Why do some people get everything and I got nothing?" she asks. "Why? Why was that?" Through the undead Bernie, Saunders unleashes the fury of the unfulfilled, the yearnings of America's damned.

In "The Barber's Unhappiness," an aging bachelor who was born without toes lives with his mother (in Saunders's world, this always signals male abjection). He spends his time "ogling every woman in sight" and fantasizing about each one. An uncle's cruel comments about his bachelorhood spark even more obsessive thoughts, which are both hilarious and miserable.

Saunders crosscuts between the lives of two anxious men in "The Falls." There's Morse, who is "too ashamed of his own shame," and Aldo Cummings, "an odd duck who, though nearly 40, still lived with his mother." To Cummings, Morse is "a smug member of the power elite in this conspiratorial Village"; to Morse, Cummings is a nut he fears will "collar him. When Cummings didn't collar him . . . Morse felt guilty for having suspected Cummings of wanting to collar him."

Saunders pulls out all the parodic stops in "The Falls." Cummings, a secretive writer, concocts rhapsodies in his head and also corrects them, hoping to remember and write it all down later. Morse, a family man, carries Saunders's version of the paradigmatic American disease. "His childhood dreams had been so bright, he had hoped for so much, it couldn't be true that he was a nobody." Both wind up at the falls, witnesses to an accident, where they fear taking action and dream of heroism, two solitary fighters in an ethical boxing match. Uncharacteristically, both "The Falls" and "The Barber's Unhappiness" end ambiguously— with hope, maybe. Given Saunders's generally ironic stance, it's hard to tell but intriguing to consider.

In all of his unsentimental stories, Saunders commiserates with the disspirited, the weak, the flawed. His engagement with have-nots is a kind of return, like Aunt Bernie's, a visit to the worlds of John Steinbeck, Sinclair Lewis, Thornton Wilder and the Theodore Dreiser of "An American Tragedy"—small-town, small-city, little-people writers. Impoverishment in Saunders's work includes economic inequality, but he focuses more on deprivations that foreclose possibilities for expansive experiences, limiting perception and imaginative thinking. His eccentrically poignant fictions speak, in part, to the concerns Max Weber raised in 1921 in "The Protestant Ethic and the Spirit of Capitalism": "In the United States, the pursuit of wealth, stripped of its religious and ethical meaning, tends to become associated with purely mundane passions, which often actually give it the character of sport. No one knows who will live in this cage in the future, or whether at the end of this tremendous development entirely new prophets will arise, or there will be a great rebirth of old ideas and ideals, or, if neither, mechanized petrification, embellished with a sort of convulsive self-importance."

Saunders avoids righteousness and pleading. He understands Mary McCarthy's observation in "A Charmed Life," "Nobody can have a permanent claim on being the injured party," and his earnestness and seriousness propel him instead, as they did McCarthy, to satire and parody. Imagine Lewis's Babbitt thrown into the back seat of a car going cross-country, driven by R. Crumb, Matt Groening, Lynda Barry, Harvey Pekar or Spike Jonze. That'd be a story Saunders could tell.

T is for What Would Lynne Tillman Do

I wrote a first novel. I spent years on it, and, when it came out, it was just a book. I had worried about its cover, but it was just a cover. When I went into a bookstore, I saw it was just a book among many others, or it wasn't even there. Its dwarfed presence or absence made me think: Why add another book, I haven't even read all the books here? Or, narcissistically: Why publish a book if even I can't find it? When it was reviewed, the reviews were just words, often the wrong words. I spent months in bed, overwhelmed by my naïveté and folly. All my suppressed hopes acted like a tsunami and reduced me to nothing; my wishes were too big for any book, especially a first book. Later, I discovered it was the book that readers knew, if they knew any of mine, and no others. It was also the book whose existence made me realize that writing before publication was sweeter. Then I could think about my work the way I wanted: It didn't exist for others, and nothing about it could be disputed, including its presence.

Write your first novel, put everything you know and don't know into it, and stow it in the back of a drawer. Do this with your agent's cooperation. Ask her or him to spread the word in the industry that your first novel is explosive, revealing, scandalous, so brilliantly written that you are the new Pynchon, Morrison,

Austen, Beckett, Joyce, Woolf, Burroughs. You have created—no, invented—an entirely new novel, whose time has not yet come; it cannot be exposed to the public. Instead, the manuscript on offer is your second novel, which is even better, as it is more mature.

Your second novel is not roman à clef or a bildungsroman, not thinly disguised or outright autobiography. It is not based on your terrible past, whose egregious trials mock the reality of childhood innocence. The protagonist is not you. If the secondary characters appear to be you, they are cleverly achieved. The reader will not look for you, the author. You have skipped all the troubles of the first novel by presenting your second, first. Let others wonder about the first. Someday, you suggest, you may allow it to be published. But only after everyone, including you, has died.

In the beginning, there seems just one way to write, the way it comes out, and then that way becomes a debate, contested, most essentially, in and by its writer. Hopefully, a writer reads and reads and will become more conscious of decisions in style and form. Some writers make these choices more consciously than others, the decisions mark differences in fiction, though whether they might be experiments can't be assumed, certainly not by their authors.

The term "experimental" and others that characterize or categorize writing have, for me, lost their explanatory power. Mainstream, conventional, innovative, progressive, whatever value they hold or once held, the notions are vague, and they lack agreed-upon meanings among writers, readers and critics. Rather than being descriptive, the characterizations are predictive and can mark expectation, both writers' and readers'. Also, they are outmoded and unhelpful, even as heuristic tools; still, they survive, like the human appendix, without usefulness. Lacking other terms, we writers are their hapless recidivists.

If a writer has an idea about how writing should act, or what a reader should experience, it can occupy the writing, which then might foreground the writer's beliefs and a priori aesthetic preoccupations, which then might preclude a sensation, for a reader, of its "newness" (even when writing is not technically "new," as most isn't). A writer's discovering or discerning a way to write "it," whatever that is, finding a style, structure, subject to realize "it" through his or her capacities and sensibilities, lies outside of proscription. It's not that any of us can, with clairvoyance, recognize our ensnarement in and by language or in the grand, middling and small narratives that construct our lives, but it is a writer's most essential work to be conscious of the act of writing, of enabling words to do as much as possible, for instance.

> Our business is to see what we can do with the old English language as it is. How can we combine old words in new orders so that they create beauty and that they tell the truth. That is the question. . . . [Words] hate anything that stamps them with one meaning or one attitude. What is our nature, but to change. It is because the truth they try to catch is many-sided, they convey it by being many-sided, dashing this way and that. Thus they mean one thing to one person, another thing to another person.
> —Virginia Woolf, from "A Eulogy to Words," BBC Radio broadcast 1938

Sometimes finding the best word, best way of saying it, at least to the writer's mind, can be less accommodating to a reader; difficulty is always relative. But how a writer's trials, errors and successes add, or not, to a body called literature draws consensus in one time that might be denied in another. Believing in how it should be written, a way to write, also bedevils reasons to write; for me, the necessity to figure out how to accomplish a story or novel pushes me on. Many writers talk about sensing necessity in fiction, feeling it in a story, in its writing, which does not imply subject, psychology, relevance or reason, since nonsense can have necessity in the way it's written. Harry Mathews once remarked, and I paraphrase, It's not what you write about, it's how you write it. This is the ineffable which makes writing about writing so hard.

Unquestioned adherence to any dictates—about arcs, character development, fragmentation, dramatic tension, use of semicolons or adjectives, closure, character development or assassination, resolution or anti-closure—to any MFA workshop credos, or their antitheses, for a novel, story, poem, essay, will generate competent, often unexciting work, whether called mainstream, conventional, progressive or experimental; these products will have been influenced by or derived from, almost invariably and without exception, "established" or earlier work, their predecessors. In writing, "derivativeness," except in extreme cases, is a cagey issue, since all things flow from others; discontinuities emerge from a writer's objections, conscious and unconscious, to earlier literary approaches. But contemporary art and writing can be thoughtless or mindful re-inventions, dull or highly creative imitations, resonant and generative reworkings; new work can also glide, skip or jump off of culture's secure bases and revamp them remarkably, keeping the racquet, just restringing it. It's assumed there's less conformity in "experimental fiction." But what constitutes a genuine experiment in an "experimental" text? An argument might go: A true paradigm shift will model what follows, and these accumulate and accrete to the next. So, a convention results from earlier breaks or reformulations—Gertrude Stein's, Jane Bowles', Henry James' with the novel—and, augmented over time and by practice, the "experimental novel" becomes recognizable, no longer really an experiment but in the spirit or school of such. "Innovative" is used instead of "experimental," and that's often allied with "fresh," "edgy," "inventive," "novel," "groundbreaking." Then there's "unique," but how many formulations can be? The "literary novel"—what is it? Uncommercial? Conventionally experimental? And, how is "literariness" measured? And then there's "progressive." What is progressive writing, is it in its subject matter, politics or style? Or all three? Can there be a measure for it, whatever it might be, in its own time or before readers experience it?

The indeterminate and indefinable, elemental to fiction, complicate any naming. Inexorably, all writing fits into genres, like the genre-bending novel, which has itself become a genre. Wishing for scientific and technological discoveries or an avant garde to save and advance society and culture is futile; it supports, in the sense Modernism did, the idea of more advanced and superior articulations in writing, of a loftier civilization, less bellicose, more civilized, and an expanded human consciousness—progress. But the machinations and machines of the 20th century should have eviscerated this understandable illusion, since, by midcentury, progress ate its babies alive. So, no progress in literature or art, only differences and changes, contemporary responses and aesthetic variations: *Mrs. Dalloway* is not better than *Middlemarch*, Zeno's *Conscience* isn't better than Augustine's *Confessions*. And the other way around.

If the reader accepts, as I do, that no object has inherent value, that it is re-made by passing generations of readers and viewers —the erratic history of the worth and reputation of authors' work attests to this—no form can be privileged, no judgment eternal. Consciousness, in all its manifestations, will come to be represented variously by each generation for their different days and nights; since what is around people, what we see, hear, watch, exist in, affects our being and becoming, our reactions and what we make, as our psychologies shift within parameters of basic needs, new hungers and expanded wants.

Human beings are fantastic and horrifyingly adaptive creatures, fashioning tools or re-tooling, making nice, making war, building up and tearing down. Things change, they stay the same, the world changes and doesn't, simultaneously. Writers rue rewriting old narratives, despair that there's nothing new under the sun, except, say, a depleted ozone level, which will engender a plethora of apocalyptic myths. Still, an object can be shaken up and turned on its head, a word set beside another can create a shattering collision, like John Milton's use of "gray" as an adjective in his poem, "Lycidas." Still, fiction will thrive primarily through readers' imaginative capacities, which means that how and what we read is ultimately more crucial than how and what we write.

Those of us who are practicioners live in interesting times. Writing now is like doing laps without a pool. Maybe we wail in an aesthetic void or shout in a black hole, life's empty or dense; we can't know what we're in—fish probably don't know they're in water (who can be certain, though). But uncertainty is not the same as ignorance, it may point writers toward other registers of meaning, other articulations. Complacency is writing's most determined enemy, and we writers, and readers, have been handed an ambivalent gift: Doubt. It robs us of assurance, while it raises possibility.

Fiction is the enemy of facts, facts are not the same as truths. Fiction is inimical to goals, resistant to didacticism, its moralities question morality, its mind changes, while explanations crash and burn, mocking explicability. Fiction also claims that seeming lies can be true, because everything we say and don't say, know and don't know, tells and reveals. Novels and stories are not training manuals, their "information" is gleaned by readers in their terms and for their own uses, often not easily comprehended in part or whole, or never. Knowing the plot of *Oedipus Rex*, say, doesn't change its powerful effects, for its enunciation of the unspeakable, the way it's written and its evocation of the mystery and tragedy of human desire overwhelm any one of its parts. A great story is necessarily greater than its plot.

Call these statements a polemic or rant or a partial theoretical background to my own writing, my catholic or promiscuous inclinations. I'm for generative types of contemporary writing, not for proscriptions about writing. I don't have a secure or immovable position, my various notions on writing might include contradictions, I'm sure they do. I don't want to take A Position. Not taking a position is a position that acknowledges the inability to know with absolute surety, that says: Writing is like life, there are many ways of doing it, survival depends on flexibility. Anything can be on the page. What isn't there now?

U is for Unheimlich

A *Conversation with Peter Dreher*

In 1994, I visited the Museum für Neue Kunst in Freiburg. My host, artist Dirk Gortler, showed me a thick, gray book with page after page of gray-toned reproductions—all paintings of the same water glass. Dirk told me Peter Dreher did the same painting every day—there are now over 2,500 of them—and taught in the art academy there. I bought the book, then asked Dirk to send me two more copies. Recently Dreher was in New York for his opening at the Monique Knowlton Gallery. I went and asked if I could interview him. We talked the next morning at the gallery. When I was leaving, he graciously said, "Even if nothing else happens, it was good to talk with you," which turned out to be portentous. I walked up Broadway, rewound the tape, and started to play it back. There was nothing on it. "Even if nothing…" I phoned him, told him there was nothing on the tape, made another appointment for later that night—he was leaving New York in a day—and bought a new tape recorder. I was intent upon doing this, obsessed, in a way. There were some differences between the first and second interviews—it's extremely difficult to have exactly the same conversation twice. I think we laughed more the second time.

Lynne Tillman: You paint the same object every day. You have since 1974. That fascinates me.

Peter Dreher: Is this the question?

LT: Do whatever you want with it.

PD: It's difficult to say the second time . . .

LT: You paint the same thing every day, this should be easy for you. In fact, if I had planned it . . .

PD: Did you plan it?

LT: No. But if I had, I'd have been more Machiavellian than I ever thought myself.

PD: Many ideas came together. When I was sitting in a bathtub—I love to sit in hot bathtubs, I have all my ideas there—I had the idea to paint the most simple thing I could imagine. Before that I painted large, gray paintings which showed a sort of optical illusion. I thought they were something very simple. But you could identify them as pieces of art only in a museum or gallery. Outside, in the streets, nobody would recognize them as art. I thought it should be more simple than just painting a wall white like Yves Klein did. And what is more simple than to take something usual, like a glass—I mean, something invisible—and place it on a white table before white walls, a white, white glass. Something you could see everywhere, everybody's used it. It's something like Hitchcock's idea of hiding a diamond in a chandelier, which is more simple in the mind than in the form. That was one idea, and I thought the next step would be to do this simple thing, with its simple motive, again and again and again. I had the idea to paint it five or six times. I did one, two, three, then five, then seven, then 10, then 100. I couldn't stop, and it became fascinating. I think the whole history of art—no, let's say the history of the problems in painting—came to me in the last 22 years.

LT: As you were doing this.

PD: Yes.

LT: It's interesting you mention Hitchcock. The viewer can see a little window in the glass. When you look closely at your paintings, you see minute details, minute changes. The window is made with just a few, tiny strokes of different colors. And you—the painter—are in the window. Hitchcock made *Rear Window*; and in your paintings, the window's at the rear of the glass. You said you wanted something that could be recognized as a piece of art not only in a gallery . . .

PD: Yes, everywhere.

LT: I wonder what that means to you.

PD: I think painting should be open or recognizable to everybody.

Everybody. These little paintings of a glass, everybody can under-stand. You see a glass, you say, "It's a glass, it's a nice painting, it's realistic." You don't feel that you didn't understand it. But if you want to learn more about it, you can. If you begin to deal with this concept, I think a whole world opens to you.

LT: Many artists, since Duchamp, have been very concerned with: Why is this art?

PD: Yes.

LT: You started from a different premise: This is art.

PD: I thought, first, I'm an artist, I like painting. Maybe my paint-ings are art, or they aren't, but this is not something I can force. I cannot make art just by my will. I can only say, "I feel I'm an art-ist, and I want to put as much energy, sensibility into my paintings as I can." What I wanted to do was to show that I have a great desire to paint. I wanted the most simple way to show that. Without any other ideas in my paintings than just this desire, this addiction.

LT: Does it make your life easier or simpler to have chosen one ob-ject to paint and to know that you'll always paint it? Do you think you'll ever not paint it? Can you imagine…

PD: I ask myself every day if it still has sense to do this. The day I must say to myself, "No, it's not necessary, there's no more sense in it," I'll stop it. But now, it's 22 years, and I'll do it as long as I can, as long as I can paint. As long as I live.

LT: We were talking earlier about when you were teaching in 1968 and '69, of the effect of that time and its politics on your work and thought.

PD: I was 35, a young teacher, and I was interested in the ideas of my students. At first we appeared to be on different sides. After some time, my students learned that we had some of the same interests. Their idea was that painting wasn't necessary anymore, at least not as long as the revolution and the development of society didn't succeed. As long as that struggle was going on, you had to do that work—revolution—and not paint. When revolution fulfilled its aims, its goals, you could paint again, make art again; but then, it wouldn't be necessary anymore because people wouldn't have any frustrations.

LT: Could you ever imagine an absence of all frustration?

PD: At that time I didn't really believe it, but I thought it was a nice idea, it was a good idea. A human idea. We have lots of human ideas that never come to reality. But it's necessary to have ideas. I respected their ideas. I tried not to paint anymore, but I couldn't.

LT: How long did you try not to paint?

PD: I realized I couldn't stop painting, that my desire was too big. I tried to find a way to show that I must paint, that there are people in the world who have this desire and cannot deny it.

LT: So you're making a continuous statement by painting this glass. No matter what the social conditions are, someone might just have to paint? Even if other people think it's no longer necessary, some will still need to do it? It's interesting that you've chosen to paint an object that's considered a necessity.

PD: The object, the glass, is a simple, simple thing. An abstract painting is something much more difficult to understand. You have to have a certain education to understand it.

LT: If it were just one glass, I'd agree with you. But when you produce and show hundreds of them, it does become abstract and conceptual. It raises many issues. You can think about the glass as a kind of container of ideas, you can think about the glass being half full or half empty, a kind of philosophical statement. The project's also about art history—painters have been painting still lifes for a very long time.

PD: Yes.

LT: There's the way you demonstrate your desire for painting, and there's also an emphasis on the artisanal quality of painting, because you have to be able to know how to paint glass; that's not easy.

PD: It's easy. That's not the problem.

LT: It's not a problem?

PD: It's just to look at it, to paint what you see.

LT: Do you think anybody could do that?

PD: Yes. I think so.

LT: Have you ever taught a class how . . .

PD: How to paint a glass? No. They can do it if they want, but they don't. They see it as a project which is so special they don't imitate it. I'm really lucky to have this project…

LT: Because nobody else wants to do it.

PD: Right. When I began the project, Berswort, who is a famous gallerist in Germany, saw it. He's a very intelligent man. He said, "Beware of somebody who steals your idea, maybe he does it more intelligently or better." I thought, yes, maybe he's right. But nobody tries to imitate me. The glass—if you do it once, everybody says, "OK, how nice, what is he doing?" But if you do it a lot of times—do you know the game, saying "table, table, table" a hundred times?

LT: The word becomes garbage.

PD: Yes, it becomes something else, it's no longer the word. I think that's the same with the glass. Again, if you're trying to do something very simply only to show that you love to paint, it's good if the glass after a time goes out of the painting; then its meanings and its philosophy, and so on, become apparent . . .

LT: Do you think that if you look at it long enough, the painting becomes empty?

PD: If you do it a hundred times, people will ask themselves, "If he does it a hundred times, it cannot be to portray the glass. It must be something else. And what is it?" It's just what I see, and I don't see a glass, I see a painting. I see the work of a painter.

LT: In our first, lost conversation, we discussed seriality; Warhol, Pop Art. Was that an influence on your thinking? Were you thinking about Walter Benjamin's ideas about photography?

PD: When I started, in the '50s and the beginning of the '60s, the Abstract Expressionists, Jackson Pollock, reigned over the whole art world. You were asked, "What do you paint?" If you said, "I'm a realistic painter," they went away.

LT: Nobody was interested.

PD: You were not an artist anymore if you painted realistically. Then in Venice in 1964, at the Biennale, I saw Pop Art for the first time, and I was happy, you can't imagine. It was quite late. I didn't know the work before—and I loved Jasper Johns, Oldenburg. Great, great experience. But it had come from America, which I adored since I was a child. They were great things that Warhol did. I think he was a great artist. Then, on the other hand, there's On Kawara and Opalka. Some people compare me with them. Opalka writes millions of numbers. It's something else because On Kawara and Opalka are working with signs. I'm working with reality. My idea was only to paint something in the way painters did 35,000 years ago, say they painted elephants. Then, when the work was finished, it was forgotten. They had to do the painting again and again and again. So it was one, then five, then a thousand. But the idea was not a series. The idea was just a lifetime, doing something in your lifetime, doing it with concentration, and showing that it's not necessary to change the reason, the motive.

LT: I remember you said, not changing the object, your desire in doing that, related to your history. Having been 12 when World War II ended, you felt uprooted, unstable. Your father was dead, shot at the Russian front. You were in your mid-forties when you decided to paint a glass forever. Before that you felt you were wandering around in your work.

PD: Maybe I couldn't think so simply as to get to this point. After a while I figured out this idea about floating and building a home, not by building a certain place, which I did. When I was 29 I built a little house by myself.

LT: Where?

PD: Near Hamburg. In the countryside. It was cheaper then to do that. I spent one year of my life at it. I learned this was not the way to get home or to get a home.

LT: It wasn't the physical place.

PD: Right. I came to the conclusion that you have to build it by something you do or think, or something you paint. When I was a boy, after my father died, his house was destroyed. I had to leave Mannheim, my hometown. I told you I felt uprooted. But maybe, more important, is a feeling that perhaps I was born with, that everybody is born with: that one is somehow floating between thoughts, between literature, speaking, continents, races, and so on. I think, more or less, each of us today, maybe more than a hundred years ago, has this feeling.

LT: Of floating.

PD: Of being homeless somehow. Everybody has to find out how to deal with this, how to get around it.

LT: When you're painting the glass each day, do you feel in a place? Or do you feel like you're floating with it?

PD: It's very funny to say, it's the only place and the only hours in my life when I really feel quiet. Maybe I don't make the impression of being unquiet, but I am.

LT: You're anxiety-ridden?

PD: Yes.

LT: You've had many shows in Germany, and since '74, this is what you've exhibited. What's the response been?

PD: At the first show, I saw people come in, and they looked around for half-a-minute, and said, "Oh, it's all the same." I remember a story the director of the Baden Baden Kunsthalle told me about a very famous German art critic, who came in and said to him, "Do you want to cheat me? Make fun of me?" That was 1975. But, at the same time, half of the people came and stayed three hours, looking at the work. When they left, they said, "I have to return tomorrow." These are the two reactions. And from art critics—I really never had bad criticism. I don't know why. Germans understand it somehow if they are familiar with art, opera, philosophy, ideas, and so on.

LT: You're going against the grain of what other painters of your generation do and have done. How does that feel, to you?

PD: To me? It makes me happy.

LT: You don't feel the need for their approval?

PD: No, but I have it from some. At my opening here, for instance. Wolfgang Laib came. He's a very good artist. I was very happy he was here, because he's the person who's possibly closest to my ideas. He's doing something else, though. By doing what I do, I have the distance to be friends with lots of artists, because we don't touch each other. I really like seeing the work of other painters, other artists, my students, discussing, learning what they're thinking about art. I'm very happy because I'm like a frog to them.

LT: A frog?

PD: A frog, or a dog, or something…

LT: Just a sort of odd creature to them.

PD: I saw a film of a Zen Buddhist master. The interviewer asked him, "What is your task?" He said, "To become a dog." I think that's a great idea. Because a dog has no intention of influencing anybody. I think you know what I mean.

LT: Yes, I do. There's a joke going around: "In cyberspace, nobody knows if you're a dog."

PD: Today I told Lucio Pozzi a story of "the frog who fell into the milk." The frog was afraid to drown. He was working with his feet, very fast, to keep his head above the milk. So he made butter and then he had an island he could sit on. That's what we, I, do.
LT: I'm still fascinated by the idea that you paint the glass every day.

PD: 14 days after I began the glass, I got in contact with a woman who was very familiar with Zen Buddhism. She lived in a Zen cloister in Japan for three years. She told me that a tape I'd recorded off the radio was a Zen Buddhist ceremony. She told me exactly what it meant, and what she told me—it was like coming home. I'm not a Buddhist. I'm a Christian. But these ideas made me very happy—I learned that there are thoughts in the world which try to express what I try to express with the painting of the glass.

LT: The idea of doing a simple thing that shows you're in the world, doing something every day, not more, not less?

PD: The Buddhists say everything has the same value. The grass and the king. I say, "That's right. I feel that too." But also, if you do it again and again and again, it's worth the same, and the thing is new every day. It's as worthwhile as anything else, but—it's difficult for me to express—it's also worthwhile to look at it again and again and again. The glass is the glass is the glass is the glass. Gertrude Stein!

LT: Why don't you consider yourself a Buddhist?

PD: I'm European. I'd like to be a Buddhist, but it's not my culture, it's not my heritage. When I lived in New York in 1980, I thought I'd find the sources of Pop Art, and on every corner would be Pop Artists; I'd meet Warhol, which I could have, but I didn't. When I was here, I realized I'm a European. I can do what I want to, but I will never be a New Yorker. I will never learn how to think like a New Yorker. I have to deal with that. There's something else I wanted to tell you. Do you know the German painter Otto Dix?

LT: Yes, I do.

PD: The Nazis didn't allow him to paint his social satires, so he had to paint landscapes, and he said, "I look to the landscape like a cow." That's good. I would say, "I look to the cat like a dog." I try. I'm not good enough to really do it, but I try.

V is for Virtual

Ordinary people get the news, they don't make it. Mediacs report, repeat, spin, repeat and pummel non-ordinaries with self-serving rhetorical questions, and, except for dead people and "undecideds," or the living dead, Americans are addicted. Media junkies, by definition, can't stop: They need more of that blah-blah powder. Obama himself, the public recently learned, had to go cold turkey off his BlackBerry—and the world sympathized. He too needs instantaneity, to be connected, like most 21st-century characters.

Once the dramatic presidential race reached its historic conclusion, the news was suddenly less tantalizing. Instant by instant, the yawning gap widened. O'Reilly, Matthews, Olbermann, Blitzer et al. chewed over Obama's cabinet picks, happily eviscerating Hillary Clinton again, but their hyperbole only exacerbated the emptiness left at election's end. Like Bush, the mediacs had become lame ducks too.

The man who had just won the globe's most visible job dominated America's attention. President-elect Barack Obama: Intelligent, witty, knowledgeable, eloquent, telegenic, photogenic, aurally pleasing. Gone, the faulty neologisms of the past eight years. Gone, the irrationality of God-directed foreign policy. Gone, the ramblings and the wacky syntax.

Obama's timely intervention into the abyss began on November 15, just 11 days after the election, when he streamed on YouTube from his website. The video opened on a modified version of the presidential seal, zooming out to reveal the words change.gov (his website's handle), and underneath, the office of the president-elect. Then it scrolled down to the approximated presidential seal again, with these words beneath: Your weekly address from the president-elect. November 15th, 2008.

This "weekly" address was in fact Obama's very first, but enjoining "weekly" creates a faux continuity: Past activities fuse with future ones. And by issuing the podcast as the president-elect, Obama created a new, unprecedented, even extraconstitutional, national office. Still, his screen presence felt familiar, comforting. He played a role that corresponds to ones Americans have long watched on TV—from Robert Young in *Father Knows Best* to Sam Waterston in *Law & Order* (or, even more apt, Waterston in his TV ads for TD Ameritrade). The role requires unflappability, which Obama exudes like Verbena cologne, and it is his aim, in this video, to quiet America's erratic pulse, its arrhythmic financial markets, its frightened workers, its bankrupt home owners.

The president-elect is seated behind a desk on a black leather chair, his head cushioned against its back. He's in medium shot and part of a cozy composition; nothing seems out of place. He almost appears tucked into the image, which divides into discrete elements. On the left, an American flag hangs the length of the frame, the one and only element taller than he. The background is a medium-brown wood-paneled wall. To the left of Obama, shoulder-high, three dark-blue volumes: *Public Papers of the Presidents: John F. Kennedy (1961–1963)*. The tomes lend a somberness to the image, representing the popular, fallen president, while associating JFK's New Frontier with Obama's upcoming variation on the New Deal. On the far right, also shoulder height, another volume, its title blurred, and a basketball, like a Pop art sculpture, signed by Lenny Wilkens of the US Olympic basketball team. A plant's green leaves drape over the ball.

Though it's video, it's basically a still image. Obama wears a dark red tie and a flag pin on his gray lapel. His head moves up and down gently, for emphasis, and occasionally it subtly shifts from side to side. His expression is serious, sober, nearly unchanging, and the new gray at his temples does no harm. The sonorous Obama voice stays steady, on course, with none of the rise and fall heard in his campaign speeches, but he doesn't shy away from unsettling language, like "the greatest economic challenge of our times." Still, he's not running anymore, so he's transmuted his stump speech into a Fireside Chat, in which the screen is the hearth and his voice the melody in the air. "I know that we can steer ourselves out of this crisis. . . . I am more hopeful than ever that America will rise once again." He has checked his radiant smile, since these are not happy times, but he reassures the American public that happy days are here to come.

From this initial video message to his preinauguration press conferences to more recent YouTube clips and weekly talks, Obama has transformed the function of the president-elect, just as he transfigured the presidential campaign into an Internet phenomenon. Streaming from the Office of the President-Elect, a nonplace or anyplace, Obama proclaims his virtual presidency. The easy acceptance by the public and the media of this novel authority—after some initial "Where's the president?" "Nowhere"—attests to the way people live today, in online encounters and communities. They connect as if they were face-to-face.

Barack Obama keeps making history. He has now also affected the English language, specifically the word *virtual*. Through his prestidigitations, he has helped along a linguistic shift: Virtual is the new actual. And, in that sense, Obama is president, news maker and commentator. He can explain himself, by himself. Since he knows what he's thinking—and why—before the mediacs do, he scoops them effortlessly. In comparison with his skills, their responses seem increasingly thin, redundant, more obviously ill-informed and excruciatingly superficial. Obama's capacity to think and answer should force the "cult of personality" pundits to stop shouting and start reading. But it won't

W is for Wharton

A Mole in the House of the Modern

Edith Wharton's passion for architecture was foundational, evidenced by her very first book, *The Decoration of Houses*, a work of notification. Wharton disdained the merely decorative in rooms and buildings, as she disdained it in her fiction. Her writing is severe, deliberate in its attacks and restraints, and lives in every detail and in the structure. Wharton's novels and stories move from small moments to big ones (she manages to merge the two), from openness of opportunity and hope, to inhibition and tragic limitation, from life's transitory pleasures and possibilities, to its dull and sharp pains and immobilizations. Traps and entrapment, psychological and societal, life's dead ends become the anxious terminals for Wharton's literary search for freedom and pleasure. (In her book, pleasure is freedom's affect.)

The architect Wharton is always conscious of the larger structure, with her meaning central in each scene. She meticulously furnishes a room, so that all the pieces and lines in it function as emotional or psychological props, conditions or obstacles. Like cages or containers, her interiors keep characters in a place, often an internalized place. They enter rooms, meet, sit, talk, then Wharton lets them find the walls, the limits. She observes them in houses or on the street in chance meetings, and they fix each other—the gaze is her métier—to a moment in time, to a truth (about the other or themselves), to a seat in the social theater. Everything that happens with effect, building her edifice. Wharton selected her words with a scalpel, as if with or without them her patient would live, die; she was precise in her renderings, otherwise the construction might fall, and other such metaphors. Her writing is never labored, though. Yet nothing's simple, or simply an object, and never just an ornament. The ornament is redolent and may even be causal. (Think of "The Bunner Sisters," those poor women whose fate hung on the repair of a timepiece. A twisted tale, but then Wharton is perverse, and sophisticated and surprising in her perverseness.)

Wharton's stately, measured rhythms let the reader linger over a sentence, then move along languidly. One may be stopped dead by some piece of psychological astuteness, a blunt idea by brutal clarity, or staggered by an almost excessive, because perfect, image. Slowly, Wharton draws beautiful portraits, deceptive pictures. (I sometimes wonder if Wharton ever felt rushed by anything, then I remember Morton Fullerton and her love letters to him, that rush late in her life). Beautiful language serves—like tea, an elegant service—ironic and difficult ends. It lures one into a network of sinister complications and, transformed, beauty leads to dreariness and viciousness. The reader will be torn by the loss of that plenitude, by failure, by hopelessness.

But Wharton is economical about elegance, stringent about lushness, display, every embellishment. Rarely extravagant. Maybe it's because she understood position and space, knew she didn't really have much room, no room for profligacy. She couldn't run from reality, even if she wanted to (and I think she did), so she had no room to waste, certainly no words to waste. The inessential might obscure the clarity she sought. She wouldn't let herself go, let her writing go. She understood the danger, she understood any form of complicity. Her often privileged protagonists fatally conspire with society against themselves, become common prey to its dictates, helpless to disown or resist what they despise in themselves and in it. Wharton was profoundly aware that, seen by others, she was free to do what she pleased, a privileged woman, perhaps explained early on in *The House of Mirth*. Lily Bart "was so evidently the victim of the civilization which had produced her, that the links of her bracelet seemed like manacles chaining her to her fate" (I, 1, 8).

***

> *I have sometimes thought that a women's nature is like a great house full of rooms; there is the hall, through which everyone passes in going in and out; the drawing room, where one receives formal visits; the sitting room, where the members of the family come and go as they list; but beyond that, far beyond, are other rooms, the handles of whose doors perhaps are never turned; no one knows the way to them, no one knows whither they lead; and in the innermost room, the holy of holies, the soul sits alone and waits for a doorstep that never comes.* —The Fullness of Life *(1891)*

In Wharton's scheme, Lily Bart's fate was to be beautiful, to become poor and unmarriageable, and to die a suicide, a tragic heroine. Like bread crumbs, Wharton scatters clues to Lily's predicament. "[S]he likes being good and I like being happy," Lily says of poor Gerty Farish to Lawrence Selden. Some of the clues correspond to Selden's grand idea, proposed once to Lily, that there is a "republic of the spirit" she might enter. Lily's conflict—her wish for freedom but her sense "that I never had any choice"—conspires to keep her from the independent or idiosyncratic life Selden represents. (His republic of the spirit is an imaginary structure, perhaps the house of mirth itself.)

Wharton's use of architecture operates in the traditional way—as built structure, as expression of the symbolic order, as place, as evidence of the hierarchical order—but it is exercised for fictive ends. The novel begins in a terminal, Grand Central Station, and terminates in a rented room. The "house" is first a capacious, modern public building, a place anyone may enter and pass through, and last a cramped space open to the public but required only by the poor. Lily journeys, like Richard II, from bigness to smallness, from a magnificent building that seems infinite—kingdom, modern world—to small rented room of desperate finitude—cell, deathbed. Space and place change with Lily Bart, or change her.

***

Lawrence Selden makes Lily happy or sad whenever they meet. It is Selden whom Lily encounters by chance in Grand Central Station, and it's Selden who finds Lily dead at the novel's end. His presence frames Lily's life, ghosts and subverts it, as the rooms, scenes and encounters Wharton sets Lily in structure it. What the reader knows of Lily's thoughts about her impossible position is gleaned primarily in her discussions with Selden, her foil and confidante. Selden is a fitting comrade, a modern flawed hero or antihero. He arouses the dubious sprite fortune and its reversals, and with its partner hope and possibility, plagues Lily. No one underwrites Lily's placelessness, or lovelessness, more than Selden.

Wharton had a keen interest in ghost stores and the supernatural, and Selden flits through *The House of Mirth* as if it were a Gothic tale and he were its elusive hero. Selden is a haunted and haunting figure who magnifies Lily's unfitness and increasing inappropriateness whenever he appears. Her double in drag, he even impedes her so-called progress with other suitors, fulfilling his double-agent, phantom-lover mission as the budding star in a magnificent sense of plot points. His last appearance at Lily's bedside makes her death more pointedly tragic and beautiful, since we see her through his shattered vision. At that deadly moment Selden becomes a character—or an ornament—Wharton might have borrowed from Poe.

The House of Mirth was originally titled "A Moment's Ornament." Lily Bart could have been its temporary decoration. Though from Lily's point of view, the occasional ornament could have been Selden. But then Wharton enjoyed symmetries. Her house, the Mount in Lenox Massachusetts, which she designed and had built, has three front doors, one of them fake; Wharton wanted the façade to be symmetrical. Selden is symmetrical to Lily and does balance her even as he unbalances her. (Symmetry to Wharton, "the answering of one part to another, may be defined as the sanity of decoration" [*Decoration*, 7].) The uncoupled couple, the two-faced couple, articulates Wharton's comprehension of how women's changed, conflictual desires are met by changed, conflicted men. Both are, in a way, misfits, though Selden's eccentricity and inappropriateness, including his bachelorhood, have value while Lily's spinsterhood and virginity daily lose theirs.

***

Wharton's enclosures house conflicts and conflicted characters, created not just by ordinary walls. The author constructs walls, limits, that are both real and metaphorical. Wharton's central and most sustained trope, architecture always alludes to Lily's physical or mental space, her environment or psychological condition. The decor—couches, paintings, fireplaces, bric-a-brac—becomes evidence of the state in which she exists or of the character of the characters she meets.

> [Mrs Dorset] could have been crumpled up and run through a ring, like the sinuous draperies she affected. . . . she was like a disembodied spirit who took up a great deal of room. (I, 2, 21-2)

> There was nothing new to Lily in these tokens of a studied luxury; but though they formed a part of her atmosphere, she never lost her sensitiveness to their charm. Mere display left her with a sense of superior distinction, but she felt an affinity to all the subtler manifestations of wealth. (I, 4, 34)

> Look at a boy like Ned Silverton—he's really too good to be used to refurbish anybody's social shabbiness. (I, 6, 56-7)

The exterior suggests the interior or, rather, is the manifestation, the visible order, of an inner world.

Since architecture also defines space by what is not built and what lies outside, the trope allows Wharton to delineate the un-bounded, permeable relationship between outside and inside, the flow and inevitable transmission between the so-called inner life and outer life. Lily contends with the limits of public life and space, with propriety and sensibility, with street life, the places without walls that are bounded and limited, to women.

> *All good architecture and good decoration (which it must never be forgotten is only interior architecture) must be based on rhythm and logic. (Decoration, 13)*

For Lily Bart, leaving rooms and being on the street is hazard-ous; it's when many of her most devastating and decisive encoun-ters occur. Leaving Selden's apartment, she accidentally meets Mr. Rosedale in front of the Benedick (bachelor) Apartments. She tells a lie that propels the novel's story—and her undoing—into motion. Lily instantly realizes her error. (Rosedale's ap-pearance has been foreshadowed by an unkempt charwoman on the Benedick stairs, who unsettles Lily and with whom Lily com-pares herself. The charwoman also returns to plague her, black-mail her.)

> *Why must a girl pay so dearly for her least escape from routine? Why could one never do a natural thing without having to screen it behind a structure of artifice? (I, 2, 19)*

Her comings and goings are not easy; she doesn't make smooth exits; and there are certainly no escapes.

Ironically, Lily identifies with the man who can undo her, Simon Rosedale, a noveau riche Jewish businessman initially sketched by Wharton with the brush of conventional anti-Semitism. He is, like Lily, "a novelty" (I, 2, 16). She "understood his motives, for her own course was guided by nice calculations" (I, 2, 16). Within a very few pages, Wharton serves up two male characters, dissimilar to each other and to her, as well as a dissimilar female, against whom to judge Lily. All balance our view of her, creating a kind of symmetry or the rhythm and logic fundamental to Wharton's idea of design in architecture and fiction.

Later in the novel, "as [Selden and Van Alstyne] walked down Fifth Avenue [to Mrs. Fisher's] the new architectural developments of that versatile thoroughfare invited Van Alstyne's comments" (I,14,126). (Wharton may be commenting upon her techniques for outlining the "redundant" manners and modes she must contend with in society and in constructing, "corseting," her fictions.) Then Van Alstyne remarks about Mrs. Bry's architect:

What a clever chap . . . how he takes his client's measure! (1, 14, 126)

Architecture, to Wharton's thinking, can reveal the whole of a character. When Van Alstyne and Selden reach the Trenor house, Van Alstyne reports it's empty and remarks offhandedly that Mrs. Trenor is away.

The house loomed obscure and uninhabited, only an oblong gleam above the
door spoke of provisional occupancy. (I, 14, 127)

At this moment, whose consequences also loom obscure, Lily is discovered in the doorway with Gus Trenor. She has just fought him off and is leaving. Her provisional presence, not inside, not outside, endangers her. Compromised, in the wrong place at the wrong time, seen by Selden, whose heart has recently turned more decisively toward her, and by her relative, Van Alstyne, her fortune is immediately reversed. But her name is never used; she has entered the realm of the unspeakable.

Wharton deploys a discourse on houses, about how an architect (maker/writer) can expose the character of the persons whose house he designs, to position Lily. When she appears in a place where she should not be, her presence there says something about her. Though this was not her design, many of the things Lily does are designed, and many that appear designing and manipulative are not. Ineluctably, Lily becomes ensnared in patterns not of her making that are not provisional enough.

***

To conform to a style, then, is to accept those rules of proportion which the
artistic experience of centuries has established as the best, while within those
limits allowing free scope to the individual requirements which must inevitably
modify every house or room adapted to the use and convenience of its occu-
pants. (Decoration, 15)

True originality consists not in a new manner but in a new vision. (Writing, 17)[2]

The distrust of technique and the fear of being unoriginal—both symptoms of a certain lack of creative abundance—are in truth leading to pure anarchy in fiction. (Writing, 15)

In *The Decoration of Houses* (1897) and *The Writing of Fiction* (1924), Wharton argues for conformity to style and tradition against originality for its own sake. The rhythm and logic of the past must be observed or at least taken into account and regarded, if not entirely followed. Wharton even claims that stream of consciousness and slice of life are the same idea; stream of consciousness is slice of life "relabeled" (*Writing*, 12). Her aesthetics and views on morality and convention form the underlying arguments in the novel and contain within them the seeds of conflict planted and harvested in Lily Bart.

Enshrined in Lily is a contest between new and old, tradition, innovation and the hazards of change. On the first page of the novel, Wharton efficiently marks her territory when Selden thinks to himself: "There was nothing new about Lily Bart, yet he could never see her without a faint movement of interest" (I, 1, 5). To him she was so "radiant" she was "more conspicuous than a ballroom" (I, 1, 5). (The scale is striking, so disproportionate.) But not bold enough or too principled to marry for money and live any way she chooses, she cannot strike out on her own and exist on her meager income, like Gerty Farish. She is not a new woman. Wharton does not allow her a wholly new manner, which the author disdains, but she also does not provide Lily with vision for a new life.

(Lily is more like a new woman manqué. It's as if Wharton invented her to put on trial and test her principle of "conform[ing] to a style . . . [that] artistic experience of centuries has established as the best, while within those limits allowing free scope to the individual requirements." How one holds to tradition and style and discovers within them "free scope" is at the crux of Wharton's contradictory, ongoing argument with the modernists and the social order.)

Lily contains within her traces and pieces of the old order and longings for the new. Wharton drops Lily between the two worlds, on the frontier, where no place is home or safe. Habitually, Lily pays the price for not being able to realize a new way and for needing the largesse of others whom she despises or for whom she has contempt.

> *That cheap originality which finds expression in putting things to uses for which they were not intended is often confounded with individuality. Whereas the latter consists not in an attempt to be different from other people at the cost of comfort, but in the desire to be comfortable in one's own way, even though it be the way of a monotonously large majority. It seems easier to most people to arrange a room like someone else's than to analyze and express their own needs.* (Decoration, 19-20)

Lily's difference from the "monotonously large majority" hangs her on a cross constructed from an opposition between novelty and individuality. She feels superior and wants to discover and "express [her] own needs," as Selden does. She must find a way to "use" herself, not as a "cheap experiment" but in the intended way. But there is no intended way, not for her.

***

Men, in these matters, are less exacting than women, because their demands, besides being simpler, are uncomplicated by the feminine tendency to want things because other people have them, rather than to have things because they are wanted. But it must never be forgotten that everyone is unconsciously tyrannized over by the wants of others.

. . . The unsatisfactory relations of some people with their rooms are often to be explained in this way. They have still in their blood the traditional uses to which these rooms were put in times quite different from the present. . . . To go to the opposite extreme and discard things because they are old-fashioned is equally unreasonable. (Decoration, 19-20)

Desire is a strange brew, Wharton knew, concocted of the desires of others. Her psychological acumen suffuses *The House of Mirth*, in which Lily is "unconsciously tyrannized over by the wants of others." Lily has "in her blood" the uses for which she was made but is unwilling to go to "the opposite extreme" and "discard things" because they are "old-fashioned."

Once more the haunting sense of physical ugliness was intensified by her mental depression, so that each piece of the offending furniture seemed to thrust forth its most aggressive angle. (I, 9, 86)

Lily does want to get rid of ugly things. The effects of physical ugliness—disproportion—and mental depression intermingle in her. Their symmetry or dissymmetry serves Wharton's notion of the interior as inextricable from the exterior. Lily's internal conflicts are displayed in the outer world, where she is a beautiful but tormented trophy in its display case. Her inner struggles show themselves as much by what she does not do as by what she does.

> *It must be pure bliss to arrange the furniture just as one likes, and give all the horrors to the Ashman. If I could only do over my aunt's drawing room I know I should be a better woman.* (I, 1, 8)

Lily's longing to clean out her aunt's room is a wish to change herself, to throw out her own horrors. In a better room, she might become better—setting and place affect character. But Lily can't throw out the horrors, she cannot change the conditions in which she lives that have made her the kind of woman she is. When she strikes out against convention or her interests, by spending time with Selden and avoiding her rich, boring suitor, Percy Gryce, her revolt takes the shape of inaction, temporizing. She may want to remove horrors but she does not act or cannot. Cleaning her aunt's room of horrors could also be another clever reference to the Gothic, but from the Gothic, which preceded Freud, with its insistence on the darkness in human beings and the cauldron of murky, unconscious desires that drive behavior, other ideas march in. They enter through a side door—call it the unarticulated or the unconscious—of Wharton's subtle fiction.

***

. . . she was not meant for mean and shabby surroundings, for the squalid compromises of poverty. Her whole being dilated in an atmosphere of luxury, it was the background she required, the only climate she could breathe in. But the luxury of others was not what she wanted.

. . . Now she was beginning to chafe at the obligations it imposed, to feel herself a mere pensioner on the splendor which had once seemed to belong to her. There were even moments when she was conscious of having to pay her way. (I, 3 23)

Lily pays by being charming and by trying to keep her reputation intact. A twentieth-century Clarissa, who even fights off a rape, Lily's chastity is a series of questions. Purity? Property? Repression? Inhibition? Architecture is, among other things, about bodies living within structures built for bodies by bodies. Lily is subject, even prey, to assaults within two kinds of structures—external or social and internal or psychological. The exterior holds, conditions and is manifested in the interior, interiority inhabited and penetrated by the social. (If houses and ornaments are mated, psychologies are married to societies.)

She had always hated her room at Mrs. Peniston's—its ugliness, its impersonality, the fact that nothing in it was really hers. To a torn heart uncomforted by human nearness a room may open almost human arms, and the being to whom no four walls mean more than any others, is, at such hours, expatriate everywhere. (I, 1 5, 118)

She had tried to mitigate this charmless background by a few frivolous touches . . . but the futility of the attempt struck her as she looked about the

room What a contrast to the subtle elegance of the setting she had pictured
for herself—an apartment which should surpass the complicated luxury of
her friends' surroundings by the whole extent of that artistic sensibility which
made herself feel their superior. (I, 9, 86)

Lily wants her accommodations to fit her sense of superiority. But they usually don't. She may even want a house or room, with its "almost human arms," more than a man and marriage, a desire for which society traditionally punishes women. Living at her aunt's, Mrs. Peniston—penal, penurious, penis—Lily must sleep and dream in a bedroom that's "as dreary as a prison" (I, 9, 86). Since Wharton's prisons are real spaces and metaphors, Lily's mind and body are trapped not only in dreary rooms but also in the society whose customs shape her.

***

The survival of obsolete customs in architecture, which makes the study of
sociology so interesting, has its parallel in the history of architecture.
(Decoration, 5)

Excremental things are all too intimately and inseparably bound up with sexual
things . . .The genitals themselves have not undergone the development of the rest
of the human form in the direction of beauty; they have retained their animal
cast; and so even today love, too, is in essence as animal as it ever was.[3]

Sigmund Freud and Edith Wharton were contemporaries. They lived during approximately the same years, Freud from 1856 to 1939,

Wharton 1866 to 1937. Freud was as interested in archeology as Wharton was in architecture; it was foundational for his thought. He mined it for metaphors and used it as analogues to human psychology. Wharton obviously had an interest in psychology, though it's unlikely she read Freud. She was aware of him as every educated person would have been then, and wrote in a letter to Bernard Berenson, "Please ask Mary not to befuddle her with Freudianism and all its jargon"[4] Though she eschewed Freud's "jargon," Wharton understood the terms, the ground on which she built her characters. Wharton had a sophisticated understanding of psychology, and her treatment and development of Lily Bart shows her exploring some issues that Freud did. Differently, of course.

Beneath the customs of society lie what the Gothic, and ghost stories, point to: human anxieties and fears, needs and motives drive by desires and instincts not governable by reason. The vicissitudes of sex and sexuality, duty and morality, wreak havoc on Wharton's characters, whether in this novel, *The Age of Innocence*, or *Madame de Treymes*. Wharton is the poet of oppression and repression, and attending to her project, she presents Lily with obstacles. Freud might call them neuroses. Whatever one calls them, "things" are in the way of Lily Bart's ability to thrive.

The preciousness of Lily's reputation reflects the irrational foundations of her world. Taboos about virginity mark both so-called primitive and civilized societies. They mask, Freud theorized, universal human fears about female sexuality and sexuality itself. Wharton's female characters dwell and flail about in a troubled, transitional period (a very long moment that continues to the present). Like Freud, Wharton was nurtured in a Victorian culture and then lived on into a newer, modern world. Like him, she studied the psychological effects on people resistant to, and transformed by, great cultural and social changes. (In *The Mother's Recompense*, the mother flees her marriage, abandons her young daughter for her lover. Years later, the daughter whom she hasn't seen since she ran away, will become engaged to that same man. It's a cautionary Oedipal tale about what can happen if women chase after their desires. When the social order is overturned, duty and obligation ignored for siren freedom, Wharton intimates, incest is a possibility.)

> Seated under the cheerless blaze of the drawing room chandelier—Mrs. Peniston never lit the lamps unless there was "company"—Lily seemed to watch her own figure retreating down vistas of neutral-tinted dullness to a middle-age like Grace Stepney's. (I, 9, 80)

Inside this narrow world of prohibition and inhibition, Lily's possibilities are limited. If Selden embodies Lily's hopes, her Utopian vision, Grace Stepney personifies her fears of the nightmarish future—poverty, spinsterhood, social ugliness. The fear of turning into Grace alarms Lily as much as Selden's freedom entices her.

> Ah, there's the difference—a girl must, a man may if he chooses . . . Your coat's a little shabby—but who cares? It doesn't keep people from asking you to dine. If I were shabby no one would have me: a woman is asked out as much for her clothes as herself. . . Who wants a dingy woman? We are expected to be pretty and well-dressed until we drop—and if we can't keep it up alone, we have to go into partnership. (I, 1,12)

***

The social constraints for women are as clear as the crystal in the houses Wharton describes. But she proposes less obvious or visible constraints. Rarely insistent or repetitive, she is both about Lily's beauty and her terror of dinginess. (Two sides of the same coin, they may constitute her fatal flaw.) Lily's dread—"who wants a dingy woman?"—renders her incapable of happiness, even of living within her means. Even if one supposes one understands how Lily's beauty works—as surface or appearance, as a manifestation of the sublime, as her difference from others, as artistic perfection and imperfection (the human golden bowl)—dinginess is still trickier, more obscure and difficult to grasp. But both refer to the liminal, mostly unseen relationship between interiors and exteriors.

Beauty and dinginess, beauty and the beast, depend upon each other. Dinginess isn't brilliant, sublime, perfect, but dirty, tainted, dark, discolored, worn, or spoiled, used and disgusting. (The word "dingy" may come from the word "dinghy," a small boat or vessel that sails by the side of larger vessels.) Lily's mother instills the terror of it in her. Mrs. Bart's greatest "reproach" to her husband is that he expected her to become dingy or "live like a pig" (I, 3, 26), one of Freud's animals. (Anality comes to mind.) Treated with indifference and contempt, Mr. Bart's a cash machine to his wife and to Lily, who has more sympathy for him. After he loses his money, his failure and inadequacy in Mrs. Bart's eyes are made complete when he dies and leaves them poor, ruined.

After two years of hungry roaming, Mrs. Bart had died—of a deep disgust. She had hated dinginess, and it was her fate to be dingy. Her visions of a brilliant marriage for Lily had faded after the first year. (I, 3, 30)

To Miss Bart, as to her mother, acquiescence in dinginess was evidence of stupidity; and there were moments when, in the consciousness of her own power to look and be so exactly what the occasion required, she almost felt that other girls were plain and inferior from choice. (I, 8, 70)

Mrs. Peniston's opulent interior was at least not externally dingy. But dinginess is a quality that assumes all manner of disguises; and Lily soon found it was as latent in the expensive routine of her aunt's life as in the makeshift existence of a continental pension. (I, 3, 31)

Dinginess isn't ever simple wear and tear. Contrasted again and again to brilliance, light, the sun, glow (as if Wharton were a Manichee), the dark and dirty that Lily fears and names dinginess emanates from what she doesn't know and can't see. There's no clarity, no bright light by which to see these appalling, unconscious forces that threaten her every step. Stupidity, as dullness, is also dinginess (though for her to shine too brilliantly could attract unwanted attention and failure). But Lily is stupid before the irrational. Wharton knew everyone was.

In an extraordinary passage, Lily worries that Mrs. Peniston ("To attempt to bring her into active relation with life was like tugging at a piece of furniture which has been screwed to the floor" [I, 3, 32]) has been "too passive," has not helped her enough socially; but Lily also fears she herself has "not been passive enough" and too "eager" (I, 3, 33).

> Younger and plainer girls had been married off by the dozens, and she was nine and twenty and still Miss Bart.
>
> She was beginning to have fits of angry rebellion against fate, when she longed to drop out of the race and make an independent life for herself but what manner of life would it be? . . . She was too intelligent not to be honest with herself. She knew that she hated dinginess as much as her mother had hated it, and to her last breath she meant to fight against it, dragging herself up again and again against its flood till she gained the bright pinnacles of success which presented such a slippery surface to her clutch. (I, 3, 33)

She fights against being ruined. It's a struggle to the death that she loses, one beyond her control, fought blindly, unconsciously. For a smart girl, Lily often acts impulsively and against her interests. But Wharton sometimes confounds the reader who is attempting to decide what is in her interest. Maybe nothing is. Even if Lily knew what her interests were, she might not be able to stop herself or control herself, for reasons she cannot know.

***

The question persists: If plainer and stupider girls could marry, why can't Lily? Marriage's promise is not just economic and social partnership, but also sexual union. Terror of sex and sexuality, of being made dingy, may be a piece of Lily's unmarriageability, inscribed in her body as attenuated virginity. Intent upon weaving surface and foundation, Wharton lets Lily's body and interior speak society's prohibitive customs and conventions.

(Imagining a character's psychology can be as "slippery" as the "bright pinnacles of success" Lily can't reach. But Wharton looks hard at Lily, as a condition, as a symptom of social injustice, restriction, inhibition, repression, oppression, as an unstable object in an uncertain structure. She scrutinizes her with a kind of clinical neutrality.

> The chief difference between the merely sympathetic and the creative imagination is that the latter is two-sided, and combines with the power of penetrating into other minds that of standing far enough aloof from them to see beyond, and relate them to the whole stuff of life out of which they partially emerge. Such an all-round view can be obtained only by mounting to a height; and that height, in art, is proportioned to the artist's power of detaching one part of his imagination from the particular problem in which the rest is steeped.
> (Writing, 15)

Her very sharp pen, held high, is dipped in the ink of ambivalence—fascination, contempt, compassion, anger, fear. Like all writers, Wharton works as much from what she knows as from what she doesn't. The unconscious presents mysteries and allows pleasures, pains and pathologies a visibility that one can't plan or control.)

Lily's unlovableness and sense of unworthiness is disguised by her beautiful, impenetrable exterior. She's valued for it alone.

One thought consoled [Mrs. Bart], and that was the contemplation of Lily's
beauty . . . it was the last asset in their fortunes . . . She watched it jealously as
if it were her own property and Lily its mere custodian . . . (I, 3, 29)

The dinginess of her present life threw into enchanting relief the existence to
which she felt herself entitled. To a less illuminated intelligence Mrs. Bart's
counsels might have been dangerous, but Lily understood that beauty is only
the raw material of conquest, and that to convert it into success other arts are
required. She knew that to betray any sense of superiority was a subtler form of
the stupidity her mother denounced, and it did not take her long to learn that a
beauty needs more tact than the possessor of an average set of features.
(I, 3, 30)

Lily can't manipulate what's inside her, her feelings about who
she is or isn't. Her beauty is unassailable and absolute; no one
touches it—or her. But its scale triggers alarms, calls too much
attention upon her and maybe isn't a good enough cover story.
She manages it, like her intelligence, though it's inconvenient and
ill-fitting—"more conspicuous than a ballroom." Lily's "passion
for the appropriate" (I, 6, 51) may be oxymoronic.

***

In *The Decoration of Houses*, Wharton claims that "structure
conditions ornament, not ornament structure" (*Decoration*,
14). Lily's an ornament that can be betrayed, deformed, in the
wrong setting. Her beauty will turn ugly if nothing else around
it, or within her, supports it, makes it function or harmonize

with the structure that conditions it. Inappropriate and out of context, beauty can be empty, a thing, nothing but a facade, a fake. When Selden thinks he "see[s] before him the real Lily Bart," she is a tableau vivant, an image, "Mrs. Lloyd" of the Reynolds painting (I, 12, 106). He suddenly perceives her "divested of the trivialities of her little world and catching for a moment a note of that eternal harmony of which her beauty was a part" (I, 12, 106).

It's a singular moment. Lily blends in, in the right setting, and is embraced by Selden for her perfection. Selden's revelry is shattered, though, when Ned Van Alstyne trivializes her, and he becomes indignant.

This was the world she lived in, these were the standards by which she was fated to be measured! Does one go to Caliban for a judgment on Miranda? (I, 12, 107)

He's sympathetic to her; but she's an idealized image. Wharton extols her beauty in this highly artificial, artful scene. She freezes Lily and portrays her as a living picture, so there's something grotesque about it, and about her, too. She's not quite human. But Selden, an aesthete, can adore her and suspend his harsh judgment of her. He can almost love her.

Selden's no less harsh about her, and society, than she is. There's dogged reason in Wharton's pairing of these cool characters, each of whom mirrors the other's desires and lacks. The differences between them elucidate differences based on sex, but through them, Wharton plays with balancing the unbalanced sexes.

If he did not often act on the accepted social axiom that a man may go where he pleases, it was because he had long since learned that his pleasures were mainly to be found in a small group of the like-minded. But he enjoyed spectacular effects, and was not insensible to the part money plays in their production. All he asked was that the very rich live up to their calling as stage managers, and not spend their money in a dull way. (I, 12, 103-4

Like Lily, Selden isn't rich, but unlike her he works for a living. Like Lily, he abjures dullness, appreciates beauty and the finer things, has a pronounced and cultivated sensibility, and recognizes and is repulsed by vulgarity. He feels above most people; he wants to avoid being bored. His lack of chastity isn't, of course, an obstacle. Lily often talks with him about her chances for marriage. But she rarely thinks about or mentions love. (When Lily loves and thrills, it is to rooms and places. Her sensitivity to a room and decoration is as excessive as her beauty.) One of the times she considers love is when she thinks about Selden.

(Lily) could not herself have explained the sense of buoyancy which seemed to lift and swing her above the sun-suffused world at her feet. Was it love, she wondered, or a mere fortuitous combination of happy thoughts and sensations? How much of it was owing to the spell of the perfect afternoon, the scent of the fading woods, the thought of the dullness she had fled from? Lily had no definite experience by which to test the quality of her feelings. She had several times been in love with fortunes or careers, but only once with a man . . . If Lily recalled this early emotion it was not to compare it with that which now possessed her; the only point of comparison was the sense of lightness, of emancipation, which she remembered feeling . . . that glow of freedom; but now it was something more than blind groping of the blood. (I, 6, 52)

Earlier in the scene, Lily wails for Selden to come to her, surrounded by nature, with which she "had no real intimacy" (I, 6, 51). Nature is another one of *The House of Mirth*'s uneasier foundations. What is woman's nature? With freedom, will Lily Bart be "womanly," capable of giving herself in marriage, having babies and conforming to social obligations? Or will she become too new, unusable?

She's been "in love with fortunes and careers, but only once with a man." Nature and love aren't natural to Lily, and she doesn't conform to feminine proscriptions that link women with nature, women with love. Lily thinks she knows Selden's nature, since it's like hers. His "air of friendly aloofness ... [is] ... the quality which piqued Lily's interest" (I, 6, 53). Selden's aloofness sets Lily up, off and down. She doesn't know what to expect from him, never knows if he loves her or might be serious about marrying her.

> Everything about him accorded with the fastidious element in her taste, even to the light irony with which he surveyed what seemed to her most sacred. She admired him most of all perhaps, for being able to convey as distinct a sense of superiority as the richest man she had ever met. (I, 6, 53)

She admires him for an irony that keeps him at a distance. Like her his passions are oxymoronically reserved for the appropriate. Wharton's odd couple are dedicated to controlling themselves. But love jeopardizes control; forces one to become involuntarily subject to another, even lost in the other. Selden's suspicious of losing himself, and he's so suspicious of Lily he thinks that "even her weeping was an art." (I, 6, 58)

That which he projects ahead of him as his ideal is merely his substitute for the lost narcissism of his childhood—the time when he was his own ideal. [5]

When Selden thought he saw the real Lily Bart, she was a living doll. Maybe he loved her most then as a lost part of himself, the illusory ideal he once imagined himself to be or have. They're both difficult characters, wary of love, looking for perfection. Not finding it in themselves or others, they don't lose themselves.

In a recent TV advertisement for a men's perfume called Contradiction, a young man declares, "I don't want her to need me. I want her to desire me. Need isn't desire." Lily needs Selden more than she desires him; Selden's idea of freedom entails being wanted, not needed. Their attraction to each other is unstable and compelling, living, dying, again and again. The contradictory logic that might make them lovers—both are ambivalent, both want freedom—is precisely what makes them unfit for each other.

***

In this thwarted romance, star-crossed lovers want to love but can't, do in some ways love themselves and each other, but also share in self-loathing, an effect, too, of narcissism. Freud wrote that loving oneself is not a "perversion but the libidinal complement to the egoism of the instinct of self-preservation, a measure of which may justifiably be attributed to every living creature" ("Narcissism," 105). Selden's self-regard appears less compromised than Lily's; she worries too much about becoming clingy.

But both suffer from narcissistic wounds and lick them throughout the novel, sparing themselves the pain of further injury.

> *The effect of the dependence upon the love object is to lower that feeling [of self-regard]: the lover is humble. He who loves has, so to speak, forfeited a part of his narcissism, which can only be replaced by his being loved.*
> ("Narcissism," 120)

> *There is, in the act of love, a great resemblance to torture or to a surgical operation.*[6]

Selden and Lily never stop preserving and defending themselves from imagined or real injuries and threats. Love—relinquishment of control—might be torture for them. When Lily visits Selden for the last time, she is finally able to articulate it.

> *Do you remember what you said to me once? That you could help me only by loving me? Well—you did love me for a moment; and it helped me. But the moment is gone—it was I who let it go. And one must go on living. Goodbye.*
> (II, 12, 241)

Love's dead, but "something lived between them also. . . . it was the love his love had kindled, the passion of her soul for his" (II, 12, 241). Her idea of love colludes with Wharton's understanding of desire that arises from the desire to be desired. Even more abstractly, Lily understands that "she could not go forth and leave her old self with him; that self must indeed live on in his presence, but it must still continue to be hers" (II, 12, 241). Even when love is dead, no longer capable of causing pain, surgery—amputation—won't be allowed. Lily's fear of losing herself, giving herself up to him, certainly may be her magnificent desire to be herself. But what Wharton suggests is that her impassioned need to preserve herself at all costs may be an implacable obstacle to happiness; for it she will pay the ultimate price.

***

Not coincidentally, the most exquisite or maybe the only love scene in *The House of Mirth* is not between Selden and Lily, but between mother and child—with Lily playing the mother and becoming the child in a kind of self-love scene. (It's also the only scene in which one character holds another with passion or for any length of time.) After the devastating last meeting with Selden, Lily bumps into Nettie Crane Struthers, one of Gerty Far-ish's "girls," on the street.

> *Nettie Struther's frail envelope was now alive with hope and energy; whatever fate the future reserved for her, she would not be cast into the refuse heap without a struggle.* (II, 13, 243)

Though poor, Nettie's not rubbish, not dingy. Nettie invites Lily home: "it's real warm in our kitchen" (II, 13, 244). In another of Wharton's relatively few underscorings and repetitions, she italicizes "was" in Lily's repeated thought: "It *was* warm in the kitchen" (II, 13, 244). (*Warm* or *warmth* occurs several more times in this hearth-and-home kitchen scene.) Nettie's life, though different from Lily's, has its similarities. She was about to give up, having been jilted, but unlike Lily, Nettie found a man, George, married, and had a baby. Nettie's reputation doesn't stop George from marrying her; Lily's stops everyone. Nettie's success as a traditional woman, playing traditional roles, is severely contrasted to Lily's failures, her flawed femininity and fatal unmarriageability. This extreme pairing, before Lily's suicide, seems to enunciate the author's ambivalence toward Lily and the allure and demands of femininity. And maybe it also addresses Wharton's own maternal deprivation, since through the veil of fiction one writes what one wants as much as what one doesn't.

When Lily holds Nettie's baby, at first the child

seemed as light as a pink cloud or a heap of down, but as she continued to hold it the weight increased, sinking deeper, and penetrating her with a strange sense of weakness, as though the child entered into her and became a part of herself. (II, 13, 245-6)

Wharton fashions another *tableau vivant*, a *Madonna and Child* (by Bellini, let's say), and paints the badly mothered Lily Bart into it. In a moment of devastating psychological revelation, Lily is transformed as the infant enters her. The baby becomes a lost part of her, an adult still so little, so undeveloped, she's as weak as a baby, or she is the baby.

[Nettie:] "Wouldn't it be too lovely if she grew up to be just like you?"
[Lily:] "Oh she must not do that—I should be afraid to come to see her too often." (II, 13, 246)

351

Now Wharton's gone Gothic again, writing a ghost story. Lily foresees her death, and, as a ghost, could return to visit the real Lily Bart, who has never actually existed. The baby could become the person she might have been, had she been loved and able to thrive. At Nettie's warm hearth, Lily's heartless mother is a spectral presence, with Lily's pathetic, beaten-down father hovering in the corner where her mother placed him. (What kind of man could Lily love after him? Or, even, could Lily really love a man after him?)

***

> One may distinguish the novel of situation from that of character and manners by saying that, in the first, the persons imagined by the author almost always spring out of a vision of the situation, and are inevitably conditioned by it, whatever the genius of their creator; whereas in the larger freer form, that of character and manners (or either of the two), the author's characters are first born, and then mysteriously proceed to work out their destinies. (Writing, 89)

In writing and design, Wharton strove for clean lines and economy, to remove excess. Lily's excessive, a disturbance within the social structure. It's rotten, but she's a character formed inside its rooms. Lily wanted to be an original, and Wharton, conflicted and ambivalent about the new, gave her enough rope to hang herself— trapping her between the novel of situation (or circumstance and circumstantial evidence) and the novel of character. Through her imperfect heroine, Wharton proclaimed the vivacious allure of freedom, the voracious seductiveness and promise of modernity and change, with all its destructive potential, and the helplessness of individuals before the claims and blind dictates of society in which women and men lived. But she didn't allow them a talking cure, and her characters have very little room in which to negotiate happy endings.

***

Another unsettling element of modern art is that common symptom of immaturity, the dread of doing what has been done before; for though one of the instincts of youth is imitation, another, equally imperious, is that of fiercely guarding against it. (Writing, 17)

Original vision is never much afraid of using accepted forms [*my emphasis*]; *and only the cultivated intelligence escapes the danger of regarding as intrinsically new what may be a mere superficial change, or the reversion to a discarded trick of technique.* (Writing, 109)

There is one more thing to be said in defence of conformity to style; and that is, the difficulty of getting rid of style. Strive as we may for originality, we are hampered at every turn by an artistic tradition of over two thousand years. Does any but the most inexperienced architect really think he can ever rid himself of such an inheritance? He may mutilate or misapply the component parts of his design, but he cannot originate a whole new architectural alphabet. The chances are that he will not find it easy to invent one wholly new moulding. (Decoration, 15)

When I read the last quote to Laura Kurgan, an architect, she said, "You could get rid of the molding entirely." It's what the modernists did.

> I have discovered the following truth and present it to the world: cultural evolution is equivalent to the removal of ornament from articles in daily use . . . Don't you see the greatness of our age lies in its inability to produce a new form of decoration? We have conquered ornament, we have won through the lack of ornamentation. . . . for ornament is not only produced by criminals; it itself commits a crime, by damaging men's health, the national economy and cultural development.[7]

Adolf Loos wrote his famous essay, or manifesto, "Ornament and Crime," in 1908. Wharton's work on houses and decoration preceded it by a decade. She was in line with Loos, and the modernists, to a point.

> It is the superfluous gimcrack—the "ornament"—which is most objectionable, and the more expensive these items are the more likely they are to harm. (Decoration, 177)

> The supreme excellence is simplicity. Moderation, fitness, relevance . . . There is a sense in which works of art may be said to endure by virtue of that which is left out of them, and it is this "tact of omission" that characterizes the modern hand. (Decoration, 192)

Wharton appreciated simplicity and omission. But she could see the reason, rhythm, and logic of certain kinds of decoration.

While plain paneling, if well-designed, is never out of keeping, the walls of a music-room are especially suited to a somewhat fanciful style of decoration. . . . Fewer changes are possible in the "upright" [piano]; but a marked improvement could be produced by straightening its legs and substituting right angles for the weak curves of the lid. The case itself might be made of plainly paneled mahogany, with a few good ormolu ornaments; or of inlaid wood, with a design of musical instruments . . . (Decoration, 146-7)

Slavoj Zizek, lecturing at New York University, once urged the audience I was in to throw out the baby but keep the bathwater. Wharton wanted to keep the bathwater. Her disinclination to throw out everything—except what she called the "horrors"—makes her a vital candidate for rereading and rethinking. Wharton relentlessly forced her characters to live, and die, struggling against or submitting to conventions, acknowledging their contradictions, while trying to create paths through or around rigid social customs. They were usually blocked. She did not imagine a utopia. She didn't see a way of divorcing the past from the present. She didn't see the necessity of abandoning all traditions or styles. Even molding, in proportion to the room, could be beautiful.

It is a curious perversion of artistic laws that has led certain critics to denounce painted architecture or woven mouldings. As in imaginative literature the author may present to his reader as possible anything that he has the talent to make the reader accept, so in decorative art the artist is justified in presenting to the eye whatever his skill can service to satisfy its requirements nor is there any insincerity in this proceeding. (Decoration, 40)

Her ideas were modern—she wanted to clear house of nine-teenth-century vestiges, stuffed chairs and stuffed shirts, to question conventions and numbing, absurd traditions, but she was far from being a card-carrying modernist. Wharton was skeptical about the new, not positive that progress was progress, not sanguine about the future of the joys of speed and flight, as the futurists were; she took off and looked back over her shoulder at the past. She doesn't fit comfortably into the modernist canon and has suffered for it.

Architecture articulates space, the movement within walls and without them, delineates the relationships of the built to the unbuilt and surroundings. Wharton's prose makes its own particular space, its complex borders pierced by new and old. It's one of those uncanny pieces of fate—less colloquially, historical overde-termination—that her reputation, her literary place, is inflected not just by her idiosyncratic relationship to Modernism but also by three biographical facts: She was female, upper-class and Henry James's younger friend. Not mentioning James in relation to her is like not mentioning the elephant in the room, a room which she did not, of course, design. Her critical reputation stands mostly in his large shadow. (Her primary biographer R.W.B. Lewis's first sentence in his introduction to the *House of Mirth* begins "Henry James . . .")[8] Few U.S writers who are women make it, as the song goes, to standing in the shadows of love, critical love. (And her books were about love, its promise and seductiveness, its inevitable impossibility within a harsh, prohibitive world.)

The ironist Wharton might have appreciated, in her perverse way, the secondary or minor position she has attained. (Perhaps in the way Deleuze and Guattari appreciate minor literature) Ironically, undidacitally, Wharton teaches that separate isn't equal; difference shouldn't be but usually is hierarchical, and change in any establishment or tradition is like her sentences, slow.

ACKNOWLEDGEMENTS

The author would like to thank Gregg Bordowitz and Kenneth Frampton for their invaluable help in the writing of this essay.

A brief, preliminary version of this essay appeared in Conjunctions: 29, Tributes, Fall 1997 *(pp. 122-125); it was entitled "Edith Wharton: A Mole in the House of the Modern."*

NOTES

1. *Edith Wharton and Ogden Codman, Jr.,* The Decoration of Houses *(New York: Classical America and Henry Hope Reed/Norton, 1998); first published in 1897.*

2. *Edith Wharton,* The Writing of Fiction *(New York: Touchstone, 1997); first published in 1924.*

3. *Sigmund Freud, "Contributions to the Psychology of Love," in* Sexuality and the Psychology of Love, *ed. Philip Rieff (New York: Collier Books, 1963), 63.*

4. *Edith Wharton,* The Letters of Edith Wharton, *ed. R.W.B. Lewis and Nancy Lewis (New York: Scribner's, 1988), 450-1.*

5. *Sigmund Freud, "On Narcissism: An Introduction," in* A General Selection from the Works of Sigmund Freud, *ed. John Rickman, M. D. (New York: Doubleday, 1957), 116.*

6. *Charles Baudelaire,* Intimate Journals, *trans. Christopher Isherwood (London: Picador, 1990), 14.*

7. *Adolf Loos, "Ornament and Crime," in* Adolf Loos: Pioneer of Modern Architecture, *ed. Ludwig Munz and Gustav Kunstler (New York: Prager, 1996), 226-8.*

8. *R.W.B. Lewis, "Introduction" to Edith Wharton,* The House of Mirth *(New York: Bantam, 1984), viii.*

X is for X-rated

A cesspool is not just a metaphor. In the suburbs, it's under the driveway or front lawn, and, sometimes, during long, hot summers, it seeps. What escapes is an olfactory embarrassment that reminds the neighborhood of stuff no one wants to talk about. Dominique Laporte's *History of Shit* reveals and revels in dirty, unmentionable stuff, digging beneath the beautiful to find the unspeakable it hides. Laporte sniffs bad smells, waxes rhapsodic about the odoriferous body and explores the division between private and public.

The story of shit is older than human beings, of course, but Laporte begins his account in 1539, with the proclamation, in France, of two edicts. One, the Ordinance of Villers-Cotterets, stated that "henceforth justice would be administered and civil documents and notarized acts registered in the French language." The other edict, Laporte writes in characteristically florid style, "we need exhume . . . for its substance, and in so doing, may as well abandon ourselves, albeit briefly, to the strange beauty of its language." It forbade "all emptying or tossing out into the streets and squares of [Paris] and its surroundings of refuse, offals, or putrefactions, as well as all waters whatever their nature . . ." Of the coterminous moves toward purging "maternal French" of Latin and Parisian streets of shit, Laporte comments: "We have known since Barthes that 'when written, shit does not smell.' . . . No doubt beautiful language has more than a little to do with shit, and style itself grows more precious the more exquisitely motivated by waste."

This playful treatise, wryly translated by Nadia Benabid and Rodolphe el-Khoury, links asshole to mouth, excrement to language. Laporte claims that efforts to contain, deodorize and sanitize the body's products have shaped language and consciousness. "To touch, even lightly, on the relationship of a subject to his shit," Laporte writes, "is to modify not only that subject's relationship to the totality of his body, but his very relationship to the world and those representations that he constructs of his situation in society." Representations, such as language, must be censored, elegant phrases and stylistic flourishes invented to cover and disguise, like literary kitty litter, the human capacity to foul and be foul. "But the incapacity of this system to manage its own filth is lucidly betrayed by its intrepid fantasy of an elimination so complete it leaves no trace of waste."

To this futile end—the fantasy of wastelessness in which "the hygienist is a hero"—excrement was taxed, by emperors Vespasian and Constantine; urine was drunk; and feces were turned into medicine and cosmetics. What streamed out of us could make money or make us healthy and beautiful. (The truism "Waste not want not" finds its supreme explicator in Laporte.) In a wackily convincing way, *History of Shit* traces society's efforts to legislate and handle human waste, to reduce the shame produced by what leaks from our orifices, even to transform shit into gold. "The place where one 'does one's business' is also the place where waste accumulates. . . . To each his shit! proclaims a new ethic of the ego decreed by a State that entitles each subject to sit on his own ass on his own heap of gold."

Laporte, a French psychoanalyst, died in 1984 at the age of thirty-five. Along with Barthes, not surprisingly, his guiding lights were Freud and Lacan. The former "defined order, cleanliness, and beauty . . . as the cornerstones of civilization," while the latter stated: "Civilization is the spoils: the cloaca maxima." For these two theorists, the terror of our own mucky, dark holes, the abject fear of never climbing out of the primeval sewer, propelled the march to civilization—the costuming of human animality.

As a character from the anarchic '60s should, Laporte maintains an ironic posture toward the civilizing drive. "The privatization of waste," he proclaims in his inimitable fashion, "a process whose universality is not a historical given, made it possible for the smell of shit to be bearable within the family setting, home to the closest social ties." In other words, the family, the basis of society, established an enduring bond only after first being able to stand each other's shit—something R.D. Laing failed to mention in his critique of that neurotic social unit.

Reading *History of Shit* is both pleasurable and disgusting—and it is also about that ambivalent duo, pleasure and disgust. Laporte, who studied the hidden mission of style, also had style in abundance—a definite way with words—and his tongue is often in his cheek. My recourse to that flaccid metaphor drolly underscores his idea that language and the body are bound together—often gagged—in secret, inviolable secretions or nuggets. See, it's nearly impossible to discuss *History of Shit* without sliding into bathroom humor, which is by definition immature. A baby's interest in its shit precedes its ability to speak. So if eschatology is the study of last things, scatology should be the study of first things, since shit precedes language and death. In any case, *History of Shit* could transform all language scholars into Howard Stern. It certainly confirms this reader's sense that it would be less embarrassing to admit to having murdered someone than to having farted in a "good" restaurant.

Twee Kamers

It's very difficult to find apartments in Amsterdam, an old and small city. Sidonie and her friend were trying to find a place to live and they placed an ad in the newspaper, giving my place of work to call. They asked if I would mind taking calls for them. I said I wouldn't.

My Dutch was hardly adequate; it enabled me to buy food and panic when times called for it. They had advertised for two rooms. I knew two rooms to be *twee kamers*.

I was alone in the office when the telephone rang. A Dutch male voice asked, "*Advertitie voor twee kamers?*" *Ya*, I replied, not me (or *may*, as it would be pronounced in Dutch), my friends, *twee persons voor twee kamers*. I felt quite proud of myself, two people for two rooms. *Aah*, he said, *twee persons*. *Ya*, I said, do you have them? *Twee kamers*, he said. *Ya, ya*, I said. Slowly, and partially in English, he said, "I am holding my *pemel*." Oh, *ya*, I said, thinking he might mean he was holding a pencil, not knowing the world for pencil in Dutch, though curious as to why he would tell me that at all. "*Momentje*," he called out. I imagined he was writing something down and waited. "*Ik kom*," he cried. I hung up.

Y is for Yearning

It's Independence Day, the Fourth of July, and America is 236 years old. I've been pondering the tortuous coupling, "art and politics." Each partner resists easy definition, especially "art" ("Is it art?" and "What is art?" are jokes); I can't imagine Ludwig Wittgenstein countenancing their murky conjunction. It's hard to avoid the couple's traps.

Art is not usually measured by its utility (the school of "relational aesthetics" attempts to call that hand), while politics is. What usefulness is believed to be is also a matter of contestation. In 1972, in Amsterdam, with artist Jos Schoffelen, I ran a cinema with an eclectic program, the first in the Netherlands to feature double-headers and to screen an Andy Warhol movie, *Bike Boy* (1967). A rogue film collector approached us with a 16mm print of *Tarzan Escapes* (1936). He screened it for us: Its white supremacy and brutal racism were shockingly casual. Black African men fell off steep cliffs, while their white British masters exclaimed about the loss of precious equipment.

Jos and I wanted to pair it with a documentary about the Black Panthers. Amsterdam's Communist Film Club distributed it, but wouldn't rent it unless we organized a protest march. "Why do we have to organize a march?" "Because it's a political film," they said. I said, "If people want to march afterward, they can."

Juxtaposing the two was art and politics; "Art could be a dialogue," we said, "which is political activity." "No way," they said.

The cinema wasn't considered "serious" because of its emphasis on art; soon their club vetoed the cinema getting funding from Amsterdam City Council. Maybe this is too strident or absurd an example of conflict between, and in, art and politics. Generally, I proffer the idea that all art is political, though I'm not satisfied by it. It seems subtle, yet too broad, and because of this not convincing. But I may be trapped in it, not having a better argument.

Writing novels and stories, I've become convinced that narratives concern themselves with justice or adjudication. Writing fiction, I might be able to avoid mental traps, habits of mind. I try to be vigilant about how I write—style, form—to trample complacency of all types; in concert with a writer's lacks, it generates truisms and stereotypical characters.

I often recall other artists' choices. Ad Reinhardt drew political cartoons and made non-referential paintings. The American poet George Oppen stopped writing poetry for 30 years, after he became a member of the Communist Party in the 1930s, because he wouldn't write Party poems. When he started again, he produced an exceptional poetics.

In a performance I once saw, the artist Bob Flanagan hammered a nail into his penis. I put my head in my hands, covering my eyes (one man fainted); but I wouldn't think of stopping him. It was his penis. Was this a political act? Flanagan was born with cystic fibrosis and was told he'd die at 20. He'd been a cystic fibrosis poster boy at 13. His art fought his genetic identity, and what the disease didn't cruelly claim, he tormented. For his exhibition

"Visiting Hours" at the New Museum, New York, in 1994, Flanagan built a hospital room and lay on a hospital bed, attached to an oxygen tank.

Viewing Flanagan installed as a piece in a museum, knowing him since the 1980s, I felt disorientated—installed momentarily in his hell. "Voyeuristic" pales as a description of my looking. Was his métier disorientation? Flanagan's conflation of art, body and disease bewildered me, rebelling against any modifier, such as progressive or regressive, which might characterize the politics of an art practice.

Some say artists should make work for an audience, that anything else is indulgent; art should be "accessible." To whom is never clear. Recently, in various newspapers and literary magazines, a debate about so-called "difficult books" has been unfolding. Writers should remember their readers, one side insisted, by making books enjoyable. For one thing, "difficulty" and "pleasure" are relative terms; without foundation, the argument lacked cogency and drifted into nowheresville.

Filmmaker Trinh T. Minh-ha reckoned with the concept of audience differently. Minh-ha was present at the New York premiere of *Naked Spaces—Living is Round* (1985), at the Museum of Modern Art. The film pictured women working, walking, socializing. No narrator explained the women or the spaces they inhabited. Instead, words shaped and suggested more impressions, ways of seeing.

The first question to Minh-ha came from a man, who asked, vehemently: "Who is this film for? Who's the audience for this film?" Minh-ha took a moment, then said: "I make films for sensitive people." Her audience fell silent, maybe stunned by her brilliant tactic, which leaped over patterned responses. Minh-ha allowed for the contemplation of positions, by escaping the usual discursive traps. It's the hardest thing to do, and in art and politics the most imaginative and stimulating.

Z is for Jonze

Life's tough as a street-art puppeteer, but when Craig Schwartz (cunning John Cusack) starts a deadbeat day job in an office where the ceiling's so low everyone has to bend over, he discovers a way out—a secret tunnel into the mind and body of John Malkovich (playing himself, sort of). Spike Jonze's first feature *Being John Malkovich* renders identity as the playground and prison it is. When everyone wants to be known, rather than to try to know, celebrity is the pinnacle of success. To the star-obsessed, being known might mean not having to know yourself, and if you don't like yourself, this must be freedom. Dropped into the body of someone else, though, might allow for the ironic discovery that others are just as limited as you are. I laugh every time I think of Cameron Diaz—so thoroughly unglamorous she's a sight gag—in a cage with a monkey; and Malkovich at home halfnaked, his paunch smiling at the fantasy of celebrity perfection.

Acknowledgments

The publisher and author would like to acknowledge and thank Stephen Frailey, artist/photographer and chair of Undergraduate Photography Department (The School of Visual Arts), for providing the title for this collection. Frailey edits a photography magazine, *Dear Dave*, and for its advertising campaign, several years ago, chose to run, in every issue, a powder-blue page, with white letters: "WHAT WOULD LYNNE TILLMAN DO?" (This was a great surprise to LT.) On the side of the page, it says: Subscribe to Dear Dave, WWW.DEARDAVEMAGAZINE.COM. We heartily recommend you do.

Credits

"The Last Words are Andy Warhol," in *Grey Room* 21, Grey Room Inc. and M.I.T., Fall 2005, pp. 38-44.

"Blame it on Andy: The Problems of Acting Natural," In these Intemperate Times, *Frieze Magazine*, Issue 141, Sept. 2011, London.

"Nothing is Lost or Found: Desperately Seeking Paul and Jane Bowles," *Tin House*, Vol. 1, number 3, New York: Winter 2000, pp. 122-29.

"Adieu, American Abroad," *Tin House*, Vol. 12, number 2. Ed: Rob Spillman, pp. 70-79.

"Cut Up Life," Introductory essay in *Water from a Bucket: Diary 1948-57*, by Charles Henri Ford, Turtle Point Press, 2001, pp. vii-xiii.

"Object Lesson" (on Fred Hughes's house and art collection), *Nest*, New York: Summer 2000, pp. 54-61.

"White Cool," *Elle* 4:86, New York: May 1989, p. 86.

It's About Time: Definitions, in *The Future Dictionary of America*, McSweeney's Books, 2004.

"There, Not There: How our attitudes betray us," In these Intemperate Times, *Frieze Magazine*, Issue 147, May 2012, London.

This interview, Paula Fox by Lynne Tillman, was commissioned by and first published in *BOMB Magazine*, from BOMB 95/Spring 2006. © *Bomb Magazine*, New Art Publications, and its Contributors. All rights reserved. *BOMB* can be read at www.bombmagazine.org.

"*Borrowed Finery*," (memoir by Paula Fox), *Bookforum*, Winter 2001, p. 27.

"*The Coldest Winter*," (novel by Paula Fox), *Bookforum*, WORD: The Literary Magazine, ed. M Mark, June 1995, New York.

"The Regulation of Pleasure," *Voice Literary Supplement*, 1989.

"A New Chapter of Nan Goldin's Diary," in the Sunday *New York Times*, Arts and Leisure, Nov. 16, 2003, p. 36.

Interview with Harry Mathews, commissioned by and first published in *BOMB Magazine*, from BOMB 26/Winter 1989. © *Bomb Magazine*, New Art Publications, and its Contributors. All rights reserved. *BOMB* can be read at www.bombmagazine.org

"SLANT," *Artforum*, April 1990.

"Try Again," In these Intemperate Times," *Frieze* Magazine, Issue 145, March 2012, London.

"Of Its time," In these Intemperate Times, *Frieze Magazine*, Issue 151, November-December 2012, London.

"The Final Plot," *The Inevitable: Contemporary Writers Confront Death*, pp 275-280. Ed: David Shields, Bradford Morrow. W.W. Norton & Company inc, New York 2011.

"Downtown's Room in Hotel History" in *Downtown Film, TV and Video Culture 1975-2001*. Ed. Joan Hawkins. Intellect Press: London, 2014

"Boss of Bosses—The Fall of the Godfather: The FBI and Paul Castellano," by Joseph F. O'Brien and Andris Kurins (review), *Voice Literary Supplement* 36:28, New York: July 9, 1991, pp. 6-7.

"The Real McCoy: I Should Have Stayed Home" (Horace McCoy), *Voice Literary Supplement* 35:17, New York: September 11, 1990, pp. 15-16.

"Guide for the Misbegotten:" Lynne Tillman on John Waters's Role Models, *Art Forum International*, 2010.

"Point of View," In these Intemperate Times, *Frieze Magazine*, Issue 143, Nov. 2011, London.

"The Rolling Stones, The Academy of Music," in *The Show I'll Never Forget*, ed. Sean Manning, Da Capo Press, Cambridge, MA., 2007, pp. 22-25.

"Great Expectations: *Underworld* by Don DeLillo," *Bookforum*, New York: Winter 1997, p. 17.

"Future Shock" (review of George Saunders's *Pastoralia*), *New York Times Book Review*, May 28, 2000, p. 8.

"Reconsidering the Genius of Gertrude Stein," *New York Times Book Review*, January 27, 2012, p. 13.

"First Novel," in *Bookforum*, July/August/September 2006, New York, p. 37.

"Doing Laps Without A Pool," Chapbook, New Herring Press, Brooklyn, 2011. Reprinted: Best Offense 2009.

interview with Peter Dreher, commissioned by and first published in BOMB *Magazine*, from BOMB 57/Winter 1996. © *Bomb Magazine*, New Art Publications, and its Contributors. All rights reserved. BOMB can be read at www.bombmagazine.org

"The Virtual President," *Art Forum*, January 2009.

"A Mole in the House of the Modern," in *The American Novel: The House of Mirth*, ed. Deborah Esch, Cambridge University Press, Cambridge, Winter 2001, pp. 133-58.

"*History of Shit,*" (review of Dominique LaPorte's *History of Shit*), *Bookforum*, New York: Summer 2000, p. 9.

"The Hardest Thing," In these Intemperate Times, *Frieze Magazine*, Issue 149, September 2012, London

"Stars in their Eyes: Fame is a Frame" (on Spike Jonze's Being John Malkovich), Frieze, #49, London: Fall 1999, p. 58.

About the Author

Lynne Tillman is the author of five novels, four collections of short stories, one collection of essays and two other nonfiction books. She has collaborated often with artists and writes regularly on culture. Her novels include *American Genius, A Comedy* (2006), *No Lease on Life* (1997), a New York Times Notable Book of 1998 and a finalist for the National Book Critics Circle Award; *Cast in Doubt* (1992); *Motion Sickness* (1991); and *Haunted Houses* (1987). *Someday This Will Be Funny* (2012) is her most recent short story collection. Her nonfiction books include *The Velvet Years: Warhol's Factory 1965-1967*, with photographs by Stephen Shore (1995); *Bookstore: The Life and Times of Jeannette Watson and Books & Co.* (1999), a cultural history of a literary landmark, and *The Broad Picture*, an essay collection.